The Mediterranean Vegan Kitchen

88 - rice Salad

The Mediterranean Vegan Kitchen

Meat-Free, Egg-Free, Dairy-Free Dishes from the Healthiest Place under the Sun

Donna Klein

HPBooks

HPBooks
Published by The Berkley Publishing Group
A division of Penguin Putnam Inc.
375 Hudson Street
New York, New York 10014

Cover design by Dorothy Wachtenheim
Cover photograph © Stock Food/Brauner

First edition: May 2001

Published simultaneously in Canada.

The Penguin Putnam Inc. World Wide Web site address is
http://www.penguinputnam.com

Library of Congress Cataloging-in-Publication Data

Klein, Donna (Donna M.).
The Mediterranean vegan kitchen / Donna Klein.
p. cm.
Includes bibliographical references and index.
ISBN 1-55788-359-9
1. Vegan cookery. 2. Cookery, Mediterranean. I. Title.

TX837 .K545 2001
641.5'636'091822—dc21

00-049931

Printed in the United States of America

10 9 8 7 6

To my parents, Ruth and Joe Blong,
for a lifetime of encouragement

Contents

Acknowledgments

Grateful thanks to my literary agent, Linda Konner, for her support and belief in this project from the start.

Sincere thanks to John Duff, and to Jeanette Egan for her guidance and skillful editing of the manuscript.

Loving thanks to my daughters, Emma and Sarah, for their willingness to try many new and delicious foods, and most of all to Jeff, my patient husband and official taste tester, who, after sampling countless pesto recipes, never once asked, "Where's the cheese?"

Introduction

The Legendary Mediterranean Diet: Almost Too Good to Be True

Once upon a time in a far-off land bordered by the Mediterranean Sea and blessed by year-round sun, people discovered that a diet plentiful in fruits, vegetables, grains, and legumes, dressed with little more than olive oil, garlic, and fresh herbs, was as healthful as it was delicious. They gathered daily around a table with family and friends to share in their abundance, toasting each other's health and good fortune with a glass or two of red wine.

Thousands of years passed and the people continued to enjoy their good food and good health in relative obscurity. Then in the early 1960s a distinguished medical researcher named Ancel Keys began to examine the relationship between diet and disease. The eyes of the scientific community became increasingly focused on the people of the Mediterranean and their diet and their relatively low rates of coronary heart disease, stroke, cancer, and diabetes. Always quick to spot health trends, Americans took notice. Bottles of imported olive oil, jars of marinated artichokes, and tins of sardines began appearing on pantry shelves. Pasta no longer boiled down to just spaghetti with meat sauce, as busy home cooks added linguine with clam sauce to their weekly menus. The ambitious purchased paella pans and revealed the magic of Spain's most famous rice dish to their dinner guests. At fancy French restaurants, sophisticated diners, watching their cholesterol, supped from giant bowls of bouillabaisse. Outside, on street corners, vendors hawked felafel sandwiches dressed with tahini and sold them regularly to the fast-food crowd and vegetarians. Inside, on kitchen counters, hippies and vegans soaked bulgur wheat they'd purchased from the lone health-food store and turned it into a Middle Eastern meze, or appetizer, known as tabbouleh. They scooped it up with lettuce leaves and called it lunch. With some hummus—another meze—and pita on the side, they called it dinner. Indeed, there was something for everyone from the bountiful land of the Mediterranean.

By 1993, the headline news was almost too good to be true: the International Conference on Diets of the Mediterranean, based on the work of Keys and his many associates, backed the Mediterranean diet as the best one for overall good health. America's whetted appetite turned ravenous. At the start of the new millennium, its hunger seemingly knows no bounds.

Home cooks pressed for time now boil tagliatelle until al dente and sauce it with ricotta salata for a quick weeknight supper. The ambitious purchase *couscousières* and reveal the magic of Moroccan cuisine by serving couscous de poisson to impressed dinner guests. At upscale bistros, sophisticated diners, now watching their "sat fat," sup from giant bowls of seafood stew called bourride and go easy on the aioli. Panini, Italy's favorite grilled sandwiches, are currently all the rage—corner bakeries sell roasted vegetable with smoked mozzarella specials to the fast-food crowd and vegetarians, who reheat them in their microwaves. The hippie crowd, though aging, is still going strong; the vegan numbers, meanwhile, have increased tenfold. But alas, both have been left behind at the meze table, still scooping tabbouleh with wilted lettuce leaves.

The Vegan Dishes of the Mediterranean: A Matter of Chance, Not Design

Yet travel to the Mediterranean, and a panoply of meat-free, dairy-free dishes awaits the hungry vegan. Since Homeric times, small amounts of red meat, and low to moderate amounts of fish, poultry, eggs, and dairy, have been consumed there. That meat is used sparingly is not so much a matter of choice, but of environmental conditions and economic constraints. The rocky, sandy, rather dry terrain of much of the Mediterranean, in which olive trees thrive, is not suitable for grazing; consequently, meat—red in particular—is in short supply and expensive.

Although fish, poultry, eggs, and dairy products are generally abundant, they have often proved perishable during much of the region's turbulent and poverty-stricken history. In times of war, famine, drought, plague, and other hardships that have afflicted many Mediterranean countries throughout the millennia, it was the dried beans, whole grains, salted nuts, and preserved fruits and vegetables, mainly olives, that sustained them. Furthermore, the Lenten fast leading up to Easter, when eating meat is prohibited, is observed by many Christians who live in the region. The traditional Orthodox Lenten fast is particularly strict—downright vegan, in fact—as no animal products of any kind, including eggs and dairy, may be consumed. As a result, there are enough naturally vegan Mediterranean recipes to fill a book—and this is it.

Mediterranean Cuisine: Always a Place in the Sun

But this is not another Mediterranean diet cookbook. Indeed, even this seemingly idyllic way of eating, with its uncanny fusion of good flavor with good health, is literally too good to be true in certain circles—a few doubt its very existence. Some say it's all in the genes. Others say it's a question of lifestyle. Still others say that while the diet may be beneficial for native Mediterranean peoples, there's no guarantee that those benefits are transferable to Americans. Given the differences in the air we breathe, the water we drink, the soil in which our fruits and vegetables grow, and the chemicals we add to our foods during growth and processing, diet alone could not reasonably be the only factor. And so it goes. Yet even the doubting Thomases—save for a few caught up in current food fashion—will readily admit that there's nothing wrong and everything right with the Mediterranean diet's basic premises of lots of fruits, whole grains, and vegetables, with small amounts of meat, fish, dairy products, and saturated fats.

Fortunately, our ongoing passion for the Mediterranean and its food is more than a mere modern health trend. The Mediterranean is a land of inspiration. Throughout history the beauty of Provence's lavender fields, Spain's citrus trees, Italy's terra-cotta roofs, Morocco's sandy beaches, and the region's ubiquitous olive groves, blue sea, and bluer sky has enchanted visitors and inspired art, from breathtaking still life to soulful poem to sonorous song. For centuries, the heady aromas of rosemary and thyme, mint and basil, the pungent flavors of garlic and olive oil, wine and tomatoes, all ripened by the incandescent Mediterranean sun, have fired the imaginations of home cooks and restaurant chefs alike to create one of the world's greatest cuisines. They fill up our senses, these intoxicating foods of the sun. In spring, they urge us to plant gardens; in summer, they prompt us to plan picnics; in fall, they beckon us to forage; in winter, they simply lift our spirits. That they are essentially healthful is, like life itself, a gratuitous gift. While other food fashions may come and go, Mediterranean cuisine, by its very nature, will always have a place in the sun.

About the Ingredients

Is there a place for animal product and by-product substitutes, especially for cheese, in Mediterranean cooking?

In the developing stages of this book, I spent considerable time pondering this question. While my original concept of including only vegan recipes that really exist in Mediterranean cuisine never wavered, I also knew that on the Mediterranean some of these recipes—pesto is a prime example—typically contain cheese. I must confess to a weakness for cheese. I also must confess to a fear of irate cooks, having opened to the pesto recipe on page 107, demanding "Where's the cheese?" As a compromise, I was very tempted to list a cheese substitute as an optional ingredient in these particular recipes. But written in this fashion, the recipes I had developed appeared as if something were missing, when in truth I knew the recipes tested quite well on their own. On the other hand, I wanted to make this book as user-friendly as possible. Then there was the problem of cheese substitutes themselves, which not only tend to taste overly strong, but often contain casein, a milk by-product. And so it went. Finally, I asked myself what a Ligurian cook of modest means, set on making pesto to sauce the potatoes and green beans she planned on serving with pasta later that day, would do with a thriving patch of basil in the garden, a good olive oil in the pantry, and lots of garlic in the cellar, only to discover that she had used her last scraps of Parmesan rind (perhaps the oldest cheese "substitute" of all) in yesterday's minestrone? The answer was simple: like her mother and grandmother before her, she would make do with what was at hand. So, too, would I, and leave the matter of cheese substitutes in the cooks' hands.

If you do choose to use cheese substitutes in the recipes throughout this book, particularly in the pasta recipes not containing pesto, please note that they have been included in this book specifically because the majority of Italian cooks traditionally serve them without cheese. Indeed, a sprinkling, let alone a showering, of grated cheese is generally considered inappropriate on pasta tossed with the following sauces: marinara sauce, arrabbiata and other hot red pepper sauces, olive and caper sauces, mushroom or truffle sauces with an olive oil base, most olive oil and garlic-based vegetable sauces (such as those using green beans, zucchini, sweet peppers, roasted tomatoes, broccoli, broccoli rabe, cauliflower, asparagus, artichokes, and potatoes), most olive oil–based fresh herb sauces (with or without garlic), most olive oil–based nut sauces (with or without garlic), and any sauce containing saffron or dried fruit. Risotto, on the other hand, when made with butter, as it often is in northern Italy, is usually finished with a generous addition of grated cheese. However, when prepared with olive oil or with the addition of saffron, as in the recipes included in this book, it is typically omitted.

What about anchovies? Aren't they an integral part of Mediterranean cuisine, used to flavor countless otherwise vegetarian dishes, particularly in Italian and Provençal cuisine? Yes, in fact, they are, but contrary to popular belief, not everyone who lives there is a fiend for anchovies, namely children, who need time to acquire a taste for these salty creatures. While they would never be absent from a dish such as the infamously named "streetwalker-style" spaghetti alla puttanesca (just as ricotta salata cheese would never be missing from the popular pasta alla Norma), they are occasionally omitted from tapenades (Provençal olive pastes) and certain pizza and pasta dishes. Therefore, I decided that listing a substitute for anchovies (miso sauce is a common one) for the recipes in this book was not necessary.

What about butter? Isn't it used more frequently than one might expect in such major olive-producing areas, especially in baked desserts? Yes and no. With its higher price tag and shorter shelf life, butter is considered a luxury item in many households and is often reserved for special occasions. While baklava is almost exclusively made with butter, or, at the very least, a mix of butter and olive oil, many baked desserts now derive their fat from extra-light olive oil, canola oil, or vegetable shortening. Consequently, a butter substitute simply isn't necessary for the recipes in this book.

What about honey? Isn't it used frequently as a sweetener, particularly in fruit desserts? Yes, but in a contest, sugar easily wins, at least among my various reference sources. Figs are a major exception; with their natural affinity for honey, they are commonly roasted or cooked in compotes with this by-product of bees. Substituting corn syrup, barley malt, or even vegan honey always seemed odd to me. Aside from a suggested variation (namely, the fresh fig substitution for plums in the Plum Tart in Phyllo on page 219), you will find no recipes using fresh figs in this book. But as fresh ripe figs are probably one of the most delicious fruits on earth, they hardly need honey, let alone a honey substitute, anyway. On the other hand, panforte (a highly spiced Italian sweet bread similar to fruitcake), traditionally made with honey, can easily be made using light corn syrup, as it is on page 220. While I've no proof that Italian cooks in Italy ever make it with corn syrup, I know they do here—with all the spices in this highly seasoned cake, one hardly notices a difference.

A final note regarding any of the ingredients in this cookbook: Because nowhere are individual tastes and preferences more evidenced than in the act of eating, whatever you think works best for your taste buds and dietary needs, by all means use them.

About the Nutritional Numbers

All of the nutritional analyses in this book were compiled using MasterCook Deluxe 4.06 from SierraHome. However, as certain ingredients (wheat berries, broccoli rabe, Niçoise olives) were unknown to the software's authors at the time of compilation, substitutes of equivalent caloric and nutritional value were used in their place. Also, approximations based on the analysis of total ingredients used have been given for a few of the strained recipes, namely the vegetable broths, whose solid ingredients are overwhelmingly discarded after cooking.

All of the recipes using broth have been analyzed using low-sodium canned vegetable broth. All the recipes using beans such as chickpeas and cannellini beans have been analyzed using freshly cooked dried beans. However, if thoroughly rinsed and drained canned beans have been used in the recipe, the nutritional value and sodium content should be equivalent to the freshly prepared dried beans. Unless salt is listed as a measured ingredient (versus to taste, with no preceding suggested measurement) in the recipe, no salt has been included in the analysis; this applies to other seasonings (black pepper, cayenne, nutmeg) as well. None of the recipes' optional ingredients have been included in the nutritional analyses. If there is a choice of two or more ingredients in a recipe (for example, spinach or dandelion greens), the first ingredient has been used in the analysis. When a range of number of servings is given, the analysis is done using the smaller number.

Reducing Fat Content

Keep in mind that this is not a diet book, but a cookbook of healthy recipes that are cholesterol-free, low in saturated fat, and high in fiber. With the exception of the cakes and tarts, it is generally easy to reduce the total fat of the recipes, if you so desire. The easiest method is to substitute broth or water for up to about half of the oil. For example, if a recipe that requires softening or browning chopped onions calls for sautéing them in two tablespoons of olive oil before adding other ingredients, you can use one tablespoon of oil in a good nonstick skillet, and add broth or water as necessary to prevent sticking until the onions are cooked to the desired state. Baked, roasted, and braised dishes essentially work on the same principle; add broth or water to prevent sticking, and turn or stir them more frequently. Sauces, such as pesto, and many salad dressings can also be lightened by substituting vegetable broth, preferably the Concentrated Vegetable Broth (page 37), for up to about half of the oil. While you certainly could try reducing the fat even further, I'm afraid that the recipes' authentic flavor would be greatly diminished and, so too, your enjoyment of the dishes.

The Mediterranean Vegan Kitchen

Appetizers

Meze, Tapas, Antipasti, Hors d'oeuvres, and Other Tempting Snacks and Starters

Like so many ideas about Mediterranean food, the existential purpose of appetizers relates to the moment at hand. During a hectic work week in Athens, meze, or *mezéthes,* as the Greeks say, may be nothing more than a few olives to wash down with a quick cup of coffee at a busy taverna before rushing back to the office. On a lazy Sunday afternoon at an outdoor café in Cyprus, to keep the customers lingering over their ouzo (and the café owner's coffers filled), meze can become part of a seductive table set not only with olives of varying color, size, and taste, but with hummus, baba ghanouj, and stuffed grape leaves.

Tapas are the legendary Spanish equivalent of bar food, served to fill the hunger gap between lunch and the traditional late-hour dinner. Ranging from little bowls of unadorned nuts and olives to small dishes of sautéed mushrooms anointed with garlic sauce to platters of grilled vegetables crowned with Salsa Romesco, the world-class Catalan almond sauce, tapas also have a knack for inspiring conversation and camaraderie. Indeed, should the talk and tapas prove too good to cut short, it's not unusual for a Spaniard to skip dinner altogether and go *de tapas* (tapas-romping) with friends.

Antipasto literally means "before the meal." As such, antipasti are seldom on the menu at drinking establishments in Italy; rather, like French hors d'oeuvres, they are the stuff of restaurants and special dinners, served as introductions to the main event. Classic bruschetta—thick slices of toasted bread rubbed with garlic and drizzled with olive oil—and countless olives are standard year-round favorites. In winter, at the height of the truffle season, crostini à la scheggino, or thin toasts spread with a black truffle sauce, are savored with reverence. In spring, assorted raw and lightly blanched baby vegetables such as violet artichokes, wild asparagus, and fennel root are presented with great fanfare for dipping into pinziminio—nothing more than the finest of the year's olive oil into which generous amounts of coarse salt and black pepper have been ground.

Hors d'oeuvre literally means "outside the work," the work referring to the entrée. An hors d'oeuvre's reason for being is to whet the diner's appetite, not overwhelm it. In Provence, roasted whole heads of garlic squeezed onto toasted baguette rounds are one of the more rustic methods of accomplishing this goal, while marinated vegetables, or crudités, served with eggplant "caviar" are one of the more elegant. Always there are olives. Ask a Frenchman why this is so and chances are he'll answer, *"Pourquoi pas?"* Why not, indeed!

Stuffed Artichokes, Niçoise-Style

This classic dish is a terrific method of preparing and eating medium-size artichokes. Although served as a standard hors d'oeuvre in Provence, a stuffed artichoke makes a satisfying lunch or light supper accompanied with a soup and green salad. Surrounded with the Peas Braised with Lettuce and Mint (page 150) and Wild Mushrooms in Garlic Sauce (page 22), it makes an elegant meal.

MAKES 6 SERVINGS

- 1 large lemon, halved
- 6 globe artichokes (about 8 ounces each)
- 2 tablespoons extra-virgin olive oil
- 1 large onion (about 8 ounces), finely chopped
- 6 cloves garlic, finely chopped
- 6 ounces plum tomatoes (about 3 small), seeded and finely chopped
- ¼ cup Niçoise or other good-quality black olives, pitted and finely chopped
- 1½ tablespoons finely chopped fresh flat-leaf parsley
- 1 tablespoon fresh thyme leaves or 1 teaspoon crumbled dried thyme leaves
- Salt and freshly ground black pepper, to taste
- ¾ cup unseasoned dry bread crumbs
- 1½ cups vegetable broth, preferably Basic Vegetable Broth (page 38), or low-sodium canned
- 1½ cups dry white wine

Preheat the oven to 400F (205C). Fill a large bowl with water and add the juice from a lemon half. Cut off the stem of each artichoke flush to the base so that the artichokes can stand upright. Cut 1 to 2 inches from the tops. Bend back and pull off the tough, dark green outer leaves to expose the pale green hearts. With your fingers, spread open the center of each artichoke; twist out the inner purple-tinged leaves. With a melon baller or sharp grapefruit spoon, scoop out and discard the hairy choke in the center. Drop each artichoke into the lemon water when you finish to prevent browning.

In a medium nonstick skillet, heat the oil over medium heat. Add the onion and cook, stirring often, until softened but not browned, about 5 minutes. Reduce the heat to low and add the garlic. Cook, stirring occasionally, until the onion is translucent and the garlic is fragrant, 3 to 5 minutes.

Remove the skillet from the heat and add the tomatoes, olives, parsley, thyme, salt, and pepper; stir well to combine. Stir in the bread crumbs until combined. With a wooden spoon, divide the bread crumb mixture into 6 equal mounds. Loosely stuff the centers of the artichokes with the bread crumb mixture, placing some in between the leaves, if necessary.

Place the stuffed artichokes upright in the bottom of a baking dish just large enough to hold them, gently touching each other, in a single layer. Add the broth, wine, juice from the remaining lemon half, and water, if necessary, to come halfway up the sides of the artichokes.

Cover the dish tightly and bake for 1 hour and 15 minutes, or until the artichokes are very tender when pierced near the base with the tip of a sharp knife. With a slotted spoon, transfer the artichokes to a serving platter, or individual serving plates, and keep warm.

Strain the cooking liquid into a small nonreactive saucepan. Boil the liquid over high heat until reduced to a syrupy sauce, about 6 tablespoons;

pour over or around the artichokes. Serve slightly warm or at room temperature.

Advance Preparation The baked stuffed artichokes can be held at room temperature for one hour before serving, or covered and refrigerated for up to twelve hours. Reheat, covered, in a low oven. Serve slightly warm for the best flavor.

PER SERVING

Calories 245 · Protein 8g · Total Fat 8g · Saturated Fat 1g · Cholesterol 0mg · Carbohydrate 28g · Dietary Fiber 7g · Sodium 468mg

Catalan Tomato Bread

The Catalan cousin of Italian bruschetta, tomato bread is a highly popular snack in both Spanish and French Catalonia. It's delicious and a resourceful way to use up any overripe, visually imperfect tomatoes sitting on the windowsill or languishing in the garden during the late summer and early fall. This recipe easily doubles to serve eight.

MAKES 4 SERVINGS

- ½ baguette (about 5 ounces), cut in half crosswise, then cut in half horizontally
- 1 clove garlic, halved
- 1 very ripe medium tomato (about 6 ounces), cut in half crosswise
- 2 teaspoons extra-virgin olive oil
- Salt, preferably the coarse variety
- Freshly ground black pepper, to taste

Grill or toast the bread lightly on the cut sides. Rub the grilled sides with the flat sides of the cut garlic.

Squeeze the tomato halves evenly into the toasted sides of the bread, rubbing in the tomato pulp; discard the skin. Drizzle each piece of bread with ½ teaspoon of the oil. Sprinkle each piece with a few grains of coarse salt, if using, or more if using the regular table variety, and season with pepper. Serve at room temperature.

PER SERVING

Calories 126 · Protein 4g · Total Fat 3g · Saturated Fat 1g · Cholesterol 0mg · Carbohydrate 20g · Dietary Fiber 1g · Sodium 219mg

Bruschetta with Cannellini Beans, Bitter Greens, and Tomatoes

A slightly simpler variation of Crostini with Pureed White Beans and Sautéed Wild Greens (page 9), here the beans are not pureed, nor the greens sautéed. Double the recipe, and you have a casual open-faced sandwich dish to serve six for lunch or a light supper.

MAKES 6 SERVINGS

- 2 tablespoons extra-virgin olive oil
- 2 large cloves garlic, 1 finely chopped, 1 halved
- 1 cup cooked cannellini beans (see Box, page 18) or about ⅔ (15-ounce) can cannellini, Great Northern, or navy beans, drained and rinsed

¼ cup vegetable broth, preferably Basic Vegetable Broth (page 38) or low-sodium canned
Salt and freshly ground black pepper, to taste
About 6 (½-inch-thick) slices Italian bread (about 1 ounce each), lightly toasted or grilled on one side
½ cup packed stemmed and chopped arugula, escarole, dandelion, endive, watercress, or other bitter greens
1 medium ripe tomato (about 6 ounces), seeded and chopped
Coarse salt (optional)

In a small saucepan, heat 1 tablespoon of the oil over medium-low heat. Add the chopped garlic and cook, stirring, for 2 minutes. Add the beans, broth, salt, and pepper. Bring to a simmer over medium-high heat. Reduce the heat to medium-low and cook, uncovered, stirring occasionally, until the mixture is thickened and very creamy, about 10 minutes.

Rub the toasted sides of the bread with the flat sides of the garlic halves. Top each slice evenly with the bean mixture, using about 2 tablespoons per piece; top with the greens, then the chopped tomato. Sprinkle with a little coarse salt, if using, or additional table salt and another grinding of pepper. Drizzle each piece with ½ teaspoon of the remaining oil and serve at once.

PER SERVING

Calories 177 · Protein 7g · Total Fat 6g · Saturated Fat 1g · Cholesterol 0mg · Carbohydrate 25g · Dietary Fiber 4g · Sodium 202mg

Bruschetta with Tomatoes and Basil

The popular duo of tomato and basil is in top form in this favorite bruschetta or crostini topping. To achieve its proper consistency, use a chef's knife instead of a food processor to chop the tomatoes.

MAKES 6 SERVINGS

¾ pound ripe tomatoes, preferably vine-ripened, seeded, and finely chopped
2 tablespoons finely chopped fresh basil
1 tablespoon extra-virgin olive oil
½ teaspoon balsamic or sherry vinegar
Salt, preferably the coarse variety, to taste
Freshly ground black pepper, to taste
About 6 (½-inch-thick) pieces of Italian bread (about 1 ounce each), lightly toasted or grilled on one side
1 large clove garlic, halved
About 6 small whole basil leaves (optional)

Place the tomatoes, chopped basil, oil, vinegar, salt, and pepper in a medium bowl; toss well to combine. Set aside for a few minutes to allow the flavors to blend.

Rub the toasted sides of the bread with the flat sides of the garlic halves. Top each slice evenly with the tomato mixture, using about 2 tablespoons per piece. Garnish each with a whole basil leaf, if desired. Serve at room temperature.

PER SERVING

Calories 111 · Protein 3g · Total Fat 3g · Saturated Fat 1g · Cholesterol 0mg · Carbohydrate 18g · Dietary Fiber 2g · Sodium 170mg

Variation To make crostini, either cut the Italian bread in half crosswise or substitute it with twice the amount of thin rounds of toasted baguette. Instead of rubbing the bread with the halved garlic, chop the garlic and add it to the tomato-basil mixture.

Bruschetta with Tomatoes, Black Olives, and Marinated Artichokes

This tangy topping also makes an excellent raw tomato sauce for hot pasta. Well-drained, finely chopped marinated sun-dried tomatoes can be substituted for about one-quarter of the artichokes, if desired.

MAKES 6 SERVINGS

1 medium ripe tomato (about 6 ounces), seeded and finely chopped
6 kalamata or other large good-quality black olives, pitted and finely chopped
¼ cup drained marinated artichoke hearts, finely chopped
1 tablespoon finely chopped fresh basil
1 tablespoon finely chopped fresh flat-leaf parsley
1 tablespoon extra-virgin olive oil
½ teaspoon red wine vinegar
Salt, preferably the coarse variety, to taste
Freshly ground black pepper, to taste
About 6 (½-inch-thick) pieces of Italian bread (about 1 ounce each), lightly toasted or grilled on one side
1 large clove garlic, halved

Place the tomato, olives, artichokes, basil, parsley, oil, vinegar, salt, and pepper in a medium mixing bowl; toss well to combine. Set aside for a few minutes to allow the flavors to blend.

Rub the toasted sides of the bread with the flat sides of the garlic halves. Top each slice evenly with the tomato mixture, using about 2 tablespoons per piece. Serve at room temperature.

PER SERVING

Calories 117 · Protein 3g · Total Fat 4g · Saturated Fat 1g · Cholesterol 0mg · Carbohydrate 17g · Dietary Fiber 2g · Sodium 235mg

Classic Bruschetta with Olive Oil, Garlic, and Coarse Salt

Called *fettunta* in Tuscany, the original bruschetta was nothing more than garlic bread doused with first-pressed olive oil, then sprinkled with a bit of coarse salt. After one bite, you'll never want to go back to the store-bought, garlic-salted variety again.

MAKES 6 SERVINGS

6 (½-inch-thick) slices Italian bread (about 1 ounce each), lightly toasted or grilled on one or both sides
1 large clove garlic, halved
1 tablespoon extra-virgin olive oil
¼ teaspoon coarse salt, or to taste

Rub a toasted side of each bread slice with the flat sides of the garlic halves, then brush the same sides evenly with ½ teaspoon of the oil.

Sprinkle the oiled sides with a few grains of coarse salt. Serve at room temperature.

PER SERVING

Calories 98 · Protein 3g · Total Fat 3g · Saturated Fat 1g · Cholesterol 0mg · Carbohydrate 14g · Dietary Fiber 1g · Sodium 244mg

Chickpeas with Parsley-Tahini Sauce

This addictive appetizer—rather like an unmashed hummus—is terrific with pita bread, crackers, or served in butter lettuce or radicchio leaves. Ready in just about five minutes using canned chickpeas, you simply can't beat its convenience when unexpected guests drop by.

MAKES 4 TO 6 SERVINGS

2 cups cooked chickpeas (see Box, page 18) or 1 (19-ounce) can chickpeas, drained and rinsed
½ cup packed fresh flat-leaf parsley, finely chopped
2 tablespoons sesame tahini (see Cook's Tip, page 15)
2 large cloves garlic, finely chopped
Juice of ½ large lemon (about 2 tablespoons)
Salt and freshly ground black pepper, to taste
Pita bread, crackers, or whole butter lettuce and/or radicchio leaves (optional)

In a medium bowl, toss the chickpeas, parsley, tahini, garlic, lemon juice, salt, and pepper until well combined. Serve at room temperature, or refrigerate for at least 1 hour and serve chilled, accompanied by the pita bread, crackers, or lettuce leaves, if desired.

Advance Preparation The mixture can be stored, covered, in the refrigerator for up to two days.

PER SERVING

Calories 186 · Protein 9g · Total Fat 6g · Saturated Fat 1g · Cholesterol 0mg · Carbohydrate 26g · Dietary Fiber 1g · Sodium 11mg

Provençal Chickpea Puree

This is the south of France's version of hummus, minus the tahini. It's a particularly good dip or spread with Garlic-Herb Pita Toasts (page 26).

MAKES 6 TO 8 SERVINGS

2½ cups cooked chickpeas (see Box, page 18) or about 1¾ (15-ounce) cans chickpeas, drained and rinsed
1 tablespoon extra-virgin olive oil
1 tablespoon fresh lemon juice or to taste
About 1 tablespoon vegetable broth, preferably Basic Vegetable Broth (page 38) or low-sodium canned
2 cloves garlic, finely chopped
2 tablespoons finely chopped fresh parsley
Salt and freshly ground black pepper, to taste
Sweet paprika
Pitted Niçoise or other good-quality black olives (optional)
Assorted raw vegetables and/or toasted baguette rounds

Place the chickpeas, oil, lemon juice, 1 tablespoon broth, and garlic in a food processor fitted with the metal blade or in a blender. Process or blend until smooth and pureed, adding more broth as necessary to achieve a spreadable consistency.

Transfer the mixture to a serving bowl and add the parsley, salt, and pepper, stirring well to combine. Taste and add additional lemon juice, if desired, stirring well to combine. Sprinkle with paprika and scatter the olives, if using, over the top. Serve at room temperature as a dip with raw vegetables or as a spread with toasted baguette rounds.

Advance Preparation The mixture can be covered and refrigerated for up to two days. Bring to room temperature before serving.

PER SERVING

Calories 135 · Protein 6g · Total Fat 4g · Saturated Fat 1g · Cholesterol 0mg · Carbohydrate 19g · Dietary Fiber 2g · Sodium 11mg

Provençal Chickpea Flour Pancake

Known as socca, this is the original fast food of Nice, a giant chickpea flour pancake sold on the streets throughout the region. Essentially a snack, it makes for an interesting appetizer or first course, as well. But if you are a traditionalist, be forewarned: Although a bit on the messy side, socca is eaten in Nice without benefit of a fork. Chickpea flour can be located in most health food stores and in Indian markets, but make sure it is the plain, not spiced, variety.

MAKES 4 TO 6 APPETIZER SERVINGS

⅔ cup chickpea (garbanzo bean) flour
2 cups water
3 tablespoons extra-virgin olive oil
¼ teaspoon salt
Coarse salt and freshly ground black pepper, to taste

In a medium bowl, whisk together the flour and water; strain into another medium bowl. Whisk in 2 tablespoons of the oil and the ¼ teaspoon salt. Let stand for a minimum of 30 minutes, up to 6 hours, at room temperature.

Preheat the oven to 500F (260C). Brush a 10½-inch cast-iron skillet with the remaining oil. Place in the center of the oven for 5 minutes, or until the oil just begins to smoke.

Carefully remove the skillet from the oven. Whisk the batter vigorously, then very slowly pour it into the hot skillet, taking care as the batter may splatter. Return the skillet to the oven and bake, checking often after 10 minutes, for about 15

Cook's Tip

You can use a preheated standard pizza pan if you don't own a cast-iron skillet, but the results won't be quite as satisfactory—the even-heating qualities of the latter simulate those of the huge copper pans used in Nice to a greater degree. But don't expect a pizzalike texture or an American-style pancake, for that matter. Good socca is slightly crisp on the outside and creamy on the inside, so take care not to overcook it. Also, socca by its nature tends to stick a bit to the surface. However, if your cast-iron skillet has been properly oiled and heated, the sticking will be minimal.

minutes, or until the top of the pancake is nicely browned and the mixture is bubbling.

Remove the skillet from the oven and immediately sprinkle with the coarse salt and pepper. Divide the socca into 6 wedges with a knife. Using a thin metal spatula or a pie server, gently scrape and lift each wedge out of the pan and transfer to serving plates. Serve at once.

PER SERVING

Calories 136 · Protein 1g · Total Fat 10g · Saturated Fat 1g · Cholesterol 0mg · Carbohydrate 10g · Dietary Fiber 0g · Sodium 133mg

Crostini with Pureed White Beans and Sautéed Wild Greens (La Capriata)

Dating back to Greek rule, this is a highly popular dish throughout the Apulia region of Italy. Although it is traditionally made with bitter-tasting greens such as dandelion or escarole, sweeter greens such as spinach or Swiss chard can easily be substituted. Surrounded with the optional garnishes, this makes a visually appetizing antipasto platter.

MAKES 4 TO 6 SERVINGS

- 2 cups cooked cannellini beans (see Box, page 18) or 1 (19-ounce) can cannellini, Great Northern, or navy beans, drained and rinsed
- About 3 tablespoons vegetable broth, preferably Basic Vegetable Broth (page 38) or low-sodium canned
- 2 tablespoons extra-virgin olive oil
- ½ teaspoon dried rubbed sage
- Salt and freshly ground black pepper, to taste
- ½ cup finely chopped onion
- 2 cloves garlic, finely chopped
- 8 ounces dandelion, curly endive, escarole, rapini, or other bitter greens, washed, stemmed, and coarsely chopped
- Thinly sliced red onion (optional)
- Thinly sliced radishes (optional)
- Chopped fresh tomatoes (optional)
- Chopped black olives (optional)
- Toasted baguette rounds or toasted slices of Italian bread, halved crosswise, to serve

Place the beans, broth, 1 tablespoon of the oil, sage, salt, and pepper in a food processor fitted with the metal blade. Process with on/off motions until a chunky puree is formed. Transfer to a medium saucepan and cook over low heat, stirring occasionally, until heated through. Keep warm until needed, adding more broth if the mixture appears to be drying out.

In a large nonstick skillet, heat the remaining oil over medium heat. Add the onion and garlic and cook, stirring often, until softened but not browned, about 3 minutes. Add the greens and increase the heat to medium-high. Cook, tossing and stirring constantly, until wilted, 2 to 3 minutes. Remove from the heat and season lightly with salt and pepper. Keep warm until needed.

To serve, spoon the warm bean puree into the middle of a warmed serving platter, and top with the sautéed greens. Surround with the optional garnishes, if using. Serve at once, accompanied by the toasted bread.

PER SERVING

(without bread):

Calories 222 · Protein 11g · Total Fat 8g · Saturated Fat 1g · Cholesterol 0mg · Carbohydrate 30g · Dietary Fiber 10g · Sodium 74mg

Crostini with Radicchio, Balsamic Vinegar, and Olive Oil

Probably because the differences are negligible, crostini are often confused with bruschetta, and vice versa. I've found that the toppings are used interchangeably. Usually crostini are made with toasted pieces of thinly sliced French baguette or thinly sliced Italian bread or boule, cut in half, whereas bruschetta is typically made with larger slices of toasted Italian bread that have been rubbed with a cut clove of garlic. Whichever bread you choose, so long as it's lightly toasted or grilled on at least its top side to prevent sogginess, your crostini, or bruschetta if you'd rather, will be delicious spread with this colorful and healthy topping. MAKES 4 TO 6 SERVINGS

- 2 small heads radicchio (about 4 ounces each), separated into leaves, rinsed and drained well
- 2 tablespoons extra-virgin olive oil
- 1 tablespoon balsamic vinegar
- ½ teaspoon coarse salt, or to taste
- Freshly ground black pepper, to taste
- About 16 (½-inch-thick) pieces baguette or 8 (½-inch-thick) slices Italian bread or boule, halved crosswise, lightly toasted

Place the radicchio in a food processor fitted with the metal blade; process until finely chopped. Add the oil, vinegar, salt, and pepper; pulse until just combined.

Spoon evenly over the toasted bread, using 2 to 3 teaspoons per piece, and serve at room temperature.

Advance Preparation The topping can be covered and refrigerated for up to one day. Bring to room temperature before serving.

PER SERVING

Calories 150 · Protein 3g · Total Fat 8g · Saturated Fat 1g · Cholesterol 0mg · Carbohydrate 17g · Dietary Fiber 1g · Sodium 419mg

Crostini with Tomatoes, Capers, and Thyme

The topping for this piquant crostini rossi from Tuscany is equally excellent over broiled or toasted polenta. Not surprisingly, it's also great with tortilla chips! MAKES 4 TO 6 SERVINGS

- 1 slice fresh whole-wheat bread (about 1 ounce), crust removed
- 1 tablespoon red wine vinegar
- 2 medium ripe tomatoes (about 6 ounces each), seeded and quartered
- 2 tablespoons chopped fresh parsley

- 1 tablespoon fresh thyme leaves or 1 teaspoon dried
- 1 tablespoon drained capers
- 1 tablespoon extra-virgin olive oil
- 1 large clove garlic, finely chopped
- ¼ teaspoon coarse salt, or to taste
- Freshly ground black pepper
- 12 to 16 (½-inch-thick) pieces baguette or 6 to 8 (½-inch-thick) slices Italian bread or boule, halved crosswise, lightly toasted

Place the whole-wheat bread on a small plate and sprinkle with the vinegar. With your fingers, press down until all the vinegar has been absorbed. In a food processor fitted with the metal blade, combine the soaked bread, tomatoes, parsley, thyme, capers, oil, garlic, salt, and pepper to taste. Pulse until well combined but still a bit chunky.

Spoon 2 to 3 teaspoons evenly over each piece of bread and serve at room temperature.

Advance Preparation The topping can be covered and refrigerated for up to one day. Bring to room temperature before serving.

PER SERVING

Calories 129 · Protein 3g · Total Fat 5g · Saturated Fat 1g · Cholesterol 0mg · Carbohydrate 20g · Dietary Fiber 2g · Sodium 312mg

Crostini with Black Truffle Sauce (Crostini à la Scheggino)

Truffles, indeed, are expensive, but every now and again they're worth the splurge—even for an appetizer. Fortunately, black truffles are more common and therefore more affordable than the white variety; they are available in jars or cans in most gourmet and specialty markets and some well-stocked supermarkets. **MAKES 4 SERVINGS**

- 1 tablespoon extra-virgin olive oil
- ½ ounce (dry weight) jarred black truffles (about 2 small), drained, finely chopped or grated
- 1 large clove garlic, finely chopped
- ½ teaspoon fresh lemon juice or to taste
- Salt and freshly ground black pepper, to taste
- About 8 (½-inch-thick) slices baguette or 4 (½-inch-thick) slices Italian bread or boule, halved crosswise, lightly toasted

In a small skillet, heat the olive oil over medium heat. Add the truffles and garlic and cook, stirring constantly, for 1 minute once the mixture begins to sizzle. Remove from the heat and add the lemon juice, salt and pepper, stirring well to combine.

Spoon evenly over the bread and serve warm or at room temperature.

PER SERVING

Calories 71 · Protein 1g · Total Fat 4g · Saturated Fat 1g · Cholesterol 0mg · Carbohydrate 8g · Dietary Fiber 1g · Sodium 87mg

Variations Substitute ¼ teaspoon black or white truffle–flavored olive oil for ¼ teaspoon of the olive oil. The use of a few drops of truffle-flavored olive oil, found in gourmet and specialty markets, intensifies the truffle flavor of the dish.

Pasta à la Scheggino

To serve two as a special-occasion pasta course, double the above recipe, substituting 4 ounces of spaghettini or other thin pasta, cooked according to package directions, for the toasted bread. Toss the pasta with the truffle sauce, 1 tablespoon of finely chopped fresh flat-leaf parsley, and coarse salt to taste. Serve immediately, accompanied with fresh Italian or French bread to capture any bits of truffle left on the plate.

PER SERVING

Calories 339 · Protein 8g · Total Fat 15g · Saturated Fat 2g · Cholesterol 0mg · Carbohydrate 44g · Dietary Fiber 2g · Sodium 6mg

Garlic Puree with Croutons

In Provence, this fragrant and remarkably sweet puree is used on bread like butter. Often, the intact heads of garlic are roasted in the oven and served whole for each diner to squeeze onto his or her toasted baguette rounds, but I find the following stovetop method more convenient and equally delicious. This versatile spread also makes a great topping for grilled eggplant, a filling for broiled mushrooms, and a thickener for soups or sauces. If you don't have a food mill, press the garlic through a fine-mesh sieve with the back of a large heavy spoon. The recipe easily doubles, but count on several more minutes of simmering.

MAKES 4 TO 6 SERVINGS

- 2 heads garlic, separated into cloves, skins on
- 1 cup vegetable broth, preferably Basic Vegetable Broth (page 38) or low-sodium canned
- 2 cups water
- ½ tablespoon extra-virgin olive oil
- 16 to 20 (½-inch-thick) pieces baguette, lightly toasted

In a small saucepan, combine the garlic, broth, and water; bring to a boil over high heat. Reduce the heat and simmer, uncovered, briskly for about 1 hour, or until almost all of the liquid has evaporated.

Run the garlic and remaining liquid through a food mill; discard skins. Place the puree in a small mixing bowl and blend well with the oil.

Spread about ½ teaspoon evenly on each piece of bread and serve at room temperature.

Advance Preparation The puree can be covered and refrigerated for two to three days. Bring to room temperature before serving.

PER SERVING

Calories 136 · Protein 7g · Total Fat 3g · Saturated Fat 0g · Cholesterol 0mg · Carbohydrate 22g · Dietary Fiber 2g · Sodium 306mg

Cook's Tip

To toast the baguette rounds, preheat the oven to 400F (205C). Arrange the bread in a single layer on an ungreased light-colored baking sheet and bake on the middle rack of the oven for 5 minutes, or until lightly toasted.

Wild Mushroom Spread with Croutons

This earthy and warming Provençal-style ragout makes a splendid spread for croutons, crostini, or bruschetta during the fall and winter months. Leftovers can be added to stews, soups, or pasta sauces, as well. **MAKES 4 TO 6 SERVINGS**

- 1 ounce dried porcini or other wild mushrooms
- 1 tablespoon extra-virgin olive oil
- 8 ounces white button mushrooms, cleaned, trimmed, and sliced
- 2 large cloves garlic, finely chopped
- Salt and freshly ground black pepper, to taste
- 2 tablespoons marsala, port, sherry, or Madeira
- 2 tablespoons finely chopped fresh parsley
- 16 to 20 (½-inch-thick) baguette rounds, lightly toasted

Soak the porcini mushrooms in 1 cup hot water for 15 minutes; drain, and reserve the soaking liquid. Strain the soaking liquid through a coffee filter or paper towel–lined strainer. Reserve ½ cup and set aside. (Save the remaining strained liquid for soups or stocks, if desired.) Rinse the mushrooms thoroughly; chop coarsely and set aside.

In a large nonstick skillet, heat the oil over medium heat. Add the porcini mushrooms, button mushrooms, garlic, salt, and pepper. Cook, stirring often, until the mushrooms have started to give off their liquid, 3 to 5 minutes.

Add the marsala and reserved soaking liquid to the skillet; bring to a boil over high heat. Cook, stirring constantly, until the liquids are greatly reduced and syrupy. Remove from the heat and add the parsley, stirring well to combine. Taste and season with additional salt and pepper if needed.

Serve warm with the baguette rounds.

Advance Preparation The spread, without the parsley, can be covered and held over very low heat for up to one hour before serving. It can also be stored, covered, in the refrigerator for up to twenty-four hours. Reheat over low heat.

PER SERVING

Calories 150 · Protein 5g · Total Fat 5g · Saturated Fat 1g · Cholesterol 0mg · Carbohydrate 23g · Dietary Fiber 2g · Sodium 177mg

Eggplant Roll-Ups with Pesto

While it's true that purists often pooh-pooh the use of pesto on any vegetable other than potatoes or green beans, the combination of grilled eggplant and pesto is too good to pass up. To turn this appetizer, first course, or side dish into a complete meal, serve warm over rice, orzo, or couscous. **MAKES 6 SERVINGS**

- 1 (1¾-pound) eggplant
- Salt
- 2 tablespoons extra-virgin olive oil
- ½ cup Poor Man's Pesto (page 107)

Trim both ends of the eggplant and stand it upright on its flattest end. Remove most of the skin in thin slices. Cut lengthwise into 2 equal halves. Place 1 half, cut side down, on a cutting board. With one hand resting on top of the eggplant, make 6 equal lengthwise cuts with a large sharp knife. Repeat with the other half. Sprinkle the eggplant slices with salt, and place in a colander to drain for 30 minutes. Rinse under cold running water and pat dry with paper towels. (If time doesn't permit, omit salting and draining eggplant that is to be stewed or baked with several ingredients, as any bitterness is typically masked by the other flavors.)

Meanwhile, preheat the broiler. Lightly oil 2 baking sheets and set aside.

Place the eggplant slices on the prepared baking sheets. Brush the tops evenly with 1 tablespoon of the oil. Broil about 4 inches from the heat source until lightly browned, 2 to 3 minutes. Turn the slices over, brush the tops with the remaining oil, and broil until lightly browned, 2 to 3 minutes. Remove the baking sheets from the oven; reduce the oven temperature to 425F (220C).

Brush 2 teaspoons of the pesto down the center of each eggplant slice. Starting at the narrow end, roll up. Transfer all the rolls, seam-side down, to a baking sheet. Cover the baking sheet with foil and bake for 10 minutes, or until the eggplant is fork tender and the pesto is heated through. Serve warm or at room temperature.

PER SERVING

Calories 197 · Protein 5g · Total Fat 15g · Saturated Fat 2g · Cholesterol 0mg · Carbohydrate 18g · Dietary Fiber 6g · Sodium 127mg

Roasted Eggplant Salad
(Baba Ghanouj)

Just a few years ago baba ghanouj was enjoyed almost exclusively in Middle Eastern restaurants and markets. It has since become a standard selection on several American-style menus and behind many mainstream deli counters. The following recipe uses both raw and roasted garlic, and ground and toasted cumin—the slightly smokier results are tantalizing. MAKES 8 SERVINGS

- 2 large eggplants (about 1 pound each)
- 8 large cloves garlic, peeled, 6 left whole, 2 finely chopped
- 1½ tablespoons extra-virgin olive oil
- 2 teaspoons cumin seeds
- ¼ cup sesame tahini (see Cook's Tip, page 15)
- 4 to 6 tablespoons fresh lemon juice
- ¼ teaspoon ground cumin
- ⅛ to ¼ teaspoon cayenne (optional)
- Salt and freshly ground black pepper, to taste
- 2 tablespoons chopped fresh flat-leaf parsley
- Pita bread or 2 recipes Garlic-Herb Pita Toasts (page 26), to serve

Preheat the oven to 450F (230C). Pierce the eggplant in several places with the tines of a fork. Rub the eggplant and whole garlic with ½ tablespoon of the oil. Place the eggplant and garlic on an ungreased baking sheet. Roast for 5 minutes and turn the garlic. Roast for another 5 minutes and remove the garlic; set aside. Continue cooking the eggplant, turning frequently with tongs, for 15 to 25 minutes more, or until the skin is blackened and the insides are soft. Remove the baking sheet from the oven. (Do not turn off the oven.)

Carefully stem the eggplants. Cut each eggplant in half lengthwise; drain, cut-side down, on several layers of paper towels. Meanwhile, place the cumin seeds on a dry baking sheet or in a small ovenproof skillet; cook in the oven until fragrant and lightly toasted, stirring once, about 2 minutes. Set aside.

When the eggplant is cool enough to handle, strip away and discard the skin. Transfer the flesh to a food processor fitted with the metal blade. Mash the roasted garlic with a fork and add to the eggplant; pulse until just combined. Add the raw garlic, remaining oil, tahini, lemon juice, ground cumin, cayenne (if using), salt, and pepper; pulse until thoroughly combined.

Transfer to a serving bowl and add the toasted cumin seeds and the parsley, mixing well to combine. Let stand for 30 minutes at room temperature to allow the flavors to blend. Serve at room temperature, or cover and refrigerate for at least 2 hours, and serve chilled with the pita bread or the pita toasts.

Advance Preparation The dish, without the parsley, can be covered and refrigerated for up to two days. Bring to room temperature or serve chilled.

PER SERVING

Calories 100 · Protein 3g · Total Fat 7g · Saturated Fat 1g · Cholesterol 0mg · Carbohydrate 10g · Dietary Fiber 3g · Sodium 6mg

Cook's Tip

Tahini is an unctuous and nutlike paste made from ground sesame seeds. It is available in Middle Eastern markets, specialty stores, and many well-stocked supermarkets. Be sure to stir it well before using, as the oil and solids tend to separate in the container. In a pinch, smooth peanut butter, preferably a natural variety, can be substituted.

Provençal Eggplant Caviar

I like to add a roasted onion, a little tomato paste, and a splash of sherry vinegar to this classic eggplant spread—often called "poor man's caviar" in Provence. Excellent as a topping for croutons, or as a dip for crudités or bread sticks, it's actually better the next day, but it should be consumed within a few days for the best flavor.

MAKES 4 TO 6 SERVINGS

- 1 large eggplant (about 1 pound)
- 1 medium onion (about 6 ounces), peeled, left whole with stem intact
- 2 tablespoons extra-virgin olive oil
- 2 tablespoons fresh lemon juice
- 1 tablespoon tomato paste
- 2 large cloves garlic, finely chopped
- 1 teaspoon sherry vinegar or balsamic vinegar
- ⅛ teaspoon cayenne pepper or to taste
- Salt and freshly ground black pepper, to taste
- Assorted raw vegetables, bread sticks, and/or toasted baguette rounds, to serve

Preheat the oven to 400F (205C).

Pierce the eggplant in several places with the tines of a fork. Rub the eggplant and onion with 1 teaspoon of the oil. Place the eggplant and onion on an ungreased baking sheet. Roast for 40 to 50 minutes, turning frequently with tongs, or until the eggplant is collapsed and the onion is nicely browned. Carefully remove the eggplant stem. Cut the eggplant in half lengthwise; drain, cut side down, on several layers of paper towels. Set the onion aside to cool.

When the eggplant is cool enough to handle, strip away and discard the skin. Cut the flesh into quarters and transfer to a food processor fitted with the metal blade. Remove the stem from the onion and discard. Quarter the onion and add to the eggplant, along with the remaining oil, lemon juice, tomato paste, garlic, vinegar, cayenne, salt, and pepper. Process until very smooth.

Transfer to a serving bowl; cover and refrigerate for at least 2 hours to allow the flavors to blend. Serve chilled or return to room temperature. Accompany with raw vegetables, bread sticks, or toasted baguette rounds.

Advance Preparation The dish can be stored, covered, in the refrigerator for up to three days. Bring to room temperature or serve chilled.

PER SERVING

Calories 108 · Protein 2g · Total Fat 7g · Saturated Fat 1g · Cholesterol 0mg · Carbohydrate 11g · Dietary Fiber 3g · Sodium 37mg

Caponata

There are probably as many versions of this famous sweet and sour eggplant appetizer as there are cooks in southern Italy. The following rendition is my "baked" adaptation of a Sicilian recipe that calls for frying the eggplant in copious amounts of oil. Delicious on its own or as a side dish, caponata makes a fine topping for crostini, bruschetta, and polenta.

MAKES ABOUT 3 CUPS

- 2 tablespoons extra-virgin olive oil
- 1 large eggplant (about 1¼ pounds)
- Salt
- 1 medium onion (about 6 ounces), chopped
- 1 large stalk celery, chopped
- 2 medium ripe tomatoes (about 6 ounces each), peeled, seeded, and coarsely chopped
- ¼ cup water
- 2 tablespoons red wine vinegar
- 1 tablespoon tomato paste
- 1 tablespoon sugar
- ¼ cup black olives, preferably kalamata, pitted and coarsely chopped
- ¼ cup green olives, preferably Italian, pitted and coarsely chopped
- 1 tablespoon drained capers
- Freshly ground black pepper, to taste
- 1 to 2 tablespoons chopped fresh basil (optional)

Preheat the oven to 375F (190C). Brush a large baking sheet with ½ tablespoon of the oil and set aside.

Cut the eggplant into ½-inch cubes. Place the eggplant cubes in a colander, sprinkle with salt, and drain for 30 minutes. Rinse under cold running water and pat dry with paper towels. (If time doesn't permit, omit salting and draining eggplant that is to be stewed or baked with several ingredients, as any bitterness is typically masked by the other flavors.) Arrange the eggplant in a single layer on the prepared baking sheet. Quickly brush the eggplant with ½ tablespoon of the remaining oil. Bake for 20 minutes, turning and stirring once.

Meanwhile, heat the remaining 1 tablespoon of the oil in a large nonstick skillet over medium heat. Add the onion and celery and cook, stirring often, until softened but not browned, about 5 minutes. Stir in the tomatoes, reduce the heat to medium-low, and cook, uncovered, stirring occasionally, until the tomatoes are reduced to a pulpy consistency, about 25 minutes.

Add the water, vinegar, tomato paste, and sugar; blend well. Stir in the baked eggplant, olives, and capers; season with pepper. Cook for 5 to 10 minutes, stirring occasionally, until heated through and the flavors are well blended. Serve warm or at room temperature, garnished with the basil, if desired.

Advance Preparation The dish can be covered and refrigerated for up to three days. Bring to room temperature or reheat in a low oven before serving.

PER ¼ CUP

Calories 63 · Protein 1g · Total Fat 4g · Saturated Fat 0g · Cholesterol 0mg · Carbohydrate 7g · Dietary Fiber 2g · Sodium 127mg

Polenta Crostini with Caponata

For a quick and easy appetizer, top polenta with warm Caponata.

MAKES ABOUT 12 SQUARES; 4 TO 6 SERVINGS

2¼ cups water
¾ cup instant polenta
2 teaspoons extra-virgin olive oil
Salt, to taste
About ¾ cup warm Caponata (page 16)

Lightly oil an 8-inch-square flameproof baking dish; set aside. In a medium deep-sided saucepan (important, as the polenta sputters), combine the water, polenta, 1 teaspoon of the oil, and salt. On a back burner of the stove, bring to a boil over high heat; immediately reduce the heat to medium and cook, stirring often with a long-handled wooden spoon, for 5 minutes. Immediately spoon the polenta into the prepared dish, pressing down with the back of a large spoon to form a smooth surface. Let stand 20 minutes to become firm.

Preheat the broiler. Brush the top of the polenta with the remaining oil. Broil 4 to 6 inches from the heating element until lightly browned, 3 to 5 minutes. Remove from the oven and spread the warm caponata evenly over the top. Let cool slightly before cutting into 12 squares. Serve warm.

PER SQUARE

Calories 118 · Protein 2g · Total Fat 4g · Saturated Fat 0g · Cholesterol 0mg · Carbohydrate 19g · Dietary Fiber 3g · Sodium 64mg

Hummus with Roasted Red Pepper and Cilantro

In Israel, no cook worth his or her salt is without a good recipe for hummus, a ubiquitous spread of pureed chickpeas and tahini that shows up mostly on pita bread, but is terrific with bagels and raw vegetables, as well. Though not traditional, roasted red pepper and cilantro are often added to hummus. For a more classic version, see the variation below. MAKES 6 TO 8 SERVINGS

2 medium red bell peppers (about 6 ounces each), quartered
2 teaspoons whole cumin seeds or ½ teaspoon ground cumin
2 cups cooked chickpeas (see Box, below) or 1 (19-ounce) can chickpeas, rinsed and drained
¼ cup vegetable broth, preferably Basic Vegetable Broth (page 38) or low-sodium canned
3 to 4 tablespoons fresh lemon juice or to taste
3 tablespoons sesame tahini (see Cook's Tip, page 15)
2 large cloves garlic, finely chopped
Tabasco sauce
Salt, to taste
¼ cup chopped scallions, white and green parts
2 to 3 tablespoons chopped fresh cilantro
Pita bread or 2 recipes Garlic-Herb Pita Toasts (page 26) and/or assorted raw vegetables

Soaking and Cooking Dried Beans

Although most cooks cannot dispute the convenience of canned beans, many prefer the flavor and texture of dried beans cooked from scratch. To cook dried beans, first pick through them to find any small stones, then rinse well. Soak them for a minimum of eight hours in unsalted water equaling two to three times their volume.

Quick soak method: In a large saucepan or medium stockpot, bring the beans and enough unsalted water to cover by at least two inches to a boil over high heat. Boil for two minutes. Remove from the heat, cover, and let stand for one hour.

If not proceeding as directed in a specific recipe, drain the beans and replace with fresh water to cover by at least two inches. Bring to a brisk simmer over medium-high heat, reduce the heat to medium-low, and simmer for one to two hours, stirring occasionally, or until the beans are tender, depending on the type and age of the beans. Firm beans such as chickpeas and dried beans that have been stored for over a year tend to take longer. Otherwise, proceed as directed in the recipe. Cooked beans can be stored, covered, in the refrigerator for three or four days.

As a general rule, 1 cup of dried beans equals about 2 cups cooked beans. Approximating equivalent amounts of canned and fresh beans can be tricky if you just use the label on the can as a guide, because all of the recipes in this book using canned beans require that the beans be drained and rinsed first. As a general rule, one 19-ounce can drained and rinsed beans equals about 2 cups cooked beans, and one 15-ounce can drained and rinsed equals about 1½ cups cooked beans.

Preheat the oven to 400F (205C).

Arrange the peppers, skin side up, on an ungreased baking sheet. Roast for 20 minutes, or until the skins are blistered and beginning to char, adding the whole cumin seeds, if using, to the baking sheet (away from the peppers) for the last 3 to 4 minutes of cooking. Remove the baking sheet from the oven. Carefully place the peppers in a paper bag, twist tightly to close, and leave for about 20 minutes. Set aside the cumin seeds, if used.

Meanwhile, combine the chickpeas and broth in a food processor fitted with the metal blade; process until very smooth. Peel off the skins of the roasted peppers with your fingers or with a small paring knife and add to the chickpea mixture, along with the ground cumin, if using, lemon juice, tahini, garlic, and Tabasco sauce and salt to taste; process until very smooth. Transfer to a serving bowl and add the toasted cumin seeds, if used, scallions, and cilantro, stirring well to combine. Let stand at room temperature for 30 minutes to allow the flavors to blend. Serve with the pita bread or the pita toasts and/or raw vegetables.

Advance Preparation Without the scallions and cilantro, the hummus can be covered and refrigerated for up to three days. Bring to room temperature before serving.

PER SERVING

Calories 160 · Protein 8g · Total Fat 6g · Saturated Fat 1g · Cholesterol 0mg · Carbohydrate 22g · Dietary Fiber 4g · Sodium 30mg

Variation

Classic Hummus

Omit the red bell peppers and cilantro. Use the ground cumin instead of the toasted cumin seeds. Add 1 additional tablespoon of tahini. Proceed as directed in the above recipe, garnishing the hummus with finely chopped fresh flat-leaf parsley, if desired.

Broiled Mushrooms with Pesto

This is the type of appetizer where it pays to double the recipe and hide the extra dozen to chop up and toss over hot pasta the next day. Although I prefer milder cultivated white mushrooms versus the wild variety in this particular recipe, because they allow the heady flavor of basil to shine through, any mushroom with a substantial cap can be used. To create an impressive first course, substitute four to six giant portobello mushrooms for the white mushrooms and extend the initial baking time by about ten minutes.

MAKES 4 TO 6 SERVINGS

12 to 16 large white button mushrooms (about 12 ounces), washed and stemmed, and half the stems reserved
6 tablespoons Poor Man's Pesto (page 107)
2 tablespoons finely ground soft white bread crumbs
½ teaspoon fresh lemon juice
Salt and freshly ground black pepper, to taste

Preheat the oven to 450F (230C). Lightly oil a baking sheet and set aside.

Cut off and discard the tough tips of the reserved mushroom stems. Finely chop the trimmed stems and place in a small bowl. Add the pesto, bread crumbs, lemon juice, salt, and pepper. Mix well with a fork to blend.

Dry the mushroom caps completely with paper towels and arrange, stem side up, on the prepared baking sheet. Fill the caps evenly with the pesto mixture, using about 1½ to 2 teaspoons each, and bake for 5 minutes on the middle rack. Remove the baking sheet from the oven. Place the rack on the highest position and turn the oven to broil.

Broil the mushrooms 3 to 4 inches from the heat source, or until the filling is slightly browned and bubbly, 1 to 2 minutes. Allow the mushrooms to cool slightly before serving warm.

PER SERVING

Calories 134 · Protein 4g · Total Fat 11g · Saturated Fat 2g · Cholesterol 0mg · Carbohydrate 8g · Dietary Fiber 1g · Sodium 130mg

Marinated Button Mushrooms with White Wine, Cloves, and Saffron

Stuffed, grilled or sautéed, mushrooms are seldom missing from serious tapas spreads in Spain. This sophisticated marinade of white wine and tomato sauce infused with cloves and a hint of saffron dresses the cultivated mushroom in fine style.

MAKES 4 TO 6 SERVINGS

- **2 tablespoons extra-virgin olive oil**
- **½ cup finely chopped onion**
- **2 large cloves garlic, finely chopped**
- **½ cup dry white wine**
- **About ½ cup vegetable broth, preferably Basic Vegetable Broth (page 38) or low-sodium canned, or water**
- **2 tablespoons tomato sauce**
- **4 whole cloves**
- **¼ teaspoon saffron threads**
- **Salt and freshly ground black pepper, to taste**
- **1 pound small white button mushrooms, washed and stemmed**

In a large nonstick skillet, heat the oil over medium heat. Add the onion and garlic and cook, stirring constantly, until softened but not browned, about 3 minutes. Stir in the wine, ½ cup broth, tomato sauce, cloves, saffron, salt, and pepper. Bring to a brisk simmer over medium-high heat. Reduce the heat, cover, and simmer very gently, stirring occasionally, for 40 minutes.

Add the mushrooms to the skillet, along with a few tablespoons of broth if the mixture appears too dry; bring to a brisk simmer over medium-high heat. Cook, tossing and stirring constantly, for 3 minutes. Remove the skillet from the heat, cover, and let stand for 1 hour.

With a slotted spoon, transfer the mushrooms to a shallow serving bowl. If the cooking liquids appear too watery, reduce over medium heat, stirring often, until a thin saucelike consistency is formed; remove from the heat and let cool for about 10 minutes. Remove the cloves and pour the sauce over the mushrooms, tossing gently to combine. Serve slightly warm or at room temperature. Alternatively, cover and refrigerate for at least 3 hours and serve chilled.

Advance Preparation The mushrooms can be stored, covered, in the refrigerator for up to two days before serving. Serve chilled.

PER SERVING

Calories 150 · Protein 5g · Total Fat 8g · Saturated Fat 1g · Cholesterol 0mg · Carbohydrate 14g · Dietary Fiber 5g · Sodium 152mg

Mushrooms Stuffed with Bread Crumbs, Parsley, and Garlic

The natural affinity of mushrooms and marsala is apparent in the first bite of these scrumptious stuffed mushrooms from Sicily. Use only the cultivated white variety here, as the stronger-flavored cultivated cremini or wild ones would overwhelm the sweet, nutty flavor of the fortified wine. These are casual enough for eating on cocktail napkins at parties, yet elegant enough to serve on plates as a first course. MAKES 4 TO 6 SERVINGS

- 12 to 16 large white button mushrooms (about 12 ounces), washed, stemmed, and stems reserved
- 2 tablespoons extra-virgin olive oil
- 2 tablespoons marsala, port, or sherry
- ¾ cup finely ground soft white bread crumbs
- 1 tablespoon finely chopped fresh parsley
- 2 cloves garlic, finely chopped
- Salt and freshly ground black pepper, to taste

Preheat the oven to 375F (190C). Cut off and discard the tough tips of the reserved mushroom stems. Finely chop the trimmed stems.

Heat 1 tablespoon of the oil in a medium non-stick skillet over medium-high heat. Add the chopped stems and cook, stirring occasionally, until most of the liquid released from the stems has evaporated, 2 to 3 minutes. Carefully add the marsala. Cook, stirring occasionally, until most of the marsala has evaporated, about 2 minutes. Remove from the heat. Add the bread crumbs, parsley, garlic, salt, and pepper; stir well to combine.

Lightly oil a baking sheet. Rub the rounded sides of the mushroom caps with half of the remaining oil. Arrange the mushroom caps, gill side up, in a single layer on the baking sheet. Spoon the filling evenly into the caps, then dab the tops with the remaining oil. Bake for about 30 minutes, or until nicely browned. Allow the mushrooms to cool a few minutes before serving warm.

Advance Preparation The mushrooms can be stuffed and held at room temperature up to one hour before baking. Or they can be covered and refrigerated overnight.

PER SERVING

Calories 110 · Protein 3g · Total Fat 8g · Saturated Fat 1g · Cholesterol 0mg · Carbohydrate 9g · Dietary Fiber 1g · Sodium 48mg

Wild Mushrooms in Garlic Sauce

The Spanish have a passion for mushrooms, especially wild ones. The following recipe is the most primitive method of cooking wild mushrooms and, I think, the one that best brings forth their natural essence. Although cremini are not wild, but cultivated brown mushrooms, their earthy flavor renders them well suited to this dish.

MAKES 4 TO 6 APPETIZER, SIDE-DISH, OR FIRST-COURSE SERVINGS

1 pound medium fresh wild or cremini mushrooms, washed and stemmed
3 tablespoons extra-virgin olive oil
4 cloves garlic, 3 finely chopped, 1 left whole
Juice of ½ lemon (about 1½ tablespoons)
1 tablespoon finely chopped fresh flat-leaf parsley
Salt and freshly ground black pepper, to taste

Thoroughly dry the mushrooms with paper towels. In a large nonstick skillet, heat the oil over medium heat until hot but not sizzling. Add the whole garlic clove and cook, stirring, for 1 minute. Add the mushrooms and cook, tossing and stirring constantly, until lightly browned and barely softened, 4 to 5 minutes. Do not allow mushrooms to release their own juices.

Remove the skillet from the heat and add the remaining garlic, lemon juice, parsley, salt, and pepper; toss well to combine. Transfer to a large serving platter or individual plates and serve warm or at room temperature.

PER SERVING

Calories 137 · Protein 4g · Total Fat 11g · Saturated Fat 1g · Cholesterol 0mg · Carbohydrate 6g · Dietary Fiber 2g · Sodium 6mg

Baked Black Olives with Herbes de Provence and Anise

Ready in 30 minutes, this easy yet elegant recipe is a great way to dress up plain black olives anytime of the year when unexpected company is on the way and there's no time to marinate. In fact, this is one of those few instances where the fairly inexpensive and decidedly bland canned California black olives can be used with success. Although you can pit the olives if you prefer, leaving the pits in not only helps them retain their shape during baking, but ensures that they won't disappear as soon as they appear on your appetizer or meze table. If you're lucky enough to have any left over, pit, chop, and toss them over hot pasta with a little more olive oil the next day.

MAKES 12 SERVINGS

1 pound large brine-cured black olives, pitted or unpitted, drained
½ cup vegetable broth, preferably Basic Vegetable Broth (page 38) or low-sodium canned
¼ cup extra-virgin olive oil
1 to 2 tablespoons pastis, anisette, Pernod or other anise-flavored liqueur (optional)
1 shallot, finely chopped, or 2 tablespoons finely chopped white parts of scallions
1 tablespoon herbes de Provence or dried rosemary leaves
1 teaspoon grated dried lemon peel
½ teaspoon fennel seeds
Freshly ground black pepper, to taste

Preheat the oven to 350F (175C). Arrange the olives in an 8½- or 9-inch pie plate. Combine the broth, oil, liqueur (if using), shallot, herbes de

Provence, lemon peel, fennel seeds, and pepper in a small bowl; mix well. Pour over the olives, stirring to combine. Bake uncovered for 30 minutes, stirring 3 or 4 times. Remove from the oven and let cool to room temperature before serving.

Advance Preparation The cooled olives can be covered and refrigerated for up to three days. Bring to room temperature before serving.

PER SERVING

Calories 98 · Protein 1g · Total Fat 9g · Saturated Fat 1g · Cholesterol 0mg · Carbohydrate 5g · Dietary Fiber 0g · Sodium 399mg

Black Olive Tapenade

Tapenade is perhaps the most definitive olive dish of Provence, yet curiously the word derives from *tapéno*, meaning capers. Capers must be included to make an authentic tapenade. The customary anchovies are sometimes omitted as a matter of personal taste and preference, particularly when the paste is to be used as a spread for croutons—the French equivalent of Italian crostini—and not as a condiment for lamb or fish. Leftovers are good tossed with hot pasta, couscous, rice, or steamed vegetables, namely green beans, asparagus, or zucchini.

MAKES ABOUT 1½ CUPS; 6 TO 8 SERVINGS

1⅓ cups good-quality pitted black olives, such as Niçoise, Gaeta, or kalamata
¼ cup drained capers
2 tablespoons extra-virgin olive oil
1 tablespoon brandy (optional)
2 large cloves garlic, chopped
1 teaspoon Dijon mustard
½ teaspoon herbes de Provence or ½ teaspoon dried rosemary
Freshly ground black pepper
Toasted baguette rounds

Combine the olives, capers, oil, brandy (if using), garlic, mustard, herbes de Provence, and pepper to taste in a food processor fitted with the metal blade or in a blender. Process or blend just until a coarse-textured paste is formed. Serve at room temperature, accompanied with the toasted bread.

Advance Preparation The mixture can be covered and refrigerated for up to three days. Bring to room temperature before serving.

PER SERVING

(about ¼ cup) without bread:

Calories 183 · Protein 0g · Total Fat 19g · Saturated Fat 1g · Cholesterol 0mg · Carbohydrate 4g · Dietary Fiber 0g · Sodium 900mg

Green Olive and Almond Tapenade

Sometimes referred to as "white" tapenade, this tangy variation of the traditional black olive paste from Provence is a favorite of mine. It makes a nice contrast of taste and color alongside the black version on an appetizer platter.

MAKES ABOUT 1½ CUPS;
6 TO 8 SERVINGS

- 1 cup imported pitted green Provençal, Greek, or Italian olives
- ¼ cup whole blanched almonds, coarsely chopped
- ¼ cup extra-virgin olive oil
- 2 tablespoons drained capers
- 2 tablespoons fresh lemon juice
- 2 to 3 large cloves garlic, finely chopped
- ½ teaspoon dried thyme leaves
- ½ teaspoon dried rosemary leaves
- Freshly ground black pepper, to taste
- Toasted baguette rounds

Combine the olives, almonds, oil, capers, lemon juice, garlic, thyme, rosemary, and pepper in a food processor fitted with the metal blade or in a blender. Process or blend just until a coarse-textured paste is formed. Serve at room temperature, accompanied by the toasted bread rounds.

Advance Preparation The mixture can be covered and refrigerated for up to three days. Bring to room temperature before serving.

PER SERVING
(about ¼ cup) without bread:
Calories 144 · Protein 2g · Total Fat 15g · Saturated Fat 2g · Cholesterol 0mg · Carbohydrate 3g · Dietary Fiber 1g · Sodium 219mg

Variation

Black and White Tapenade
Use equal parts black and green olives and substitute pine nuts for the almonds.

Italian Sweet and Sour Baby Cipolline Onions

Cooking vegetables in a sweet and sour sauce, or agrodolce, is an economical Italian method of both flavoring and preserving them. As the small, flat cipolline onions typically used in Italy are hard to come by here, pearl onions can be substituted. If pearl onions are unavailable, small boiling onions of uniform size—preferably no larger than 1½ inches in diameter—can be substituted.

While you can use a nonstick skillet in this recipe, the onions will not color as nicely and the sauce will take longer to caramelize.

MAKES 4 TO 6 SERVINGS

- 1 pound Italian cipolline or pearl onions, unpeeled
- 1½ tablespoons extra-virgin olive oil
- 3 tablespoons white wine vinegar
- ¼ cup sugar
- ¼ cup water
- Dried oregano (optional)
- Salt and freshly ground black pepper, to taste

In a medium stockpot or large saucepan filled with boiling water, blanch the onions for 2 to 3 minutes, depending on size. Drain in a colander and rinse under cold running water. Transfer to a cutting board; cut off the root ends and peel.

In a large nonreactive skillet, heat the oil over medium heat. Add the onions and cook, stirring often, until lightly browned, 3 to 5 minutes. Slowly pour in 2 tablespoons of the vinegar and stir quickly to coat the onions before it evaporates. Add the remaining vinegar, remove the skillet from the heat, and stir quickly to coat the onions. Sprinkle in the sugar, stirring to coat. Add the water, stirring to combine.

Return the skillet to the heat and increase the heat to medium-high. When the mixture reaches a simmer, reduce the heat to low. Cook, uncovered, stirring occasionally, until the onions are tender but still crunchy, about 20 minutes, depending on the size of the onions. The sauce should be thickened and honey-colored. If not, transfer the onions with a slotted spoon to a shallow serving bowl. Bring the cooking liquids to a boil over medium heat and reduce, stirring occasionally, until the proper color and consistency are achieved. Pour the sauce over the onions, stirring to combine. Season with the oregano (if using), salt, and pepper. Serve slightly warm or at room temperature.

Advance Preparation The onions will keep for two to three days, tightly covered, in the refrigerator. Bring to room temperature before serving.

PER SERVING

Calories 126 · Protein 1g · Total Fat 5g · Saturated Fat 1g · Cholesterol 0mg · Carbohydrate 20g · Dietary Fiber 2g · Sodium 272mg

Variation Without blanching them first, cook small, sturdy young carrots (about 2 inches long and ¾ inches wide) in the same manner.

Spanish Sweet and Sour Pearl Onions in Tomato-Raisin Sauce

This is a slightly more sophisticated Spanish variation on the Italian method of cooking baby onions in sweet and sour sauce. Here, pearl onions are not browned, but slowly cooked in a rich tomato-raisin sauce that results in a delicious chutneylike condiment, wonderful on grilled eggplant or veggie burgers. It is also a somewhat lengthier recipe, but the tomato sauce can be made a day in advance.

MAKES 8 SERVINGS

1 pound pearl onions, unpeeled
2 tablespoons extra-virgin olive oil
1 medium yellow onion (about 6 ounces), finely chopped
2 large cloves garlic, finely chopped
2 medium tomatoes (about 6 ounces each), peeled, seeded, and chopped
¼ cup vegetable broth, preferably Basic Vegetable Broth (page 38) or low-sodium canned
2 sprigs fresh parsley
2 bay leaves
½ teaspoon dried thyme leaves
Salt and freshly ground black pepper, to taste
1 cup water
½ cup white wine vinegar
¼ cup dark raisins
2 tablespoons sugar
2 teaspoons finely chopped fresh basil

In a medium stockpot or large saucepan filled with boiling water, blanch the pearl onions for 2 to 3 minutes, depending on size. Drain in a colander and rinse under cold running water. Transfer to a cutting board. Cut off the root ends, then squeeze each onion gently toward the root end until the onion slips out.

Meanwhile, in a large nonstick skillet, heat the oil over medium heat. Add the chopped onion and garlic and cook, stirring often, until softened but not browned, 3 to 5 minutes. Add the tomatoes and cook, stirring, for 2 minutes. Add the broth, parsley, bay leaves, thyme, salt, and pepper; bring to a simmer over medium-high heat. Reduce the heat, cover, and simmer gently for 20 minutes.

Add the pearl onions, water, vinegar, raisins, sugar, and basil to the skillet. Bring to a boil over high heat. Reduce the heat and simmer gently, uncovered, stirring occasionally, for 40 to 45 minutes, or until the liquids are greatly reduced. Remove the parsley sprigs and bay leaves. Cool completely before covering and refrigerating for at least 3 hours to allow the flavors to blend. Serve chilled or at room temperature.

Advance Preparation The dish can be stored, covered, in the refrigerator for up to five days. Bring to room temperature or serve chilled.

PER SERVING

Calories 108 · Protein 3g · Total Fat 4g · Saturated Fat 1g · Cholesterol 0mg · Carbohydrate 18g · Dietary Fiber 4g · Sodium 181mg

Garlic-Herb Pita Toasts

Perfect for a party, these crunchy triangles are excellent vehicles for a variety of dips and spreads. Leftovers can be used in Lebanese Bread Salad (page 84) instead of plain pita, or stirred into soups, such as the Egyptian-Style Lentil Soup (page 53). They're also a healthy snack on their own.

MAKES 32 PIECES; 4 TO 6 SERVINGS

- 3 (6-inch-diameter) pita loaves, fresh or slightly stale, preferably whole wheat, quartered
- 2 tablespoons extra-virgin olive oil
- 1 tablespoon finely chopped fresh flat-leaf parsley
- 1 tablespoon finely chopped fresh chives
- 2 large cloves garlic, finely chopped
- Coarse salt, to taste

Preheat the oven to 500F (260F). Separate each pita quarter into 2 pieces. Arrange in a single layer, rough side up, on an ungreased baking sheet. Brush evenly with the oil. In a small bowl, combine the parsley, chives, and garlic. Using your fingers, distribute the herb mixture evenly over the pita quarters. Sprinkle evenly with coarse salt.

Bake on the top rack of the oven for 3 to 5 minutes, or until the pita quarters are nicely toasted

Cook's Tip

For the best results, use a baking sheet that is not too dark for this recipe; otherwise, watch the pita bread carefully as it burns easily. If you're doubling the recipe and one baking sheet is darker than the other, keep this in mind.

and crisp, depending on the freshness of the bread. Remove from the oven and let cool to room temperature before serving.

Advance Preparation Completely cooled pita toasts can be wrapped in foil and stored for up to one day without loss of crispiness.

PER PIECE

Calories 23 · Protein 0g · Total Fat 1g · Saturated Fat 0g · Cholesterol 0mg · Carbohydrate 3g · Dietary Fiber 0g · Sodium 45mg

Tomatoes Persillade

Persillade is a ubiquitous Spanish mixture of chopped parsley and garlic; along with olive oil and red wine vinegar, it is a popular dressing for juicy slices of vine-ripened tomatoes in the summertime. From French Catalonia, this is my favorite way to eat raw tomatoes, accompanied by lots of fresh crusty bread to sop up all the wonderful juices.

MAKES 4 APPETIZER OR FIRST-COURSE SERVINGS

2 tablespoons finely chopped fresh parsley
1 large clove garlic, finely chopped
4 medium vine-ripened tomatoes (about 6 ounces each), sliced into ¼-inch-thick rounds
2 tablespoons extra-virgin olive oil
1 tablespoon red wine vinegar
Coarse salt and freshly ground black pepper, to taste
Baguette rounds or Italian bread slices (optional)

In a small bowl, combine the parsley and garlic and set aside. On a large serving plate, arrange the tomato slices in slightly overlapping circles. Drizzle the oil and vinegar evenly over the tomatoes; sprinkle with the parsley-garlic mixture. Season with salt and pepper.

Serve at room temperature, accompanied by the bread, if desired.

PER SERVING

Calories 95 · Protein 1g · Total Fat 7g · Saturated Fat 1g · Cholesterol 0mg · Carbohydrate 8g · Dietary Fiber 2g · Sodium 133mg

Catalan Grilled Vegetables with Almond Sauce (Escalivada con Salsa Romesco)

From the Catalan verb *escalivar,* which means to "cook over hot embers," escalivada is a platter of grilled or roasted vegetables especially popular in the Barcelona area of Spain as a tapa or first course in the summertime. Often, the vegetables are simply dressed with a good, fruity olive oil, red wine vinegar or lemon juice, and coarse salt. Here, they are laid out in a colorful mosaic, waiting to be enthroned on toasted slices of crusty peasant bread, then crowned with the greatest almond sauce of all, Salsa Romesco. If the optional asparagus or green beans are omitted, substitute a green bell pepper for one of the yellow.

MAKES 8 SERVINGS

1 large eggplant (about 1 pound)
2 medium red bell peppers (about 6 ounces each)
2 medium yellow bell peppers (about 6 ounces each)
2 tablespoons extra-virgin olive oil
16 to 20 pencil-thin asparagus spears or long green beans, cooked and chilled (optional)
Thin slices of peasant-style bread, lightly toasted (optional)
Salsa Romesco (opposite)

Prepare a medium-hot grill. Or preheat the oven to 450F (230C). Pierce the eggplant in several places with the tines of a fork. Rub the eggplant and peppers with the olive oil. Place directly on the grill. Cover and cook, turning frequently with tongs, for 20 to 35 minutes, or until the skins are blackened and the insides are soft. Or place on an ungreased baking sheet and roast for 20 to 35 minutes. As the peppers finish cooking, transfer to a paper bag, twist closed, and set aside for 20 minutes.

Carefully stem the eggplant, then cut in half lengthwise; drain, cut side down, on several layers of paper towels. When the eggplant is cool enough to handle, peel away and discard the skin. Cut each half into long thin strips. Set aside. With your fingers or a small sharp knife, slip the skins off the peppers. Cut each one lengthwise into quarters, removing cores and seeds. Cut each quarter in half lengthwise.

To serve, arrange the eggplant and peppers attractively on a large platter, separating and outlining the vegetables with the asparagus spears, if using, like a mosaic. Serve chilled or at room temperature with the toasted bread slices, if using, and the Salsa Romesco passed separately.

Advance Preparation The roasted vegetables can be stored, covered, in the refrigerator for up to twenty-four hours. Bring to room temperature or serve chilled.

PER SERVING

Calories 201 · Protein 4g · Total Fat 16g · Saturated Fat 2g · Cholesterol 0mg · Carbohydrate 15g · Dietary Fiber 5g · Sodium 79mg

Salsa Romesco

A Catalan sauce for fish, seafood, and vegetables, Salsa Romesco makes an excellent substitute for pesto in the Eggplant Roll-ups with Pesto (page 13). Mild to medium in spiciness, you can add one or two additional chiles to make it hotter.

MAKES ABOUT 1½ CUPS

¼ cup blanched almonds
¼ cup hazelnuts
2 large cloves garlic, chopped
1 small dried hot red chile pepper, crushed
2 medium vine-ripened tomatoes (about 6 ounces each), peeled, quartered, and seeded
1 teaspoon sweet paprika
¼ teaspoon coarse salt
¼ cup extra-virgin olive oil
1 to 1½ tablespoons red wine vinegar
2 tablespoons chopped fresh parsley

Preheat the oven to 350F (175C). Spread the nuts on an ungreased light-colored baking sheet and toast until lightly golden and fragrant, about 7 to 10 minutes, stirring once. Immediately remove from the baking sheet and let cool slightly. Rub the hazelnuts in a damp kitchen towel to remove most of their skins.

Place the nuts, garlic, and chile in a food processor fitted with the metal blade; process until finely ground. Add the tomatoes, paprika, and salt; process until a smooth paste is formed. With the motor running, add the oil in a thin, steady stream. Add the vinegar to taste, pulsing to combine. Transfer to a bowl and stir in the parsley. Cover and let stand at room temperature for 30 minutes to allow the flavors to blend. Serve at room temperature.

Advance Preparation The sauce can be stored, covered, in the refrigerator for up to two days. Bring to room temperature before serving.

PER 3 TABLESPOONS

Calories 139 · Protein 2g · Total Fat 12g · Saturated Fat 1g · Cholesterol 0mg · Carbohydrate 7g · Dietary Fiber 3g · Sodium 76mg

Tomatoes à la Provençale

From Picardy to Provence, this is perhaps the best known of all French tomato dishes, representing the finest of French provincial cooking. Be sure to select ripe but firm tomatoes here, and take care to check after the first twenty minutes of baking—the tomatoes should be tender but not at all limp or mushy.

MAKES 6 APPETIZER, FIRST-COURSE, OR SIDE-DISH SERVINGS

- 6 large firm ripe tomatoes (about 8 ounces each)
- Regular salt
- ½ cup dry unseasoned bread crumbs
- ½ cup soft white bread crumbs
- ½ cup finely chopped fresh flat-leaf parsley, plus extra for garnishing
- 3 tablespoons finely chopped fresh basil
- 3 tablespoons finely chopped shallots or white parts of scallions
- 2 cloves garlic, finely chopped
- Coarse salt and freshly ground black pepper, to taste
- ¼ cup extra-virgin olive oil

Slice off and discard ¼ inch from the top and bottom of each tomato. Cut in half crosswise. With a finger or the handle of a small spoon, scoop out the seeds. Sprinkle the insides with a little regular salt and turn them upside down to drain on paper towels for about 15 minutes.

Preheat the oven to 375F (190C). Lightly oil a shallow baking dish large enough to comfortably hold the tomato halves in a single layer. Set aside.

In a medium mixing bowl, stir together the dry bread crumbs, soft bread crumbs, parsley, basil, shallots, and garlic. Season with coarse salt and pepper. Add half of the olive oil and toss well to thoroughly combine. Fill each tomato half with about 2 tablespoons of the bread crumb mixture, patting it in and letting it mound up slightly in the center.

Arrange the tomato halves in the prepared baking dish. Drizzle evenly with the remaining oil. Bake in the upper third of the oven for 20 to 30 minutes, or until the tomatoes are tender but not limp or mushy. Serve warm. Or let cool and refrigerate, covered, for a minimum of 3 hours, and serve chilled, sprinkled with the optional parsley if desired.

Advance Preparation The cooled tomatoes can be stored, covered, in the refrigerator for up to twenty-four hours. Serve chilled.

PER SERVING

Calories 177 · Protein 4g · Total Fat 11g · Saturated Fat 2g · Cholesterol 0mg · Carbohydrate 20g · Dietary Fiber 3g · Sodium 104mg

Assorted Vegetables in Charmoula Sauce

Charmoula is a popular Moroccan sauce used to marinate both fish and vegetables. More spicy than hot, its heat can be controlled or omitted entirely according to individual taste. Zucchini, carrots, and pearl onions are always a nice medley, but feel free to experiment with other vegetables. The following recipe makes a convenient buffet appetizer, as the dish can be made a day ahead, holds up well at room temperature, and can be eaten with wooden picks. It also makes a delicious side dish or first course tossed with couscous or rice. MAKES 6 TO 8 SERVINGS

¾ pound pearl onions, peeled (see Cook's Tip opposite)
4 medium carrots (about ¾ pound), peeled, cut crosswise into ¾-inch-thick slices
2 (about 6-ounce) zucchini, unpeeled, cut crosswise into ¾-inch-thick slices

CHARMOULA:
3 tablespoons finely chopped fresh cilantro
3 tablespoons finely chopped fresh parsley
Juice of 1 medium lemon (about 3 tablespoons)
2 large cloves garlic, finely chopped
½ teaspoon sweet paprika
½ teaspoon salt
¼ teaspoon ground cumin
Pinch sugar or to taste
Cayenne pepper, to taste (optional)
Freshly ground black pepper, to taste
¼ cup extra-virgin olive oil

Bring a medium stockpot filled with salted water to a boil over high heat. Add the onions, reduce the heat to medium, and cook, partially covered, for 4 to 6 minutes, depending upon size. Add the carrots and cook, partially covered, for 10 minutes. Add the zucchini and cook, partially covered, for 5 minutes more, or until all the vegetables are tender yet still somewhat firm.

Meanwhile, prepare the charmoula: Place the cilantro, parsley, lemon juice, garlic, paprika, salt, cumin, sugar, cayenne, (if using), and black pepper

Cook's Tip

Peeling Pearl Onions For easy peeling, drop the onions in boiling water for 2 to 3 minutes, depending upon size. Drain and rinse under cold running water. Cut the root ends, then squeeze each onion gently toward the root end until the onion slips out.

in a small bowl; stir well to combine. Gradually whisk in the olive oil.

When the vegetables are done cooking, drain well and transfer to a shallow serving bowl. While they're still quite warm, add the charmoula, tossing gently yet thoroughly to combine. Cover and let stand for 15 minutes to allow the flavors to blend. Toss gently again, and serve slightly warm or at room temperature.

Advance Preparation The dish can be stored, covered, in the refrigerator for up to twenty-four hours. Bring to room temperature before serving.

PER SERVING

Calories 130 · Protein 2g · Total Fat 9g · Saturated Fat 1g · Cholesterol 0mg · Carbohydrate 12g · Dietary Fiber 3g · Sodium 334mg

Zucchini Marinated with Sherry Vinegar and Mint

On a hot summer's day, chill out with the naturally revitalizing flavors of zucchini and mint in this simple escabeche, a method of marinating foods in vinegar or lemon juice introduced to Spain by the Moors. From the sherry-producing region of Andalusia in southern Spain, the following tapa is typically made with sherry vinegar, but balsamic vinegar can be substituted.

MAKES 4 TO 6 SERVINGS

- 1½ pounds zucchini, trimmed and cut into ½-inch-thick rounds
- 4 tablespoons extra-virgin olive oil
- 6 large cloves garlic, slivered
- 3 tablespoons finely chopped fresh mint
- Salt and freshly ground black pepper, to taste
- ¼ cup sherry vinegar
- Shredded fresh mint leaves (optional)

Place the zucchini in a medium stockpot and add salted water to cover. Bring to a boil over high heat. Reduce the heat to medium-high and cook, uncovered, until just tender, 3 to 5 minutes. Drain in a colander and let cool.

Meanwhile, in a small skillet, heat 2 tablespoons of the oil over medium-low heat. Add the garlic and sauté until golden, about 5 minutes. Remove the garlic with a slotted spoon and drain on paper towels. Let the oil cool.

Place the drained zucchini between several layers of paper towels and press down gently to squeeze out excess moisture. Arrange one-third of the zucchini in the bottom of an 8-inch nonreactive pie plate. Drizzle with one-third of the cooled garlic-flavored oil; sprinkle one-third of the reserved slivered garlic and one-third of the chopped mint over top. Season very lightly with salt and pepper. Repeat the layering process two more times with the remaining zucchini, garlic-flavored oil, garlic, chopped mint, and salt and pepper. Drizzle the last layer with the remaining plain oil. Pour the vinegar over all, tilting the pie plate slightly to evenly distribute.

Cover loosely with plastic wrap. Arrange a plate over the top and weight with any 1-pound container. Refrigerate for at least 3 hours. Serve chilled, sprinkled with the shredded mint if desired.

Advance Preparation The dish can be stored, covered, in the refrigerator for up to two days.

PER SERVING

Calories 154 · Protein 2g · Total Fat 14g · Saturated Fat 2g · Cholesterol 0mg · Carbohydrate 8g · Dietary Fiber 2g · Sodium 7mg

Stuffed Zucchini, Niçoise Style

***Petits farcis,* or "little stuffed things," are popular hors d'oeuvres in the south of France. A nice party dish that can sit at room temperature for a few hours, these zucchini look especially inviting on a platter set in a sea of assorted olives and cherry tomatoes. They also make a delicious side dish or first course.**

MAKES 8 APPETIZER OR SIDE-DISH SERVINGS

- 4 (4- to 6-ounce) zucchini, halved lengthwise
- 4 teaspoons extra-virgin olive oil
- 1 medium onion (about 6 ounces), finely chopped
- 2 cloves garlic, finely chopped
- 1 medium tomato (about 6 ounces), peeled, seeded, and coarsely chopped
- ½ cup unseasoned dry bread crumbs
- ½ cup Niçoise or other good-quality black olives, pitted and chopped
- 2 teaspoons finely chopped fresh flat-leaf parsley
- 1 teaspoon finely chopped fresh basil
- 1 teaspoon fresh thyme leaves or ½ teaspoon dried
- Salt and freshly ground black pepper, to taste
- About ½ cup vegetable broth, preferably Basic Vegetable Broth (page 38) or low-sodium canned, or water

Preheat the oven to 425F (220C). Scoop out the insides from each zucchini half, leaving a ⅜-inch-thick shell. Coarsely chop the insides and set aside.

In a large nonstick skillet, heat the oil over medium heat. Add the onion and garlic and cook, stirring frequently, until softened but not browned, about 5 minutes. Add the tomato and chopped zucchini and cook, stirring occasionally, for 15 to 20 minutes, or until the zucchini is tender and most of the liquid has evaporated.

Remove the skillet from the heat and add the bread crumbs, olives, parsley, basil, thyme, salt, and pepper. Let cool for a few minutes.

Stuff the zucchini shells with the cooled filling. Arrange in a shallow baking dish just large enough to hold them; pour in enough broth or water to cover the bottom of the baking dish. Bake 20 to 25 minutes, or until the tops are lightly browned and shells are tender when pierced with the tip of a sharp knife. Serve slightly warm or at room temperature.

Advance Preparation The assembled stuffed zucchini can be held at room temperature for one hour before baking, or stored, covered, in the refrigerator for up to eight hours before baking. The baked zucchini can sit for one hour at room temperature before serving. They can also be stored, covered, in the refrigerator for up to twelve hours. Reheat, covered, in a low oven, and serve slightly warm for best results.

PER SERVING

Calories 115 · Protein 3g · Total Fat 7g · Saturated Fat 1g · Cholesterol 0mg · Carbohydrate 12g · Dietary Fiber 2g · Sodium 320mg

Variation Prepare 4 small Italian eggplant instead of the zucchini in the same fashion.

Soups

Basic Vegetable Broths, Light Soups, and Hearty Meal-in-a-Bowl Soups

Nourishing, easy to stretch, and excellent receptacles for leftovers or whatever needs harvesting in the garden, vegetable-based soups have always been the mainstay of Mediterranean peasant cooking. From refreshing Moroccan carrot soup to rib-sticking ribollita—one of Italy's many bread soups—enough recipes for meatless, dairy-free soups exist in the Mediterranean to fill another cookbook. For the scope of this chapter, however, there are three categories of soup: broths for foundation and flavor, light soups for first courses, lunches, or simple suppers (these soups generally contain under 250 calories per serving), and substantial soups for satisfying meals-in-a-bowl. While a few in the latter category could even be classified as stews, most of the stews or ragouts in this book can be found in the Vegetables and Legumes chapter.

Broth making is a veritable ritual in many a Mediterranean kitchen. Indeed, chefs and home cooks alike are often judged on the basis of how flavorful their stocks are. Vegetable broth is not only the foundation for many soups and stews, but is essential in contributing flavor to countless rice, pasta, polenta, and vegetable entrées, braised dishes, and sauces. In lesser amounts, it is even incorporated in certain pizzas, sandwiches, and salad dressings. I have included no fewer than three recipes for vegetable broth: a stove-top version producing a light, multipurpose stock suitable for all the recipes in this book; a microwave variation producing a rather rich, slightly sweet stock perfect for many of the spicier soups, stews, and casseroles, ready in just about one hour; and a reduced stock, excellent for braised dishes and sauces. But because many of us don't always have even an hour to spare to make stock from scratch, low-sodium canned vegetable broth can be used in any of the recipes throughout this book.

Light vegetable-based soups, often ladled over thick pieces of bread and accompanied by a salad, are traditionally eaten in the evening all over the Mediterranean countryside, while main-course soups and stews are generally eaten at midday. Here in the United States, of course, the situation is typically reversed. But no matter the time of day or the occasion, the following collection of recipes will taste exactly like the ingredients you use. Go for high-quality canned goods and chances are you'll be quite satisfied; select impeccably fresh vegetables and chances are you'll receive that most coveted of cooks' compliments—a request for seconds.

Microwave Vegetable Broth

This slightly sweet and incredibly aromatic broth is ready in about one hour with the help of the microwave. Although useful in all the recipes requiring vegetable broth throughout this book, its rich flavor works especially well with the spicier and more acidic dishes. Store as directed for Basic Vegetable Broth (page 38).

MAKES 1 QUART (4 CUPS)

¾ pound onion, peeled and coarsely chopped
2 small carrots (about 4 ounces), peeled and coarsely chopped
4 ounces (about 3 small) stalks celery, coarsely chopped
10 cloves garlic, crushed with the flat side of a knife, and peeled
4 teaspoons extra-virgin olive oil
4 fresh mushrooms, preferably cremini or shiitake, cleaned and quartered
½ tablespoon sugar
½ cup dry white wine
6 cups water
6 sprigs flat-leaf parsley
1 tablespoon fresh whole thyme leaves or 1 teaspoon dried thyme leaves, crumbled
1 large bay leaf
1 cinnamon stick (optional)
1 to 3 whole cloves (optional)
Salt and freshly ground black pepper (optional)

Preheat the oven to 425F (220C). Lightly oil a flameproof, microwave-safe 8-cup casserole or baking dish with a lid. Add the onion, carrots, celery, and garlic and drizzle with the olive oil; toss well to coat. Bake, uncovered, for 15 minutes. Add the mushrooms and sprinkle with the sugar; toss well to combine. Bake, uncovered, for 15 minutes, or until the vegetables are fragrant and browned around the edges.

Transfer the casserole to the stovetop and add the wine; cook over high heat until the liquids are greatly reduced and syrupy, stirring and scraping the bottom and sides of the casserole to loosen any browned bits. Add the water, parsley, thyme, bay leaf, and cinnamon and cloves, if using, and bring to a boil over high heat. Remove from the heat and cover.

Transfer the covered casserole to the microwave. Microwave on medium-high power for 20 minutes. Strain through a fine-meshed sieve into another dish or bowl, pressing down hard on the vegetables with the back of a wooden spoon to extract their liquids. Discard remaining solids. Clean the original casserole. Line the sieve with cheesecloth, and strain the broth into the cleaned casserole. Cook uncovered on the stovetop over high heat for a few minutes until the broth is reduced to 4 cups. Season with salt and pepper if desired.

PER CUP

Calories 69 · Protein 2g · Total Fat 3g · Saturated Fat 0g · Cholesterol 0mg · Carbohydrate 9g · Dietary Fiber 0g · Sodium 24mg

Variation

Concentrated Vegetable Broth

This intensely flavorful stock is used in several of the braised dishes and sauces throughout this book, although a reduction of the Basic Vegetable Broth recipe (page 38) or low-sodium canned broth can easily be substituted. You can spoon this versatile reduction over cooked vegetables and pasta, whisk it into salad dressings, or mash it into potatoes in lieu of added fat. Store as directed for the Basic Vegetable Broth.

Prepare the microwave vegetable broth as directed on page 37; do not season with salt and pepper. Reduce desired amount of broth over high heat to about one-third of its original volume. Season with salt and pepper if desired.

PER ⅓ CUP

Calories 69 · Protein 2g · Total Fat 3g · Saturated Fat 0g · Cholesterol 0mg · Carbohydrate 9g · Dietary Fiber 0g · Sodium 24mg

Basic Vegetable Broth

Light and fragrant, this multipurpose and inexpensive broth can be used in any of the recipes in this book. However, it is a particularly fine base for the more mildly flavored soups, rice, and pasta dishes.

MAKES ABOUT 3 QUARTS (12 CUPS)

- 5 teaspoons extra-virgin olive oil
- 1½ pounds onions, coarsely chopped
- 4 small carrots (about 8 ounces), peeled and coarsely chopped
- 8 ounces (about 6 small) stalks celery, coarsely chopped
- 1 garlic head, cloves separated, crushed with the flat side of a knife, and peeled
- 12 cups water
- 12 sprigs flat-leaf parsley
- 2 tablespoons fresh whole thyme leaves or 2 teaspoons dried thyme leaves, crumbled
- 2 large bay leaves
- Salt and freshly ground black pepper (optional)

In a large stockpot, heat the oil over medium-low heat. Add the onions, carrots, celery, and garlic, tossing to coat with the oil. Cook, stirring occasionally, until the vegetables have softened and are lightly colored, 20 to 25 minutes, adding a little water, if necessary, to prevent sticking.

Add the water, parsley, thyme, and bay leaves to the pot. Bring to a boil over high heat. Reduce the heat, cover, and simmer for 2 hours. Remove from the heat and adjust the seasonings as necessary. Cover and let the broth rest for 1 hour.

Strain the broth through a fine-meshed sieve into another pot, pressing down hard on the vegetables with the back of a wooden spoon to extract their liquids. Clean the original pot. Line the sieve with cheesecloth and strain the broth into the cleaned pot. Season with salt and pepper if desired.

The broth can be tightly covered and stored in the refrigerator for up to 1 week, or frozen up to 4 months. For smaller quantities, freeze the broth in ice cube trays, then pop the frozen cubes into freezer bags. Each cube is equal to about 2 tablespoons of broth.

PER CUP

Calories 30 · Protein 1g · Total Fat 1g · Saturated Fat 0g · Cholesterol 0mg · Carbohydrate 5g · Dietary Fiber 0g · Sodium 15mg

Light Soups

Asparagus Soup with Thyme

It's hard to believe that not one drop of cream has been added to this creamy and elegant soup. For an appealing contrast of color, consider garnishing with a bit of shredded carrot just before serving.

MAKES 4 SERVINGS

- 2 pounds medium asparagus, tough stem ends trimmed
- 1½ tablespoons extra-virgin olive oil
- 1 medium leek (about 6 ounces), trimmed, topped, cleaned, and chopped, white and some green parts
- 1 small carrot (about 2 ounces), chopped
- 4 cups vegetable broth, preferably Basic Vegetable Broth (page 38) or low-sodium canned
- ¼ teaspoon dried thyme leaves
- Salt and freshly ground black pepper, to taste

Cut off the tips from the asparagus and reserve. Cut the stalks into ½-inch pieces and reserve. Fill a medium bowl with ice water and set aside.

In a medium stockpot or saucepan large enough to accommodate a 9-inch steaming basket, put 1 inch of water. Arrange the asparagus tips in the steaming basket and place in the pot. Bring to a boil over high heat. Cover tightly, reduce the heat to medium, and steam until the tips are crisp-tender, 4 to 5 minutes. Carefully remove the steaming basket and refresh the asparagus tips in the ice water for 5 minutes. Drain and set aside. Reduce the cooking liquid over high heat until 1 cup remains. Reserve.

Meanwhile, in another medium stockpot, heat the oil over medium-low heat. Add the leek and carrot and cook, stirring occasionally, until softened, about 10 minutes. Add the reserved asparagus stalks, broth, reduced cooking liquid, thyme, salt, and pepper; bring to a boil over high heat. Reduce the heat, cover, and simmer gently until the stalks are very tender, stirring occasionally, about 30 minutes. Let the soup cool slightly.

Working in two batches, transfer the soup to a food processor fitted with the metal blade or to a blender; process or blend until smooth and pureed. Return the soup to a clean pot and add the reserved asparagus tips. Cover and cook over low heat, stirring occasionally, until the soup is heated through, about 5 minutes. Serve hot.

Advance Preparation The soup can be stored, covered, in the refrigerator for up to twenty-four hours; add the reserved asparagus tips once the soup has cooled. Reheat over low heat.

PER SERVING

Calories 136 · Protein 14g · Total Fat 5g · Saturated Fat 1g · Cholesterol 0mg · Carbohydrate 11g · Dietary Fiber 6g · Sodium 528mg

Sicilian Barley Soup

This wholesome, nourishing soup is frequently fed to children and convalescing adults in Sicily. The following recipe makes a hearty main course to serve four, accompanied with the Radicchio and Butter Lettuce Salad with Toasted Walnuts (page 78). **MAKES 4 TO 6 SERVINGS**

6 cups vegetable broth, preferably Basic Vegetable Broth (page 38) or low-sodium canned
2 cups water
1½ pounds ripe tomatoes, peeled, seeded, and coarsely chopped
1 cup pearl barley
Salt and freshly ground black pepper, to taste
Chopped fresh mint, basil, or flat-leaf parsley (optional)

In a medium stockpot, bring the broth and water to a boil over high heat. Add the tomatoes, barley, salt, and pepper; stir well to combine. When the mixture returns to a boil, reduce the heat to low. Stir thoroughly again, cover, and cook until the barley is plumped and tender, adjusting the heat to maintain a gentle simmer and stirring occasionally, 45 to 50 minutes.

Serve hot, garnished with the chopped herbs, if desired.

Advance Preparation The soup can be stored, covered, in the refrigerator for up to three days. Reheat over low heat. You will need to add more broth or water because the barley will absorb the liquid.

PER SERVING

Calories 284 · Protein 23g · Total Fat 1g · Saturated Fat 0g · Cholesterol 0mg · Carbohydrate 49g · Dietary Fiber 14g · Sodium 795mg

Sicilian Bread and Tomato-Basil Soup

This simple summer soup evolved as a means of using up stale bread, more so than the hearty Tuscan Ribollita (page 51), which was invented primarily to use up leftover minestrone. For the thrifty American cook, it's a great way to use up overripe or visually imperfect tomatoes. Served with a substantial salad such as the Romaine, Red Onion, and Chickpea Salad (page 79), the following recipe easily qualifies as a main course serving four. **MAKES 6 SERVINGS**

¼ cup extra-virgin olive oil
1 bunch scallions (6 to 8), white parts finely chopped, green tops thinly sliced and reserved
3 large cloves garlic, finely chopped
1 pound very ripe tomatoes, peeled and chopped, juices reserved
¼ cup dry white wine
8 to 12 large basil leaves, shredded
Pinch of cayenne pepper or to taste (optional)
4 cups vegetable broth, preferably Basic Vegetable Broth (page 38) or low-sodium canned
Salt and freshly ground black pepper, to taste
8 ounces slightly stale, dense country-style bread, preferably whole wheat, torn into small pieces
Whole basil leaves (optional)

In a large deep-sided skillet with a lid, heat the oil over medium heat. Add the white parts of the scallions and the garlic and cook, stirring, until softened but not browned, 2 to 3 minutes. Add the tomatoes, wine, shredded basil, and cayenne, if using; bring to a brisk simmer over medium-high heat. Reduce the heat and simmer gently, uncovered, for 10 minutes, stirring occasionally.

Add the broth, salt, and pepper; bring to a boil over medium-high heat. Stir in the bread pieces, reduce the heat, and simmer gently, uncovered, for 5 minutes, stirring occasionally. Stir in the reserved scallion greens, cover, and remove from the heat. Let stand for 15 minutes before serving, garnished with the whole basil leaves, if desired.

PER SERVING

Calories 238 · Protein 12g · Total Fat 11g · Saturated Fat 2g · Cholesterol 0mg · Carbohydrate 24g · Dietary Fiber 6g · Sodium 555mg

Sicilian-Style Broccoli and Parsnip Soup

A light beginning to a meal, this versatile soup can also include potatoes. If potatoes are added, the soup is pureed and served as a hearty main dish (directions are given in the variation below). If parsnips are unavailable, carrots can be substituted.

MAKES 4 SERVINGS

- 1 large head broccoli (1¼ to 1½ pounds), rinsed and drained
- 2 tablespoons extra-virgin olive oil
- 2 medium (about 8 ounces) parsnips, peeled and finely chopped
- 1 medium onion (about 6 ounces), finely chopped
- 2 large cloves garlic, finely chopped
- 4 cups vegetable broth, preferably Basic Vegetable Broth (page 38) or low-sodium canned
- ½ teaspoon dried thyme leaves
- Pinch sugar, or to taste
- Salt and freshly ground black pepper, to taste

Cut off and separate the broccoli florets, removing as much stem as possible. Coarsely chop the florets and set aside. Trim the tough ends of the stems; peel and finely chop. Set aside.

In a medium stockpot, heat the oil over medium-low heat. Add the parsnips, onion, and garlic; cook, stirring often, until the onion is very tender, about 15 minutes. Add the reserved broccoli stems, broth, thyme, sugar, salt, and pepper; bring to a boil over high heat. Immediately reduce the heat and simmer gently, covered, for 25 minutes, stirring a few times, or until the broccoli stems are very tender.

Stir in the reserved broccoli florets and bring the soup to a brisk simmer over medium-high heat. Reduce the heat and simmer gently, covered, until the florets are tender, 5 to 10 minutes. Season with additional salt and pepper as necessary. Serve hot.

PER SERVING

Calories 211 · Protein 17g · Total Fat 8g · Saturated Fat 1g · Cholesterol 0mg · Carbohydrate 24g · Dietary Fiber 11g · Sodium 563mg

Variation

Sicilian-Style Broccoli, Potato, and Parsnip Soup

Add 1¼ pounds baking potatoes, peeled and cut into 1-inch chunks, 5½ cups broth, and ¾ teaspoon thyme with the broccoli stems, sugar, and salt and pepper; cook as directed above. Transfer the soup

Cook's Tip

The secret to the success of this soup is cooking the vegetables until they're very tender.

in batches to a food processor fitted with the metal blade and puree; return to the pot, add the broccoli florets, and cook as directed.

PER SERVING

Calories 314 · Protein 23g · Total Fat 8g · Saturated Fat 1g · Cholesterol 0mg · Carbohydrate 44g · Dietary Fiber 14g · Sodium 764mg

Moroccan Carrot Soup

If you like carrots as much as I do, this refreshing soup—called a salad in Morocco—is for you. Some recipes call for squeezing the grated carrots in kitchen towels to extract the moisture before combining with the orange juice, but I prefer to include all their vitamin-packed juices. An ideal first course to serve with any of this book's spicier entrees, the soup is especially pretty garnished with the optional parsley and decidedly richer sprinkled with the optional pistachios—but as the soup is virtually fat-free, feel free to splurge.

MAKES 4 TO 6 SERVINGS

- 2 pounds carrots, peeled, cut into 1-inch pieces
- 2 cups freshly squeezed orange juice
- Juice of ½ large lemon (about 2 tablespoons)
- ½ teaspoon sugar or to taste
- Pinch cardamom or ground ginger
- Chopped fresh parsley (optional)
- Chopped pistachio nuts, toasted (optional) (see Cook's Tip, page 121)

In a food processor fitted with the metal blade, process half the carrots until finely chopped. Add the remaining carrots and process until all is pureed. Add the orange juice, lemon juice, sugar, and cardamom; process until thoroughly blended. Cover and refrigerate for at least 1 hour and serve chilled, garnished with the parsley or toasted pistachios, if desired.

Advance Preparation The soup can be stored, covered, in the refrigerator for up to twenty-four hours.

PER SERVING

Calories 147 · Protein 3g · Total Fat 1g · Saturated Fat 0g · Cholesterol 0mg · Carbohydrate 35g · Dietary Fiber 6g · Sodium 72mg

Roasted Eggplant and Red Pepper Soup

This exotic Middle Eastern–style soup, at once smoky and spicy, easily becomes a main course served with the Romaine Salad with Lemon-Date Dressing (page 80) and Garlic-Herb Pita Toasts (page 26). When roasting the vegetables, the idea is to soften and slightly char them, not completely blacken them, as they will finish cooking in the soup. MAKES 6 SERVINGS

- 2 large eggplants (about 1 pound each), quartered lengthwise
- 2 medium red bell peppers (about 6 ounces each), quartered lengthwise
- 6 large cloves garlic, peeled
- 4 tablespoons extra-virgin olive oil
- 1 large onion (about 10 ounces), finely chopped
- 1 small carrot (about 2 ounces), finely chopped
- 3 medium ripe tomatoes (about 6 ounces each), peeled, seeded, and chopped
- 2 bay leaves
- ½ teaspoon cumin seeds
- ¼ teaspoon dried oregano
- ¼ teaspoon dried thyme leaves
- Salt and freshly ground black pepper, to taste
- 8 cups vegetable broth, preferably Microwave Vegetable Broth (page 37) or low-sodium canned
- ⅛ teaspoon cayenne pepper, or to taste (optional)
- ½ cup chopped fresh cilantro (optional)
- 1 tablespoon fresh lemon juice (optional)

Preheat the oven to 400F (205C). Lightly oil 1 large or 2 medium baking sheets and set aside.

Rub the cut sides of the eggplants, the skin sides of the bell peppers, and the garlic with 1 tablespoon of the oil. Arrange the eggplants and peppers, skin side up, on the prepared baking sheet. Add the garlic.

Roast until the garlic is browned and softened, turning once, about 15 minutes; the peppers are blistered and beginning to char, about 20 minutes; and the eggplants are softened, slightly wrinkled, and beginning to char, about 30 minutes. Place the peppers in a paper bag, twist to close, and set aside for 20 minutes. Set the eggplant and garlic aside to cool.

When the eggplants are cool enough to handle, peel away the skin. Coarsely chop and set aside. Peel off the skins of the peppers with your fingers or with a small paring knife. Coarsely chop and set aside. Chop the garlic and set aside.

Meanwhile, in a large stockpot, heat the remaining oil over medium-low heat. Add the onion and carrot and cook, stirring occasionally, until very soft but not browned, 10 to 15 minutes. Add the tomatoes, bay leaves, cumin seeds, oregano, thyme, salt, and pepper. Bring to a brisk simmer over medium-high heat, stirring constantly. Add the broth and bring to a boil over high heat. Reduce the heat, cover, and simmer gently for 15 minutes. Stir in the roasted eggplant, bell peppers, garlic, and cayenne, if using. Bring to a brisk simmer over medium-high heat. Reduce the heat, cover, and simmer gently for 15 minutes.

Remove and discard the bay leaves. Working in batches, transfer the soup to a food processor fitted with the metal blade or to a blender. Process or blend until smooth and pureed. Return to the stockpot and reheat over low heat, stirring occasionally. Season with additional salt and pepper, if necessary. Stir in the cilantro and lemon juice, if using, just before serving. Serve hot.

Advance Preparation The cooked soup, without the optional cilantro and lemon juice, can be held over very low heat for one hour before serving. The cooled soup, without the cilantro and lemon juice, can be stored, covered, in the refrigerator for up to twenty-four hours. Reheat over low heat.

PER SERVING

Calories 237 · Protein 18g · Total Fat 10g · Saturated Fat 1g · Cholesterol 0mg · Carbohydrate 23g · Dietary Fiber 11g · Sodium 707mg

Garlic Soup with Potatoes, Italian Style

Variations of garlic soup abound throughout the Mediterranean, particularly in France, Spain, and Italy. With the increasing popularity of Mediterranean cuisine and an increasing interest in the healthful benefits of garlic, they are becoming rather voguish. But like so many other Mediterranean dishes, they originated as poor man's fare—indeed, the Provençal variation, aïgo boulido, is not much more than boiled water flavored with garlic and olive oil ladled over a piece of stale bread with perhaps a raw egg scrambled in for good measure. In this hearty Italian version, potatoes are used as a thickening agent. Served with Classic Bruschetta with Olive Oil, Garlic, and Coarse Salt (page 6) and Red Kidney Bean and Mixed Green Salad (page 67), the following recipe quickly serves four hungry people for dinner.

MAKES 4 TO 6 SERVINGS

- ¼ cup extra-virgin olive oil
- 1 medium onion (about 8 ounces), chopped
- 1 small carrot (about 2 ounces), chopped
- 1 stalk celery, chopped
- 1¼ pounds russet potatoes (about 2 large), peeled and cut into ½-inch cubes
- 1 large head garlic, separated into cloves, peeled
- 4 cups vegetable broth, preferably Basic Vegetable Broth (page 38) or low-sodium canned
- 2 cups water
- ½ teaspoon dried thyme leaves
- 1 bay leaf
- Salt and freshly ground black pepper, to taste
- Chopped fresh chives or the thinly sliced green tops of scallions (optional)

In a large deep-sided skillet with a lid, heat the oil over medium heat. Add the onion, carrot, and celery and cook, stirring, for 3 minutes. Reduce the heat to medium-low and add the potatoes and garlic. Cook, stirring often, until the onion is translucent and the potatoes and garlic are softened, about 15 minutes. Add the broth, water, thyme, bay leaf, salt, and pepper; bring to a boil over high heat. Reduce the heat, cover, and simmer gently until all the ingredients are very soft, about 30 minutes. Remove from the heat and let cool slightly. Remove and discard the bay leaf.

Working in batches, transfer the soup mixture to a food processor fitted with the metal blade or to a blender; process or blend until smooth. Return to a clean pot and cook over low heat, stirring, until heated through. Season with additional salt and pepper as necessary. Serve hot, garnished with the chives if desired.

Advance Preparation This soup will keep for one hour, covered, over very low heat. It can be cooled and stored, covered, in the refrigerator for up to two days. Reheat over low heat. Stir well before serving, as it tends to separate.

PER SERVING

Calories 306 · Protein 15g · Total Fat 14g · Saturated Fat 2g · Cholesterol 0mg · Carbohydrate 33g · Dietary Fiber 7g · Sodium 541mg

Gazpacho

This uncooked chilled soup relies solely upon fresh vegetables for quality. In Andalusia, many cooks would be horrified if you asked for the Tabasco sauce (and even worse, Worcestershire sauce) that often spikes gazpacho in this country. In their eyes, it's an adulteration of the pure fresh flavors of tomato and bell pepper that are the heart and soul of Andalusia's world-famous contribution to gastronomy. But if you must, offer it separately, as an option. If golden peppers are unavailable, use green instead. While this soup is not traditionally served as a meal in Spain, it easily becomes a light lunch if you include all the delicious optional garnishes.

MAKES 4 SERVINGS

2 pounds vine-ripened tomatoes, peeled, seeded, and coarsely chopped, with juices
1 medium golden bell pepper (about 6 ounces), top third cut off and reserved, remainder coarsely chopped
1 medium red bell pepper (about 6 ounces), coarsely chopped
1 bunch thinly sliced scallions, white and green parts, separated
1 slice stale Italian or French bread (1 ounce), crusts removed, soaked in water and squeezed dry
2 tablespoons sherry vinegar or balsamic vinegar
2 large cloves garlic, finely chopped
Pinch ground cumin (optional)
Pinch cayenne pepper (optional)
Salt and freshly ground black pepper, to taste
3 tablespoons extra-virgin olive oil
Pinch sugar, or to taste
Optional garnishes: croutons, diced cucumber, diced green bell pepper, toasted slivered almonds, toasted chopped hazelnuts (see Cook's Tip, page 121), and additional olive oil

In a food processor fitted with the metal blade, place the tomatoes, chopped bell peppers, white parts of the scallions, bread, vinegar, garlic, cumin and cayenne (if using), and salt and pepper. Process until smooth and foamy. With the motor running, add the oil in a steady stream. Transfer to a large bowl. Cover and refrigerate for at least 1 hour.

While the soup is chilling, cut the reserved yellow pepper top into 4 equal rings. Stir the chilled soup well. Taste and adjust the seasonings, adding sugar to taste, as necessary. Divide evenly among 4 chilled soup bowls. Float a yellow pepper ring in the middle of each and garnish with the green parts of the scallions. Serve chilled, passing the optional garnishes separately if desired.

Advance Preparation The soup can be stored, covered, in the refrigerator for up to twenty-four hours.

PER SERVING

Calories 188 · Protein 4g · Total Fat 11g · Saturated Fat 2g · Cholesterol 0mg · Carbohydrate 22g · Dietary Fiber 4g · Sodium 69mg

Variation To create a distinctively golden and sweet gazpacho, use all yellow vine-ripened tomatoes and yellow bell peppers. Garnish with diced red tomatoes and green bell peppers.

Tomato-Fennel Soup

This elegant and subtly flavored soup makes a perfect first course during the winter months, when fresh fennel is abundant in many well-stocked supermarkets but vine-ripened tomatoes are in short supply. Its consistency can be thinned with the addition of more broth or water.

MAKES 4 SERVINGS

- 2 tablespoons extra-virgin olive oil
- 1 medium fennel bulb (about 12 ounces), trimmed, cored, and chopped; 2 tablespoons of the feathery leaves reserved
- 4 medium shallots, finely chopped
- 1 small carrot (about 2 ounces), finely chopped
- 1 (28-ounce) can whole plum tomatoes
- ½ cup vegetable broth, preferably Basic Vegetable Broth (page 38) or low-sodium canned
- Salt and freshly ground black pepper

In a medium stockpot, heat the oil over medium-low heat. Add the fennel, shallots, and carrot; cook, stirring occasionally, until vegetables are very soft but not browned, about 15 minutes.

Add the tomatoes with juice and the broth; bring to a boil over high heat. Reduce the heat and simmer gently, uncovered, for 15 minutes, stirring occasionally. Transfer the mixture, in batches if necessary, to a food processor fitted with the metal blade or to a blender. Process or blend until smooth and pureed. Serve hot, garnished with the reserved fennel leaves.

Advance Preparation The soup can be held, covered, for one hour over very low heat before serving. The soup can be stored, covered, in the refrigerator for up to two days. Reheat over low heat.

PER SERVING

Calories 156 · Protein 5g · Total Fat 8g · Saturated Fat 1g · Cholesterol 0mg · Carbohydrate 21g · Dietary Fiber 5g · Sodium 539mg

Variations Add ⅛ teaspoon crushed aniseed to the recipe when you add the tomatoes and broth for a more pronounced licorice flavor. Serve the soup completely chilled.

If shallots are unavailable, use ½ cup chopped red onion or the white parts of scallions instead.

Tomato-Rice Soup

There are many, many versions of this popular soup combo throughout the Mediterranean. Some puree the tomato soup base before adding the rice, while most leave it chunky. I prefer mine pureed, but if you like yours on the chunkier side, puree just half the soup base, or skip the step altogether. Also, you can use brown rice instead of the refined white varieties to make this soup even healthier, but increase the final cooking time by about fifteen minutes.

MAKES 6 SERVINGS

2 tablespoons extra-virgin olive oil
1 medium onion (about 6 ounces), chopped
4 ounces (about 2 small) carrots, chopped
1 stalk celery, chopped
4 garlic cloves, finely chopped
1½ pounds ripe tomatoes, peeled, seeded, and coarsely chopped
½ teaspoon dried thyme
¼ teaspoon dried oregano
Salt and freshly ground black pepper, to taste
6 cups vegetable broth, preferably Basic Vegetable Broth (page 38) or low-sodium canned
1 bay leaf
½ cup arborio or long-grain white rice
Chopped fresh basil, mint, or parsley (optional)

Heat the oil in a medium stockpot over medium-low heat. Add the onion, carrots, and celery; cook, stirring occasionally, until the vegetables are softened, about 10 minutes. Add the garlic and increase the heat to medium; cook, stirring, for 1 minute. Add the tomatoes, thyme, oregano, salt, and pepper; cook over medium heat, stirring frequently, for 10 minutes.

Add the broth and bay leaf to the pot; bring to a boil over medium-high heat. Reduce the heat, cover, and simmer gently 30 minutes, stirring occasionally. Remove the bay leaf.

Working in batches, transfer the mixture to a food processor fitted with the metal blade or to a blender; process or blend until fairly smooth. Return to a clean stockpot. Bring to a boil over high heat and add the rice. Reduce the heat, cover, and simmer gently until the rice is cooked through but not mushy, 15 to 20 minutes. Garnish with the basil, if using, just before serving.

Advance Preparation The soup can be held, covered, over very low heat for 1 hour before serving. The soup can be stored, covered, in the refrigerator for up to three days. Reheat over low heat. The rice will have absorbed additional broth, so you will need to add more broth or water, and the grains will no longer be cooked al dente.

PER SERVING

Calories 191 · Protein 14g · Total Fat 5g · Saturated Fat 1g · Cholesterol 0mg · Carbohydrate 24g · Dietary Fiber 7g · Sodium 543mg

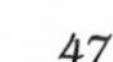

Simple Mediterranean Vegetable Soup

A simplified variation of minestrone, this makes a delicious light lunch or first course. For a more substantial soup, cooked white beans, red kidney beans, or chickpeas can be added.

MAKES 4 TO 6 SERVINGS

- 2 tablespoons extra-virgin olive oil
- 1 medium onion (about 6 ounces), chopped
- 1 small carrot (about 2 ounces), peeled and chopped
- 3 large cloves garlic, finely chopped
- 6 cups vegetable broth, preferably Basic Vegetable Broth (page 38) or low-sodium canned
- 8 ounces plum tomatoes, seeded and coarsely chopped
- 1 bay leaf
- Salt and freshly ground black pepper, to taste
- 4 ounces green beans, trimmed, cut into 1-inch lengths
- ¼ cup tubettini, ditalini, or orzo pasta
- 4 ounces coarsely chopped fresh spinach leaves (optional)

In a medium stockpot, heat the oil over medium-low heat. Add the onion and carrot and cook, stirring occasionally, until the vegetables are softened, about 10 minutes. Add the garlic and increase the heat to medium; cook, stirring, for 1 minute. Add the broth, tomatoes, bay leaf, salt, and pepper; bring to a boil over medium-high heat. Reduce the heat, cover, and simmer gently for 20 minutes.

Add the green beans and pasta; bring to a boil over high heat. Reduce the heat, cover, and simmer gently until the pasta is barely al dente, 5 to 8 minutes. Add the spinach, if using, stirring well to combine. Cook, covered, until the pasta is cooked al dente and the green beans are tender, about 5 minutes. Serve hot.

Advance Preparation The soup can be held, covered, over very low heat for one hour before serving, but the pasta will no longer be cooked al dente. The completely cooled soup can be stored, covered, in the refrigerator for up to three days. Reheat over low heat.

PER SERVING

Calories 194 · Protein 19g · Total Fat 7g · Saturated Fat 1g · Cholesterol 0mg · Carbohydrate 16g · Dietary Fiber 8g · Sodium 789mg

Meal-in-a-Bowl Soups

Persian-Style, Multi-Bean Noodle Soup

Though long on ingredients, this wholesome, delicious, and rather exotic multi-bean and noodle soup is ready in just about an hour with the use of convenient canned beans. MAKES 6 SERVINGS

- 1 small red onion (about 4 ounces), finely chopped
- 7 cloves garlic, finely chopped
- 3 tablespoons extra-virgin olive oil
- 1 teaspoon turmeric
- 2 medium yellow onions (about 6 ounces each), chopped
- 3 cups vegetable broth, preferably Microwave Vegetable Broth (page 37) or low-sodium canned
- 3 cups water
- ¼ cup lentils, rinsed and picked over
- Pinch cayenne, or to taste
- Salt and freshly ground black pepper, to taste
- 1 pound spinach with stems, washed and stems discarded, or 1 (10-ounce) bag fresh ready-washed spinach leaves, chopped
- ½ cup fresh flat-leaf parsley, chopped
- ½ cup fresh dill, chopped
- ½ cup thinly sliced scallions, green part only, or ½ cup chopped fresh chives
- 1 cup cooked red kidney beans (see Box, page 18) or about ⅔ (15-ounce) can red kidney beans, rinsed and drained
- 1 cup cooked cannellini beans (see Box, page 18) or about ⅔ (15-ounce) can cannellini or other white beans, rinsed and drained
- 1 cup cooked chickpeas (see Box, page 18) or about ⅔ (15-ounce) can chickpeas, rinsed and drained
- 4 ounces Persian-style noodles, dry linguine, or somen noodles, broken in half
- 1 tablespoon fresh lemon juice
- 1 tablespoon distilled white vinegar
- ½ cup chopped fresh mint

Preheat the oven to 425F (220C). Place the red onion and about 3 cloves of the chopped garlic in a small baking dish and toss with 1 tablespoon of the oil. Cover the dish tightly with foil and bake for 10 minutes or until softened and fragrant. Remove from the oven, sprinkle with ½ teaspoon of the turmeric, and stir well to combine. Let stand, covered, until ready to use.

Meanwhile, in a medium stockpot, heat the remaining oil over medium heat. Add the yellow onions and cook, stirring often, until lightly browned and fragrant, 5 to 7 minutes. Add the remaining garlic and cook, stirring constantly, for 1 minute. Add the broth, water, lentils, remaining turmeric, cayenne (if using), salt, and pepper; bring to a boil over high heat, stirring and scraping the bottom of the pot to loosen any browned bits. Immediately reduce the heat and simmer gently, partially covered, for 30 minutes.

Add the spinach, parsley, dill, and scallions to the pot, stirring well to combine. Bring to a brisk simmer over medium-high heat. Immediately reduce the heat, and simmer gently, uncovered, for 10 minutes, stirring occasionally. Add the beans and noodles, stirring well to combine; return to a brisk simmer over medium-high heat. Immediately reduce the heat, and simmer gently, uncovered, until the pasta is cooked al dente, about 10 minutes, stirring occasionally.

Just before serving, add the lemon juice and vinegar to the reserved red onion–garlic mixture, stirring well to combine. Serve the soup hot, garnished with the red onion–garlic mixture and chopped mint.

Advance Preparation The soup can be held, covered, over very low heat for one hour before serving, but the pasta will no longer be cooked al dente and you will need to add additional broth or water. The soup can be stored, covered, in the refrigerator for up to two days. Reheat over low heat, adding additional broth or water. Prepare the onion-garlic garnish the day of serving.

PER SERVING

Calories 359 · Protein 21g · Total Fat 9g · Saturated Fat 1g · Cholesterol 0mg · Carbohydrate 52g · Dietary Fiber 13g · Sodium 311mg

Variation If you are short on time, omit the onion-garlic garnish prepared in the first step, and add the entire amount of garlic and turmeric when they are called for. Use all the olive oil for cooking the yellow onions. Stir the lemon juice and vinegar into the soup just before serving.

Bouillabaisse of Spinach, Potatoes, Chickpeas, and Saffron

Bouillabaisse, which roughly translates into "boiling hard without stopping," is a French term applied to a whole family of soups and stews whose ingredients often bear little resemblance to the fish extravaganza so popular in American restaurants. Variations of this simple—and less costly—spinach and potato bouillabaisse are more likely to be prepared in home kitchens throughout Provence and Brittany, particularly during winter when it's too cold to fish. The Bretons, with a nod to their longtime trading partner, India, typically replace the saffron from Spain with curry powder—either way, the results are equally delicious.

MAKES 4 SERVINGS

- 2 tablespoons extra-virgin olive oil
- 1 cup chopped onion
- 3 garlic cloves, finely chopped
- 3 cups vegetable broth, preferably Basic Vegetable Broth (page 38) or low-sodium canned
- ½ cup dry white wine
- 1 pound spinach with stems, washed and stems discarded, or 1 (10-ounce) bag fresh ready-washed spinach leaves, cut into ¼-inch-wide strips
- 1½ pounds boiling potatoes, preferably red-skinned, unpeeled, cut into 1-inch pieces
- 1 bay leaf
- Salt and freshly ground black pepper, to taste
- ⅛ teaspoon powdered saffron or ½ teaspoon curry powder, or to taste

2 cups cooked chickpeas (see Box, page 18) or 1 (19-ounce) can chickpeas, drained and rinsed
4 thick slices peasant-style bread, lightly toasted (optional)

In a medium stockpot, heat the oil over medium heat. Add the onion and cook, stirring, until lightly browned and fragrant, 5 to 7 minutes. Add the garlic and cook, stirring constantly, for 1 minute. Add the broth and wine; bring to a boil over high heat, stirring and scraping the bottom of the pot to loosen any browned bits. Add half the spinach, the potatoes, bay leaf, salt, and pepper; return to a boil. Reduce the heat to medium and cook, uncovered, until the potatoes are just tender throughout, 12 to 15 minutes.

Stir in the saffron. Add the chickpeas and remaining spinach, stirring well to combine. Bring to a boil over high heat. Immediately remove from the heat, cover, and let stand for 3 minutes. Remove and discard the bay leaf. If using, place a toasted bread slice in the bottom of each of 4 serving bowls. Using a slotted spoon, divide the vegetables evenly among the bowls. Ladle in the broth and serve at once.

Advance Preparation The soup can be held, covered, over very low heat for one hour before serving, but the spinach will lose its bright green color. The soup can be stored, covered, in the refrigerator for up to three days. Reheat over low heat.

PER SERVING

Calories 388 · Protein 21g · Total Fat 9g · Saturated Fat 1g · Cholesterol 0mg · Carbohydrate 54g · Dietary Fiber 7g · Sodium 461mg

Tuscan Bread Soup with Vegetables and Beans
(Ribollita)

Ribollita means reboiled, which is exactly what is done to minestrone sandwiched between layers of peasant bread in this rustic dish from Tuscany, well known for its bread soups. Some say these soups date back to the days when unleavened breads were used for plates. Others point out their economical use of stale bread and leftover soup or less than visually perfect vegetables. Most everyone agrees these soups are rib-sticking, ribollita being perhaps the heartiest of all. The following recipe uses toasted Tuscan garlic bread, to create a firmer, soupier ribollita. For a more traditional version, see the variation below. If you have no leftover minestrone and are pressed for time, substitute a full recipe of the Quick Tuscan-Style Minestrone (page 57) for the half recipe of classic minestrone, preferably without the pasta. **MAKES 4 SERVINGS**

½ recipe Classic Italian Minestrone (page 55), freshly made or left over, preferably cooked without the pasta
4 (½-inch-thick) slices peasant-style Italian bread (about 4 ounces), lightly toasted or grilled on one or both sides
1 large clove garlic, halved
½ tablespoon extra-virgin olive oil
Coarse salt (optional)
Extra-virgin olive oil in a cruet (optional)

If using freshly made minestrone, cover and keep warm over low heat until needed. If using leftover minestrone: In a medium stockpot, bring

Cook's Tip

In a pinch, assemble the soup directly in individual soup bowls.

the minestrone to a simmer over medium-low heat, stirring occasionally. Cover and keep warm over low heat until needed.

Rub a toasted side of each bread slice with the flat sides of the garlic halves, then brush the same sides evenly with the ½ tablespoon oil. Sprinkle the oiled sides with a few grains of coarse salt, if using. Cut into quarters.

Arrange one-fourth of the bread along the bottom of a 2½-quart deep-sided baking dish or casserole, oiled sides up. Ladle one-fourth of the soup over the bread. Continue layering in this fashion, ending with the soup. Serve at once, with the additional oil passed separately, if using.

PER SERVING

Calories 369 · Protein 23g · Total Fat 10g · Saturated Fat 2g · Cholesterol 0mg · Carbohydrate 50g · Dietary Fiber 13g · Sodium 726mg

Variation To make a really rib-sticking ribollita where most of the broth is absorbed by the bread, as many Italians prefer, double the amount of bread and don't toast it, thereby omitting the garlic, the ½ tablespoon of olive oil, and the optional coarse salt. If you decide you'd like it a bit soupier, simply add some heated vegetable broth.

Tunisian Chickpea Soup

This inspiring soup gets its kick from harissa, a hot chile pepper sauce redolent of garlic, cumin, coriander, and caraway that is used in all sorts of soups, stews, and vegetable and couscous dishes throughout North Africa. Harissa is sold in tubes, cans, and jars in Middle Eastern markets and many specialty stores and is worth seeking out. However, I've found that garlicky Chinese chile paste, available in many well-stocked supermarkets, is a good substitute. Crushed hot red pepper flakes will do in a pinch.

MAKES 6 SERVINGS

- 1 small red onion (about 4 ounces), sliced into very thin rings
- 2 tablespoons extra-virgin olive oil
- 5 cups vegetable broth, preferably Microwave Vegetable Broth (page 37) or low-sodium canned
- 1¼ cups dried chickpeas, soaked overnight in 3 cups water (see Box, page 18, for the quick-soak method), drained
- 4 large garlic cloves, finely chopped
- 2 teaspoons harissa or Chinese chile paste
- ½ teaspoon ground cumin
- Salt and freshly ground black pepper, to taste
- 6 (½-inch-thick) slices peasant-style bread, lightly toasted, coarsely torn
- To serve (optional): coarsely chopped capers, thinly sliced scallions, and extra-virgin olive oil

Preheat the oven to 425F (220C). Place the onion in an 8- or 9-inch pie pan and toss with the olive oil. Cover the pan tightly with foil and bake for 15 minutes, or until softened and fragrant.

Remove from the oven and let stand, covered, until ready to use.

Meanwhile, in a medium stockpot, bring the broth to a boil over high heat. Add the chickpeas and bring to a boil. Reduce the heat, cover, and simmer gently until the chickpeas are slightly softened, 25 to 30 minutes. Add the garlic, harissa, cumin, salt, and pepper; stir well to combine. Cover and simmer for 40 minutes.

Add the reserved onion slices with oil to the chickpea mixture. Simmer, covered, until the chickpeas are very tender, 15 to 20 minutes.

To serve, divide the bread pieces equally among 6 soup bowls. Ladle the soup evenly over the bread. Serve at once, with the capers, scallions, and olive oil passed separately, if using.

Advance Preparation The soup can be held, covered, over very low heat, for one hour before serving. The completely cooled soup can be stored, covered, in the refrigerator for up to three days. Reheat over low heat.

PER SERVING

Calories 322 · Protein 20g · Total Fat 8g · Saturated Fat 1g · Cholesterol 0mg · Carbohydrate 44g · Dietary Fiber 11g · Sodium 609mg

Egyptian-Style Lentil Soup

This is my all-time favorite lentil soup. A source of nourishment in Egypt since the beginning of history, it has just recently become part of my culinary repertoire—after one mouthful, it's sure to become part of yours! **MAKES 6 SERVINGS**

- 1 small red onion (about 4 ounces), sliced into very thin rings
- 4 tablespoons extra-virgin olive oil
- 2 medium yellow onions (about 6 ounces each), coarsely chopped
- 5 ounces (about 2½ small) carrots, coarsely chopped
- 1 stalk celery, coarsely chopped
- 2 large cloves garlic, finely chopped
- 1½ teaspoons cumin seeds
- 1 teaspoon fennel seeds
- 4 cups vegetable broth, preferably Microwave Vegetable Broth (page 37) or low-sodium canned
- 4 cups water
- 1½ cups lentils, rinsed and picked over
- 1 small dried hot red chile pepper, left whole, or cayenne pepper to taste (optional)
- Salt and freshly ground black pepper, to taste
- Juice of ½ large lemon (about 2 tablespoons)
- Lemon wedges (optional)

Preheat the oven to 425F (220C). Place the red onion in an 8- or 9-inch pie pan and toss with 2 tablespoons of the oil. Cover the pan tightly with foil and bake for 15 minutes, or until softened and fragrant. Remove from the oven and let stand, covered, until ready to use.

Meanwhile, in a large stockpot, heat the remaining oil over medium-low heat. Add the yellow onions, carrots, celery, garlic, cumin, and fennel seeds and cook, stirring occasionally, until the vegetables are tender, about 15 minutes. Add the broth, water, lentils, and chile, if using; season lightly with salt and pepper. Bring to a boil over medium-high heat. Immediately reduce the heat, partially cover, and simmer gently for 30 minutes, stirring occasionally. Uncover and simmer for 15 more minutes, stirring occasionally, or until the lentils are very tender and the broth is slightly thickened.

Remove and discard the chile, if used. Stir in the reserved red onion with oil and the lemon juice. Season with additional salt and pepper as necessary. Serve hot, passing the lemon wedges separately if desired.

Advance Preparation The soup can be held, covered, over very low heat for one hour before serving, but will grow thicker, so you will need to add additional broth or water. The soup can be stored, covered, in the refrigerator for up to two days. Reheat over low heat.

PER SERVING

Calories 320 · Protein 22g · Total Fat 10g · Saturated Fat 1g · Cholesterol 0mg · Carbohydrate 39g · Dietary Fiber 19g · Sodium 367mg

Lentil and Escarole Soup

Mild, sweet-tasting lentils are cleverly paired with aggressive, bitter-tasting greens in countless dishes throughout the Mediterranean. This particular soup is my family's favorite way to enjoy escarole—in fact, it is the only way for my children, who otherwise won't touch the rather churlish, yet ever so healthy green.

MAKES 4 SERVINGS

- 2 tablespoons extra-virgin olive oil
- 1 medium onion (6 to 8 ounces), chopped
- 1 stalk celery, chopped
- 4 ounces (about 2 small) carrots, chopped
- 2 cloves garlic, finely chopped
- 2 large tomatoes, about 8 ounces each, peeled, seeded, and chopped
- 1¼ cups lentils, rinsed and picked over
- 3 cups vegetable broth, preferably Basic Vegetable Broth (page 38) or low-sodium canned
- 3 cups water
- Salt and freshly ground black pepper, to taste
- 1 large head escarole (about 1¼ pounds), washed, drained, and coarsely chopped

In a medium stockpot, heat the oil over medium-low heat. Add the onion, celery, carrots, and garlic. Cook, stirring often, until the vegetables are softened, about 10 minutes. Add the tomatoes and cook, stirring often, for 5 minutes.

Add the lentils, broth, water, salt, and pepper; bring to a boil over high heat. Reduce the heat and simmer gently, partially covered, until the lentils are tender but not falling apart, about 45 minutes. Add the escarole, stirring well to combine. Bring to a brisk simmer over medium-high heat. Reduce the heat and simmer gently, uncovered, until the escarole is tender, about 10 minutes, stirring occasionally. Serve hot.

Advance Preparation The soup can be held, covered, over very low heat for one hour before serving. The soup can be stored, covered, in the refrigerator for two days. Reheat over low heat. In either instance, if it becomes too thickened, add more broth or water.

PER SERVING

Calories 386 · Protein 30g · Total Fat 8g · Saturated Fat 1g · Cholesterol 0mg · Carbohydrate 54g · Dietary Fiber 27g · Sodium 454mg

Classic Italian Minestrone

Italian minestrone is truly the king of Mediterranean vegetable soups, a grand assortment of seasonal vegetables, beans, and pasta resulting in a perfect balance of complex carbohydrates and protein. The following recipe is essentially an assimilation of many I've collected over the years, and includes my favorite vegetables that are generally available year-round. But the possibilities are virtually endless, so feel free to add your own favorites, so long as the more delicate vegetables (tiny peas and pencil-thin asparagus tips) are added toward the end, while the stronger flavored vegetables (turnips and broccoli) are cooked separately, then also added toward the end. I've purposely supplied a recipe serving eight so that leftovers would be available for Tuscan Bread Soup with Vegetables and Beans (page 51), but the recipe can easily be halved, if you prefer. **MAKES 8 SERVINGS**

1 cup dried white beans, such as cannellini, Great Northern, navy, or borlotti (cranberry) beans, soaked overnight in 3 cups of water (see Box, page 18 for the quick-soak method), drained
8 cups vegetable broth, preferably Basic Vegetable Broth (page 38) or low-sodium canned
¼ cup extra-virgin olive oil
2 medium onions (about 6 ounces each), chopped
4 ounces (about 2 small) carrots, chopped
2 stalks celery, chopped
4 large cloves garlic, finely chopped
2 pounds plum tomatoes, chopped, all the juices included, or 1 (28-ounce) can whole plum tomatoes, drained and chopped, juices reserved
½ teaspoon dried thyme leaves
¼ teaspoon ground sage
2 bay leaves
Salt and freshly ground black pepper, to taste
8 ounces potatoes, peeled and cut into ½-inch cubes
4 ounces green beans, trimmed and cut into 1-inch pieces
2 cups shredded green cabbage
½ cup uncooked elbow macaroni or other similar small pasta
2 small zucchini (about 4 ounces each), quartered lengthwise, then cut into ½-inch pieces
2 ounces spinach (about 2 packed cups) stemmed and shredded
¼ cup finely chopped flat-leaf parsley

In a large saucepan or medium stockpot, bring the drained soaked beans and 4 cups of the broth to a boil over medium-high heat. Reduce the heat, cover, and simmer gently until the beans are tender but not falling apart, 45 minutes to 1 hour, depending on the maturity of the beans. Remove from the heat and set aside in the cooking liquid.

In a large stockpot, heat the oil over medium-low heat. Add the onions, carrots, and celery and

Cook's Tip

Cooking the beans in the broth is essential to the delicious flavor of this particular minestrone, so substituting canned beans is not recommended here. For a quick-cooking minestrone that uses cooked beans, either fresh or canned, see the Quick Tuscan-Style Minestrone Soup (page 57).

cook, stirring occasionally, until the vegetables are softened, about 10 minutes. Add the garlic and increase the heat to medium; cook, stirring, for 2 minutes. Add the remaining broth, tomatoes and their juices, thyme, sage, bay leaves, salt, and pepper; bring to a boil over high heat. Reduce the heat, cover, and simmer gently for 20 minutes.

Add the potatoes, green beans, cabbage, and pasta, stirring well to combine. Bring to a boil over high heat. Reduce the heat, cover, and simmer gently for 10 minutes. Add the zucchini and spinach, stirring well to combine. Cover, adjust the heat to maintain a gentle simmer, and cook for 5 minutes. Add the beans and their cooking liquid, and the parsley, stirring well to combine. Cover, adjust the heat to maintain a gentle simmer, and cook, stirring occasionally, until the pasta and vegetables are tender and the beans are heated through, 5 to 10 minutes. Serve hot.

Advance Preparation The soaked beans can be cooked in the broth up to two days ahead of time and refrigerated in their liquid. The soup can be held, covered, over very low heat for up to one hour before serving; decrease the pasta's initial cooking time, adding it about five minutes after the potatoes, green beans, and cabbage. The soup can be stored, covered, in the refrigerator for up to two days, but the pasta will become a bit soggy. You will probably need to add more broth or water to the soup. Reheat over low heat. If you like, cook the pasta separately and add it shortly before serving.

PER SERVING

Calories 289 · Protein 21g · Total Fat 8g · Saturated Fat 1g · Cholesterol 0mg · Carbohydrate 38g · Dietary Fiber 12g · Sodium 561mg

Variations For a Milanese rendition, substitute ½ cup of arborio rice for the pasta.

For a Spanish-style vegetable soup, use rice instead of the pasta, and add a diced roasted red bell pepper and a pinch or two of cayenne.

Omit the pasta or rice altogether, especially if the soup is to be used in Tuscan Bread Soup with Vegetables and Beans (page 51), where it is typically left out.

Provençal Pumpkin Soup with Winter Pistou

Pumpkin is a popular vegetable in Provençal cooking, although the variety grown in Provence, the Musquée de Provence, is denser and more flavorful than most grown here. Winter squashes such as butternut, acorn, or Hubbard, however, make fine substitutes. If you prefer pumpkin, try to use a cooking variety such as Sugar Pie instead of the standard jack-o'-lantern variety, which tends to be overly stringy and somewhat flavorless. MAKES 4 TO 6 SERVINGS

- 1 (3-pound) cooking pumpkin or butternut squash, peeled
- 2 tablespoons extra-virgin olive oil
- 2 large onions (about 8 ounces each), chopped
- 2 cloves garlic, peeled
- About 4 cups vegetable broth, preferably Basic Vegetable Broth (page 38) or low-sodium canned
- 1 cup cooked white rice
- 1 teaspoon ground sage
- Salt, preferably the coarse variety, and freshly ground black pepper, to taste
- ½ cup Winter Pistou (page 64)

Slice the pumpkin in half and discard the seeds and membrane. Cut the flesh into chunks and transfer, in batches, to a food processor fitted with the metal blade. Process with on/off motions until coarsely chopped. Set aside.

In a large nonstick skillet, heat the oil over medium heat. Add the onions and cook, stirring, until softened but not browned, about 5 minutes. Add the pumpkin, garlic, and 1 cup of the broth to the skillet; bring to a boil over high heat. Immediately reduce the heat to medium-low and cook, covered, for 30 minutes, or until pumpkin is very tender, stirring occasionally. Add the rice, sage, salt, and pepper. Cook, stirring, until heated through, about 3 minutes.

Transfer half the pumpkin mixture and 1 cup of the broth to a food processor fitted with the metal blade or to a blender; puree until smooth. Repeat with remaining pumpkin mixture and another 1 cup of the broth.

Transfer the mixture to a medium stockpot and add the remaining broth. Cook over low heat, stirring, until heated through, adding more broth or water as necessary to achieve the desired consistency.

To serve, divide the soup evenly among 4 to 6 soup bowls. Stir equal amounts of pistou into each and serve at once.

Advance Preparation The soup can be held, covered, over very low heat for up to one hour. The soup can be stored, covered, in the refrigerator for two days. Reheat over low heat. The Winter Pistou can be stored, covered, in the refrigerator for up to two days, but will lose a bit of its pungency.

PER SERVING

Calories 452 · Protein 18g · Total Fat 17g · Saturated Fat 2g · Cholesterol 0mg · Carbohydrate 64g · Dietary Fiber 12g · Sodium 762mg

Quick Tuscan-Style Minestrone Soup

Comforting and warm, this soup is perfect for those cold winter nights when the urge for a hot bowl of minestrone strikes, but you don't have the time to chop several vegetables, let alone soak beans. In a pinch, it's also a very respectable stand-in for the classic minestrone listed in the recipe for Tuscan Bread Soup with Vegetables and Beans (page 51).

MAKES 4 SERVINGS

2 tablespoons extra-virgin olive oil
1 medium onion (6 to 8 ounces), chopped
4 ounces (about 2 small) carrots, chopped
1 stalk celery, chopped
2 large cloves garlic, finely chopped
4 cups vegetable broth, preferably the Basic Vegetable Broth (page 38) or low-sodium canned
½ teaspoon dried thyme leaves
Salt and freshly ground black pepper, to taste
½ cup ditalini or other small pasta
½ cup diced canned tomatoes, juices included
2 cups cooked cannellini beans (see Box, page 18) or 1 (19-ounce) can canellini or other white beans, drained and rinsed
1½ cups cooked red kidney beans (see Box, page 18) or 1 (15-ounce) can red kidney beans, drained and rinsed
4 ounces fresh spinach, chopped

In a medium stockpot, heat the oil over medium heat. Add the onion, carrots, celery, and garlic; cook, stirring often, until softened, about 5 minutes. Add the broth, thyme, salt, and pepper; bring to a boil over high heat. Add the pasta and tomatoes, reduce the heat to medium-high, and simmer briskly for 8 minutes, or until the pasta is almost cooked al dente.

Reduce the heat to medium and stir in the beans and spinach. Cook, stirring occasionally, until the spinach is wilted, the beans are heated through, and the pasta is tender, about 5 minutes. Serve hot.

Advance Preparation The soup can be held, covered, over very low heat for one hour before serving; decrease the pasta's cooking time by a few minutes. The soup can be stored, covered, in the refrigerator for two days, but the pasta will become a bit soggy. You will probably need to add more broth or water. Reheat over low heat. If you like, cook the pasta separately and add it shortly before serving.

PER SERVING

Calories 387 · Protein 28g · Total Fat 8g · Saturated Fat 1g · Cholesterol 0mg · Carbohydrate 54g · Dietary Fiber 17g · Sodium 568mg

Pasta and Bean Soup
(Pasta e Fagioli)

Next to minestrone, pasta e fagioli—often pronounced "pasta fazool"—is perhaps the most widely known of Italian soups. Like the former, there are as many variations as there are cooks. However, the bean-thickened Tuscan classic is more stew than soup, and relies less on fresh vegetables for success. Even so, one serving provides over 200 percent of your daily requirement of vitamin A, 100 percent of vitamin C, 75 percent of calcium, and 50 percent of iron! Served with a crisp salad and lots of crusty Italian bread, this quick-cooking version makes an ideal wintertime meal. MAKES 5 OR 6 SERVINGS

- 3 tablespoons extra-virgin olive oil
- 1 medium onion (about 6 ounces), chopped
- 4 ounces (about 2 small) carrots, chopped
- 2 stalks celery, chopped
- 4 cloves garlic, finely chopped
- 2 (28-ounce) cans whole tomatoes, preferably plum, liquids reserved
- 4 cups vegetable broth, preferably Basic Vegetable Broth (page 38) or low-sodium canned
- 4 cups cooked cannellini beans (see Box, page 18) or 2 (19-ounce) cans cannellini or other white beans, drained and rinsed
- ¼ teaspoon dried thyme leaves
- ¼ teaspoon crushed red pepper flakes, or to taste
- 1 bay leaf
- Salt and freshly ground black pepper, to taste
- 1 cup uncooked elbow macaroni or other similar small pasta
- ¼ cup chopped fresh basil (optional)
- ¼ cup chopped fresh flat-leaf parsley (½ cup if not using basil)

In a medium stockpot, heat the oil over medium heat. Add the onion, carrots, celery, and garlic; cook, stirring often, until softened, about 5 minutes. Add the tomatoes and their liquid, broth, beans, thyme, red pepper flakes, bay leaf, salt, and pepper; bring to a boil over high heat. Reduce the heat and simmer, uncovered, for 15 minutes, stirring occasionally and breaking up the tomatoes with a wooden spoon.

Add the pasta and bring to a boil over high heat. Reduce the heat to medium and simmer briskly for about 10 minutes, stirring occasionally from

Cook's Tip

To reduce the amount of sodium to 489mg per serving, substitute no-salt-added canned whole tomatoes, available in most supermarkets, for the standard canned ones.

the bottom to prevent sticking, or until the pasta is cooked al dente. Reduce the heat to low and add the basil, if using, and parsley, stirring until just wilted. Serve hot.

Advance Preparation The finished soup can be held, covered, over very low heat for one hour before serving; decrease the pasta's cooking time by a few minutes. The soup can be stored, covered, in the refrigerator for two days, but the pasta will become a bit soggy. You will probably need to add more broth or water. Reheat over low heat. If you like, cook the pasta separately and add it shortly before serving.

PER SERVING

Calories 448 · Protein 28g · Total Fat 10g · Saturated Fat 1g · Cholesterol 0mg · Carbohydrate 66g · Dietary Fiber 20g · Sodium 1,124mg

Tomato-Lentil Soup with Brown Rice

Mediterranean cooks, who largely prefer refined short-grain white rice for risotto and long-grain white rice for pilaf, seldom use the brown variety, despite its established healthfulness. But I have found that the brown variety works well in soups with a fairly long simmering time, producing a heartier texture and slightly nuttier taste. This wholesome, mild-flavored soup is a safe choice to serve to children. MAKES 4 SERVINGS

- 2 tablespoons extra-virgin olive oil
- 2 bunches scallions (12 to 16), white parts chopped, ½ cup thinly sliced green tops reserved
- 4 ounces (about 2 small) carrots, chopped
- 1 stalk celery, chopped
- 2 large cloves garlic, finely chopped
- 4 cups vegetable broth, preferably Basic Vegetable Broth (page 38) or low-sodium canned
- 1 cup water
- 1 cup lentils, rinsed and picked over
- ¼ cup brown rice
- 1 (14-ounce) can whole tomatoes, drained, seeded, and coarsely chopped, juices reserved
- ½ teaspoon dried thyme leaves
- 1 large bay leaf
- Salt and freshly ground black pepper, to taste

In a medium stockpot, heat the oil over medium heat. Add the white parts of the scallions, the carrots, celery, and garlic; cook, stirring often, until softened, about 5 minutes.

Add the broth, water, lentils, rice, tomatoes and their juices, thyme, bay leaf, salt, and pepper;

bring to a boil over medium-high heat. Reduce the heat and simmer gently, partially covered, until the lentils and rice are tender, stirring occasionally, 50 to 60 minutes. Discard the bay leaf. Serve hot, garnished with the reserved scallion greens.

Advance Preparation The soup can be held, covered, over very low heat for one hour. The soup can be stored, covered, in the refrigerator for up to three days. Reheat over low heat. You will need to add more broth or water.

PER SERVING

Calories 374 · Protein 28g · Total Fat 8g · Saturated Fat 1g · Cholesterol 0mg · Carbohydrate 52g · Dietary Fiber 22g · Sodium 763mg

Provençal Vegetable Soup with Pistou

This thick and soul-satisfying vegetable soup is one of the best-loved dishes in Provençal kitchens. Although roasting the vegetables first is not traditional, the method allows the busy cook to enjoy the soup in just about an hour, and it lends this particular recipe a rich flavor. Lots of crusty French bread and a simple green salad round out the meal nicely.

MAKES 6 SERVINGS

- ¼ cup extra-virgin olive oil
- 4 cloves garlic, finely chopped
- 2 medium onions (about 6 ounces each), cut into ½-inch dice
- 2 small zucchini (about 4 ounces each), quartered lengthwise, then cut into ½-inch pieces
- ½ pound carrots, peeled and cut into ½-inch dice
- ¼ pound green beans, trimmed and cut into 1-inch pieces
- 1 stalk celery, cut into ½-inch dice
- 1 pound plum tomatoes, seeded and cut into 1-inch pieces
- Salt and freshly ground black pepper, to taste
- 5 cups vegetable broth, preferably Basic Vegetable Broth (page 38) or low-sodium canned
- 2 cups water
- ½ pound potatoes, peeled and cut into 1-inch pieces
- ½ cup uncooked elbow macaroni or other similar-sized pasta
- 2 cups cooked navy beans (see Box, page 18) or 1 (19-ounce) can navy, Great Northern, or other white beans, drained and rinsed
- Pistou Sauce (page 61)

Preheat the oven to 425F (220C). In a large ovenproof skillet, heat the oil over medium heat. Add the garlic and cook until slightly golden, stirring constantly, 1 to 2 minutes. Add the onions, zucchini, carrots, green beans, and celery; cook for 2 minutes, stirring and tossing constantly. Remove the skillet from the heat and add the tomatoes. Season lightly with salt and pepper and toss well to combine. Transfer the skillet to the oven and roast, uncovered, until the vegetables are beginning to brown and are just tender, 25 to 30 minutes, stirring and turning 3 or 4 times.

Meanwhile, in a large stockpot over medium-high heat, bring the broth and water to a boil. Add the potatoes, reduce the heat slightly, and boil gently for 5 minutes. Add the roasted vegetables and return to a boil over high heat. Reduce the heat and simmer for 5 minutes. Add the pasta and bring to a boil over high heat. Reduce the heat and simmer for about 10 minutes, stirring occasionally, or until the pasta is almost cooked al dente and the vegetables are tender. Stir in the beans, reduce the heat to low, and cook, stirring occasionally, until the pasta is cooked al dente and all is heated through, 5 to 10 minutes.

To serve, ladle the soup into bowls. Spoon about 2 tablespoons of pistou on top of each and serve at once.

Advance Preparation The soup can be held, covered, over very low heat up to one hour. The soup can be stored, covered, in the refrigerator for up to three days. Reheat over low heat. The pasta will no longer be cooked al dente and you might need to add more water or broth. The Pistou Sauce will keep for up to two days, covered, in the refrigerator, but will lose a bit of its pungency.

PER SERVING

Calories 368 · Protein 19g · Total Fat 15g · Saturated Fat 2g · Cholesterol 0mg · Carbohydrate 44g · Dietary Fiber 11g · Sodium 566mg

Pistou Sauce

Pistou is France's answer to Italy's pesto, minus the pine nuts. When it's headed for soup, bread soaked in the soup's broth is often added as a thickening agent. When it's used in pasta or vegetable dishes, it is often thinned with a bit of the cooking liquid. If you have coarse salt on hand, its use is highly recommended here, as many a thrifty Provençal cook has sprinkled it in his pistou in lieu of the salty and more expensive Parmesan.

MAKES ABOUT ¾ CUP

- 1 piece whole-wheat bread (about 1 ounce), crusts removed
- 3 to 4 tablespoons vegetable broth, preferably the broth from Provençal Vegetable Soup with Pistou (page 60) or low-sodium canned
- 1 cup packed fresh basil leaves
- 2 large cloves garlic, finely chopped
- 2 tablespoons extra-virgin olive oil
- ¼ teaspoon salt, preferably the coarse variety, or to taste
- Freshly ground black pepper, to taste

For use in soup: Soak the bread in the broth, using enough broth so that the bread is completely wet but not dripping liquid when lifted. Place in a food processor fitted with the metal blade and add the remaining ingredients. Process until smooth and well blended.

For use as a topping for pasta, vegetables, or pizza: Omit the bread and broth. Process the basil, garlic, olive oil, salt, and pepper in a food processor fitted with the metal blade until smooth and well blended.

PER 1 TABLESPOON

(with bread and broth):

Calories 28 · Protein 1g · Total Fat 2g · Saturated Fat 0g · Cholesterol 0mg · Carbohydrate 2g · Dietary Fiber 0g · Sodium 63mg

PER 2 TEASPOONS

(made without the bread or broth):

Calories 22 · Protein 0g · Total Fat 2g · Saturated Fat 0g · Cholesterol 0mg · Carbohydrate 0g · Dietary Fiber 0g · Sodium 39mg

Provençal Wheat Berry–Bean Soup

Available in most health-food stores, wheat berries are tiny kernels of whole wheat commonly used in soups, stews, salads, and pilaflike dishes throughout the Mediterranean. In Provence, this fiber-rich, protein-packed wheat berry soup is traditionally eaten in celebration of the fall wheat harvest. There, it is made with epeautre, a strain of wheat whose kernels are softer than most, similar to Italian farro (available through mail order from Dean and Deluca), sometimes called emmer. If you are lucky enough to find either of these soft varieties, by all means use them here. In any event, try not to use hard red spring wheat berries, as they never seem to become tender enough. Unsoaked pearl barley makes a delicious substitute, but the soup will be more porridgelike and will require additional broth or water.

MAKES 6 TO 8 SERVINGS

1 cup whole soft winter wheat berries, kamut, or spelt, soaked overnight in water to cover
2 tablespoons extra-virgin olive oil
1 large onion (10 to 12 ounces), chopped
½ pound carrots, peeled and chopped
1 medium turnip (about 6 ounces), peeled and chopped
1 celery stalk, chopped
4 large cloves garlic, finely chopped
6 cups vegetable broth, preferably Basic Vegetable Broth (page 38) or low-sodium canned
2 cups water
2 sprigs fresh flat-leaf parsley
1 large bay leaf
½ teaspoon dried thyme leaves
Salt and freshly ground black pepper, to taste
1 cup lentils, picked over and rinsed
1 pound spinach, stems discarded, washed, and chopped, or 1 (10-ounce) bag fresh ready-washed spinach leaves, chopped
1½ cups cooked cannellini beans (see Box, page 18) or 1 (15-ounce) can cannellini or other white beans, drained and rinsed

Drain the soaked wheat berries and set aside.

In a medium stockpot, heat the oil over medium-low heat. Add the onion, carrots, turnip, and celery and cook, stirring occasionally, until vegetables are softened but not browned, 10 to 15 minutes. Add the garlic and increase the heat to medium; cook, stirring, for 1 minute. Add the broth, water, wheat berries, parsley, bay leaf, thyme, salt, and pepper. Bring to a boil over high heat. Reduce the heat, cover, and simmer gently for 1 hour.

Add the lentils and return to a boil over high heat. Reduce the heat, partially cover, and simmer gently for 30 minutes. Uncover and simmer for 20 to 30 more minutes, stirring occasionally, or until the wheat berries and lentils are tender. Add the spinach and beans and cook, stirring, for 5 to 10 minutes, or until the spinach is wilted and the beans are heated through. Discard the bay leaf. Serve hot.

Advance Preparation The soup can be stored, covered, in the refrigerator for up to three days, but the wheat berries will continue to absorb the liquid. Add more broth or water and reheat over low heat.

PER SERVING

Calories 438 · Protein 32g · Total Fat 6g · Saturated Fat 1g · Cholesterol 0mg · Carbohydrate 70g · Dietary Fiber 27g · Sodium 633mg

Provençal Zucchini-Rice Soup with Winter Pistou

Zucchini-rice soup is as popular in Provence as it is in Italy. If you've never made soup from scratch before, this is an ideal one to start with—nothing could be less trouble to make. With a couple dollops of rich Winter Pistou stirred in, your simple soup becomes a satisfying meal-in-a-bowl.

MAKES 4 TO 6 SERVINGS

- 2 tablespoon extra-virgin olive oil
- 1 pound onions, chopped
- 4 cups vegetable broth, preferably Basic Vegetable Broth (page 38) or low-sodium canned
- 2 cups water
- Salt and freshly ground black pepper, to taste
- ½ cup long-grain white rice
- 1 pound zucchini, thinly sliced
- ½ cup Winter Pistou (page 64)

In a medium stockpot, heat the oil over medium-low heat. Add the onions and cook, stirring occasionally, until very tender, about 15 minutes. Add the broth, water, salt, and pepper; bring to a boil over high heat. Add the rice, reduce the heat to medium-high, and boil gently until the rice is barely tender, 8 minutes.

Add the zucchini and bring to a boil over high heat. Reduce the heat and simmer gently, uncovered, until the zucchini is tender and the rice is cooked al dente, 5 to 10 minutes, stirring occasionally.

To serve, divide the soup evenly among 4 to 6 bowls. Stir equal amounts of pistou into each and serve at once.

Advance Preparation This soup can be held, covered, over very low heat up to one hour. The soup can be stored, covered, in the refrigerator for up to three days. In both instances, however, the rice will absorb more broth, so you'll need to add more broth or water, and the rice will no longer be cooked al dente. Reheat over low heat. The Winter Pistou will keep for up to two days in the refrigerator, but will lose a bit of its pungency.

Cook's Tip

Instead of using raw rice, some recipes call for adding cooked rice to the soup at the end of cooking. While this is a good way to use up leftover rice, I've found that the starch released from the uncooked grains imparts a richer, sweeter taste to the finished soup.

PER SERVING

Calories 339 · Protein 17g · Total Fat 14g · Saturated Fat 2g · Cholesterol 0mg · Carbohydrate 39g · Dietary Fiber 8g · Sodium 708mg

Variation For a lighter soup, omit the pistou. Instead, stir in 1 tablespoon of tomato paste when you add the broth and water to the recipe, and garnish each serving with fresh chopped parsley or basil.

Winter Pistou

Italian flat-leaf parsley, generally available in bunches year-round, is the answer to a cook's prayer for good pistou—and lots of it—when the only fresh basil to be found is inside those meager (and expensive) plastic containers at the supermarket. In fact, to create a greener sauce, many gourmets will often add parsley to their summer pesto as well. This sauce is wonderful tossed with hot pasta, rice, couscous, or steamed vegetables. Thinly spread, it makes a fine topping for toasted baguette rounds or bruschetta. The recipe doubles easily. **MAKES ABOUT 1 CUP**

- ½ cup soft white bread crumbs
- 1½ cups packed fresh flat-leaf parsley
- ½ cup packed fresh basil leaves
- 2 tablespoons tomato paste
- ¼ cup extra-virgin olive oil
- 2 to 4 large cloves garlic, chopped
- ½ teaspoon coarse salt, or to taste

Preheat the oven to 350F (175C). Spread the bread crumbs in a single layer on a light-colored baking sheet (a dark surface tends to overbrown them). Bake for 2 to 3 minutes or until lightly toasted, stirring once. Set aside to cool slightly.

Combine the bread crumbs and all the remaining ingredients in a food processor fitted with the metal blade or in a blender; process or blend until a smooth paste is formed.

PER 1 TABLESPOON

Calories 47 · Protein 1g · Total Fat 4g · Saturated Fat 1g · Cholesterol 0mg · Carbohydrate 4g · Dietary Fiber 1g · Sodium 92mg

Variation

Winter Pesto

Replace half of the toasted bread crumbs with ¼ cup toasted pine nuts (see Cook's Tip, page 121).

Cook's Tip

Substituting the more astringent curly-leafed parsley for the relatively milder Italian flat-leaf variety is not recommended here; its use in such copious amounts will produce a rather bitter sauce that tastes too much of parsley. However, when shopping for flat-leaf parsley, be careful not to confuse it with fresh cilantro, which it closely resembles. If it's not labeled and your nose isn't certain, a discreet tearing and sniffing of one of the leaves is usually reliable, or ask the produce manager.

Salads

Healthful Salads before, after, and with the Meal, or as the Main Event

Salads are trendy— the fiber-rich common denominator among the various low-carbohydrate, high-protein, or sugar-free diets that are currently all the rage. Yet a quick study of Mediterranean food history reveals that salads have been in style for years. From a nutritional standpoint, Mediterranean cooks have instinctively always known that salads stimulate the appetite, aid in the digestion of large meals, round out small meals, and, all on their own, help rid the body of toxins and excess weight. As a practical matter, since they typically require more assembling than cooking—indeed, the ingredients often go straight from garden to bowl, with leftovers from the refrigerator or pantry tossed in—what could be quicker, easier, or cheaper to prepare?

The wide range and variety of greens, lettuces, vegetables, fruits, grains, and legumes guarantee endless possibilities of salad making on the Mediterranean. As a practical matter in this cookbook, the spectrum has been narrowed to include mostly salads whose ingredients are readily available in the United States, then further divided between the following two categories: first-course or side salads, and main-course salads. The first group consists primarily of combinations of greens, lettuces, vegetables, and fruits with olives, nuts, and herbs as garnishes. A few of the salads in this category feature legumes such as kidney beans and chickpeas. In larger portions, these easily become light meals. At the foundation of most of the main-course salads are grains and legumes, bread, bulgur, couscous, rice, wheat berries, chickpeas, and lentils. Depending on the serving size, most of the salads in this versatile category can become appetizers, side dishes, first courses, and light lunches as well as hearty meals. The majority of salads in both categories are dressed with simple vinaigrettes consisting of white, red, sherry, or balsamic vinegars or fresh lemon juice, and, of course, extra-virgin olive oil.

To ensure perfect salads, always purchase the freshest ingredients possible. That means selecting greens and lettuces with a good, uniform color and no wilted, dry, or yellowing leaves. Although individual vegetables by nature display different characteristics when fresh, as a general rule of thumb, avoid purchasing those that are bruised and blemished or wet and slimy to the touch. Except for tomatoes, which should never be refrigerated, if possible, it's best to store most greens, lettuces, and fresh vegetables unwashed and packed loosely in plastic bags in the refrigerator crisper drawer for use within a few days. When you're ready to prepare the salad, rinse them in cold water, and dry thoroughly with paper towels; nothing spoils a salad faster than excess moisture. If you own one, a salad spinner works splendidly for quickly drying greens and lettuces.

On a final note, you will find no pasta salads in this chapter. Apparently, they are an American invention that is not particularly popular in Italy. But if you, like me, can't imagine too many picnics or potlucks without one, you'll be pleased to know that all of the rice salads can be prepared using cooked orzo, and the delicious Provençal Couscous Tabbouleh Salad is really a type of pasta salad already.

First-Course and Side Salads

Arugula and Mushroom Salad with Lemon Vinaigrette

Arugula, a peppery, assertive green, is often paired with mild, cultivated mushrooms in salads. A slightly tangy, slightly sweet lemon vinaigrette dresses the two in a complementary style

MAKES 4 TO 6 SERVINGS

- ¼ cup extra-virgin olive oil
- 2 tablespoons fresh lemon juice (from ½ large lemon)
- ½ teaspoon sugar
- ¼ teaspoon freshly grated lemon peel
- 1 clove garlic, finely chopped
- Salt and freshly ground black pepper, to taste
- 6 cups arugula leaves, washed and dried
- 2 cups sliced fresh white mushrooms

In a large salad bowl, whisk together the oil, lemon juice, sugar, lemon peel, garlic, salt, and pepper until well blended. Let set for a few minutes to allow the sugar to dissolve.

Whisk the dressing again and add the arugula and mushrooms. Toss well to thoroughly coat with the dressing. Serve at once.

PER SERVING

Calories 222 · Protein 10g · Total Fat 15g · Saturated Fat 2g · Cholesterol 0mg · Carbohydrate 16g · Dietary Fiber 1g · Sodium 97mg

Variation For a reduced-fat version, substitute up to 2 tablespoons of vegetable broth for 2 tablespoons of the oil. Use the Concentrated Vegetable Broth (page 37) if you can, or reduce 6 tablespoons low-sodium canned broth over high heat, until it measures 2 tablespoons, and cool.

Red Kidney Bean and Mixed Green Salad

A nice balance of sweet and bitter greens, such as spinach or Swiss chard and arugula or endive, works well in this classic Italian bean salad.

MAKES 4 SERVINGS

- 2 cups cooked red kidney beans (see Box, page 18) or 1 (19-ounce) can red kidney beans, drained and rinsed
- ¼ cup finely chopped red onion
- 2 tablespoons extra-virgin olive oil
- 2 tablespoons red wine vinegar
- ½ teaspoon sugar, or to taste
- Salt and freshly ground black pepper, to taste
- 4 to 6 cups washed, dried, and torn mixed greens such as spinach, chard, arugula, escarole, endive, or dandelion greens

In a medium bowl, place the beans, onion, oil, vinegar, sugar, salt, and pepper. Toss gently yet thoroughly to combine. Let stand at room temperature for 15 minutes to allow the flavors to blend. Toss again.

Arrange the mixed greens on a serving platter or divide evenly among each of 4 salad plates. Spoon the bean mixture on top. Serve at room temperature.

Advance Preparation The bean mixture can be stored, covered, in the refrigerator for up to two days. Bring to room temperature before serving with the greens.

PER SERVING

Calories 197 · Protein 10g · Total Fat 7g · Saturated Fat 1g · Cholesterol 0mg · Carbohydrate 25g · Dietary Fiber 6g · Sodium 20mg

Tunisian Beet Salad with Harissa

The sweetness of roasted beets contrasts nicely with fiery harissa in this lovely salad from Tunisia. For a complete meal, serve over couscous. For more information about harissa see Tunisian Chickpea Soup (page 52).

MAKES 4 TO 6 SERVINGS

- 3 pounds small beets (20 to 24), trimmed and scrubbed, halved lengthwise
- 2 tablespoons extra-virgin olive oil
- 1 bunch (6 to 8) thinly sliced scallions, white and half the green parts
- ¼ cup finely chopped fresh flat-leaf parsley
- 1 large clove garlic, finely chopped
- 1 teaspoon harissa or Chinese chile paste (or crushed hot red pepper flakes, to taste)
- 1 teaspoon red wine vinegar
- Salt and freshly ground black pepper, to taste

Preheat the oven to 425F (220C). Place the beets on a baking sheet with a rim and toss with ½ tablespoon of the oil. Turn the halved beets cut side down. Cover the baking sheet tightly with foil. Bake for 30 minutes, or until the beets are very tender when pierced with the tip of a sharp knife. Remove from the oven, uncover, and let cool for 5 minutes. Peel off the skins and cut into ½-inch cubes. Set aside.

In a medium serving bowl, place the scallions, parsley, garlic, harissa, vinegar, remaining oil, salt, and pepper; stir well to combine. Add the beets, tossing well to combine. Serve slightly warm or at room temperature.

Advance Preparation The salad can be stored, covered, in the refrigerator for up to twenty-four hours. Bring to room temperature before serving.

PER SERVING

Calories 173 · Protein 5g · Total Fat 7g · Saturated Fat 1g · Cholesterol 0mg · Carbohydrate 25g · Dietary Fiber 7g · Sodium 186mg

Cook's Tip

In a pinch, you can substitute drained and rinsed canned whole beets, cubed and warmed, for the fresh. Skip the first step in the recipe, thereby omitting ½ tablespoon of the olive oil.

Persian Cucumber and Tomato Salad

Variations of this popular salad turn up everywhere in the Middle East. Stuffed in pita bread along with some black olives and chickpeas, it makes a great sandwich. **MAKES 4 SERVINGS**

- 1½ pounds ripe tomatoes (about 4 medium), cored, seeded, and chopped
- 1 large cucumber (about 12 ounces), peeled, seeded, and chopped
- 1 large red onion (about 8 ounces), chopped
- ½ cup fresh mint leaves, finely chopped
- ½ cup fresh flat-leaf parsley, finely chopped
- 1 bunch scallions (6 to 8), white and green parts, thinly sliced
- 2 large cloves garlic, finely chopped
- 3 tablespoons extra-virgin olive oil
- 2 tablespoons fresh lemon juice
- 1½ tablespoons fresh lime juice
- Salt and freshly ground black pepper, to taste

In a large bowl, place all the ingredients, tossing well to combine. Let stand for 15 minutes at room temperature to allow the flavors to blend. Toss again.

Serve at room temperature. Or cover and refrigerate at least 1 hour and serve chilled.

Advance Preparation The salad can be stored, covered, in the refrigerator for up to twenty-four hours. Serve chilled or slightly below room temperature.

PER SERVING

Calories 122 · Protein 3g · Total Fat 7g · Saturated Fat 1g · Cholesterol 0mg · Carbohydrate 14g · Dietary Fiber 4g · Sodium 26mg

Fennel, Orange, and Black Olive Salad

Here is a refreshing winter salad when fresh navel oranges are in season and fennel is readily available in most well-stocked supermarkets. If Niçoise, kalamata, or other high-quality black olives can't be found, however, omitting them is preferable to substituting with the tasteless canned California variety.

MAKES 4 TO 6 SERVINGS

- 2 medium fennel bulbs (about 12 ounces each), trimmed, cored, and coarsely shredded, 2 tablespoons of the feathery leaves reserved
- 2 large navel oranges, peeled (all white pith removed), cut into thin rounds
- ½ cup pitted Niçoise or other good-quality black olives, coarsely chopped
- 5 tablespoons fresh orange juice
- 1 tablespoon fresh lemon juice
- 2 tablespoons extra-virgin olive oil
- Salt and freshly ground black pepper, to taste

Arrange the fennel, orange rounds, and olives in a shallow serving bowl. In a small bowl, whisk together the orange juice, lemon juice, oil, salt, and pepper until well blended. Add to the fennel mix-

Cook's Tip

While fennel is regularly stocked in most major supermarkets throughout the fall and winter, it is often mislabeled anise—an annual herb grown mainly for its similar licorice-flavored seeds.

ture, tossing gently yet thoroughly to combine. Cover with plastic wrap and let stand for 20 minutes at room temperature to allow the flavors to blend. Or refrigerate at least 1 hour and serve chilled.

Sprinkle with the reserved fennel leaves just before serving.

Advance Preparation The salad can be stored, covered, in the refrigerator for up to twelve hours. Serve chilled.

PER SERVING

Calories 233 · Protein 3g · Total Fat 15g · Saturated Fat 1g · Cholesterol 0mg · Carbohydrate 25g · Dietary Fiber 7g · Sodium 561mg

Green Bean and Chickpea Salad

The ubiquitous chickpea, along with red onion, finds its way into all sorts of Mediterranean salads. The following one featuring fresh green beans makes a nice summer side dish.

MAKES 4 TO 6 SERVINGS

- ¾ pound green beans, washed and trimmed
- 1½ cups cooked chickpeas (see Box, page 18) or 1 (15-ounce) can chickpeas, rinsed and drained
- 1 small red onion (about 4 ounces), peeled, quartered, and very thinly sliced, soaked in cold water to cover for 10 minutes, drained
- 2 tablespoons extra-virgin olive oil
- 2 tablespoons vegetable broth, preferably Concentrated Vegetable Broth (page 37), or 6 tablespoons low-sodium canned broth reduced over high heat to 2 tablespoons, cooled
- 1 tablespoon balsamic vinegar
- 1 tablespoon fresh thyme leaves or 1 teaspoon dried
- Salt and freshly ground black pepper, to taste

Prepare a large bowl of ice water and set aside. In a medium stockpot or saucepan large enough to accommodate a 9-inch steaming basket, put 1 inch of water. Place the steaming basket in the pot and add the green beans. Bring to a boil over high heat. Cover tightly, reduce the heat to medium, and steam until crisp-tender, 5 to 7 minutes. Carefully remove the steaming basket and refresh the green beans in the ice water for 5 minutes. Drain well.

Cut the beans diagonally into 2-inch lengths and place in a large shallow bowl, along with the chickpeas and onion. In a small bowl, whisk together the oil, broth, vinegar, thyme, salt, and pepper. Add to the green bean mixture, tossing thoroughly to combine. Let stand at room temperature for 15 minutes to allow the flavors to blend. Toss again.

Serve at room temperature. Or cover and refrigerate at least 1 hour and serve chilled.

Advance Preparation The salad can be stored, covered, in the refrigerator for up to twenty-four hours. Serve chilled or return to room temperature before serving.

PER SERVING

Calories 204 · Protein 8g · Total Fat 9g · Saturated Fat 1g · Cholesterol 0mg · Carbohydrate 26g · Dietary Fiber 4g · Sodium 59mg

Salad of Bitter Greens and Pine Nuts with Classic Italian Vinaigrette

Italian cooks traditionally make a paste of garlic and salt before whisking in the oil and vinegar, following the theory that the salt further minces the garlic and the garlic juice dissolves the salt, thereby producing truly flavorful vinaigrette. Not surprisingly, it works!

MAKES 4 TO 6 SERVINGS

- 1 clove garlic, finely chopped
- ¼ teaspoon salt
- ¼ cup extra-virgin olive oil
- 1 tablespoon red wine vinegar
- 1 teaspoon balsamic vinegar or fresh lemon juice
- Freshly ground black pepper, to taste
- 8 cups washed, dried, and torn mixed bitter greens, such as dandelion, escarole, chicory, and/or radicchio
- 2 tablespoons toasted pine nuts (see Cook's Tip, page 121)

In a mortar and pestle, or with the back of a teaspoon in a small bowl, mash together the garlic and salt until pastelike. Transfer to a large salad bowl. Whisk in the oil, red wine vinegar, balsamic vinegar, and pepper until well blended.

Add the greens to the bowl and toss thoroughly to coat with the dressing. Sprinkle with the pine nuts and additional pepper, if necessary. Serve at once.

PER SERVING

Calories 190 · Protein 4g · Total Fat 17g · Saturated Fat 2g · Cholesterol 0mg · Carbohydrate 10g · Dietary Fiber 5g · Sodium 205mg

Variation For a reduced-fat version, substitute up to 2 tablespoons of vegetable broth for 2 tablespoons of the oil. Use the Concentrated Vegetable Broth (page 37) if you can, or reduce 6 tablespoons low-sodium canned broth over high heat, until it measures 2 tablespoons, and cool.

Mixed Green Salad with Fresh Herb Vinaigrette

Tossed with a crisp medley of salad greens, nothing beats the taste of this simple vinaigrette, redolent of herbs fresh from the garden. Use any combination of fresh herbs you have on hand if the listed ones are unavailable.

MAKES 4 TO 6 SERVINGS

- ¼ cup extra-virgin olive oil
- 1 tablespoon red wine vinegar
- 1 tablespoon fresh lemon juice
- 1 clove garlic, finely chopped
- ½ teaspoon Dijon mustard
- 1 teaspoon chopped fresh parsley
- 1 teaspoon chopped fresh basil
- 1 teaspoon chopped fresh tarragon
- 1 teaspoon chopped fresh chives
- Salt and freshly ground black pepper, to taste
- 8 cups washed, dried, and torn mixed salad greens

In a large salad bowl, whisk together the oil, vinegar, lemon juice, garlic, mustard, herbs, salt, and pepper until well blended. Add the mixed greens and toss well to thoroughly coat with the dressing. Serve at once.

PER SERVING

Calories 144 · Protein 2g · Total Fat 14g · Saturated Fat 2g · Cholesterol 0mg · Carbohydrate 4g · Dietary Fiber 2g · Sodium 39mg

Variation For a reduced-fat version, substitute up to 2 tablespoons of vegetable broth for 2 tablespoons of the oil. Use the Concentrated Vegetable Broth (page 37) if you can, or reduce 6 tablespoons low-sodium canned broth over high heat, until it measures 2 tablespoons, and cool.

Mesclun Salad with Classic French Vinaigrette

Mesclun is a Provençal blend of bitter, sharp, and mild young salad greens that typically includes arugula, radicchio, oak leaf lettuce, romaine lettuce, curly endive, escarole, chervil, and dandelion greens. These days, more and more well-stocked supermarkets are offering such blends, often labeling them "spring mixes" or "spring blends." If yours doesn't, any combination of young greens will do, so long as there is a balance of bitter (curly endive, radicchio), peppery (arugula, watercress), and mild (Bibb lettuce, oak leaf lettuce) and, most importantly, they are fresh. Traditionally, mesclun is dressed simply in classic French vinaigrette, which often contains not a hint of garlic, so that none of the delightful, contrasting flavors are masked.

MAKES 4 TO 6 SERVINGS

- **4 tablespoons light olive oil or 2 tablespoons fruity olive oil and 2 tablespoons mild vegetable oil, such as canola or safflower**
- **1 tablespoon sherry vinegar or balsamic vinegar**
- **½ teaspoon Dijon mustard**
- **1 small clove garlic, finely chopped (optional)**
- **Salt and freshly ground black pepper, to taste**
- **8 cups mesclun, washed and dried, or a combination of young salad greens**

In a large salad bowl, whisk together the oil, vinegar, mustard, garlic (if using), salt, and pepper until well blended. Add the mesclun or other lettuce greens and toss well to thoroughly coat with the dressing. Serve at once.

PER SERVING

Calories 140 · Protein 2g · Total Fat 14g · Saturated Fat 2g · Cholesterol 0mg · Carbohydrate 4g · Dietary Fiber 2g · Sodium 37mg

Variation For a reduced-fat version, substitute up to 2 tablespoons of vegetable broth for 2 tablespoons of the oil. Use the Concentrated Vegetable Broth (page 37) if you can, or reduce 6 tablespoons low-sodium canned broth over high heat, until it measures 2 tablespoons, and cool.

Warm Wild Mushroom and Frisée Salad

The woods of Provence yield abundant wild mushrooms in the fall, with cèpes (the French equivalent of the Italian porcini), girolles, and chanterelles among the most highly prized. As they are hard to come by here in their fresh state, a mixture of cultivated fresh button, shiitake, cremini, or portobello mushrooms can be used. Either way, this popular first course or side salad is delicious.

MAKES 4 SERVINGS

- 1 tablespoon finely chopped shallot
- 2 tablespoons red wine vinegar
- 4 tablespoons vegetable broth, preferably Basic Vegetable Broth (page 38) or low-sodium canned
- 8 ounces fresh mixed wild mushrooms such as cèpes (porcini), girolles, and chanterelles, cleaned, trimmed, and coarsely chopped
- Salt and freshly ground black pepper, to taste
- 4 teaspoons extra-virgin olive oil
- 1 teaspoon Dijon mustard
- 8 cups torn frisée (chicory), washed and dried

Heat a large nonstick skillet over medium heat. When droplets of water can sizzle on the bottom, add the shallot, 1 tablespoon of the vinegar, and 2 tablespoons of the broth; cook, stirring constantly, for 1 minute. Add the mushrooms and increase the heat to high; cook, stirring constantly, just until the mushrooms have softened, about 1 minute more (do not allow mushrooms to release their liquid). Remove the skillet from the heat and season with salt and pepper. Cover and keep warm.

In a large mixing bowl, whisk together the remaining vinegar and broth with the oil and mustard; season with salt and pepper. Add the frisée and toss thoroughly to coat.

To serve, divide the frisée equally among 4 serving plates; top evenly with the warm mushroom mixture and juices. Serve at once.

PER SERVING

Calories 87 · Protein 4g · Total Fat 5g · Saturated Fat 1g · Cholesterol 0mg · Carbohydrate 7g · Dietary Fiber 3g · Sodium 61mg

Cook's Tip

The chicory family includes curly endive, Belgian endive, escarole, and radicchio. Any of these greens, or a combination, can be used in this salad.

Moroccan Orange and Black Olive Salad

Some versions of this popular salad omit the red onion, use parsley or cilantro instead of the mint, or replace the red wine vinegar with lemon juice. Whichever way you go, you're bound to make one delicious salad so long as you use seasonal oranges, top-notch black olives, and a good olive oil.

MAKES 4 TO 6 SERVINGS

6 navel oranges, peeled (all white pith removed), sliced into thin rounds
1 small red onion (about 4 ounces), peeled, quartered, and very thinly sliced, soaked in cold water to cover for 10 minutes, drained
½ cup pitted oil-cured Moroccan black olives or other good-quality black olives, coarsely chopped
¼ cup fresh orange juice
1 tablespoon red wine vinegar
2 tablespoons extra-virgin olive oil
1 clove garlic, finely chopped
Pinch ground coriander
Pinch sugar
Salt and freshly ground black pepper, to taste
Lettuce leaves (optional)
2 tablespoons finely chopped fresh mint

Arrange the orange rounds, onion, and olives in a shallow serving bowl. In a small bowl, whisk together the orange juice, vinegar, oil, garlic, coriander, sugar, salt, and pepper until well blended. Add to the orange mixture, tossing gently yet thoroughly to combine. Cover with plastic wrap and let stand for 20 minutes at room temperature to allow the flavors to blend. Or refrigerate at least 1 hour and serve chilled.

Serve over lettuce leaves, if desired. Sprinkle with the mint just before serving.

Advance Preparation The salad can be stored, covered, in the refrigerator for up to to twelve hours. Serve chilled.

PER SERVING

Calories 255 · Protein 3g · Total Fat 15g · Saturated Fat 1g · Cholesterol 0mg · Carbohydrate 31g · Dietary Fiber 4g · Sodium 475mg

Orange, Cucumber, and Red Onion Salad with Aniseed

This unusual and colorful salad can open a meal on a festive note. As a side dish, its refreshing citrus and licorice tones provide a pleasant counterpoint to many of the book's spicier entrees.

MAKES 4 TO 6 SERVINGS

4 large navel oranges, peeled (all white pith removed), cut crosswise into ¼-inch-thick slices
1 large seedless cucumber (about 12 ounces), peeled and sliced into ¼-inch-thick rounds
1 small red onion (about 4 ounces), very thinly sliced, soaked in cold water to cover for 10 minutes, drained
2 tablespoons extra-virgin olive oil
2 tablespoons red wine vinegar

2 tablespoons fresh orange juice
¼ teaspoon whole dried aniseed, crushed
Salt and freshly ground black pepper, to taste
2 tablespoons chopped fresh mint

Arrange the oranges, cucumber, and onion in a large shallow serving bowl.

In a small jar or pitcher, whisk together the oil, vinegar, orange juice, aniseed, salt, and pepper. Drizzle over the salad mixture, tossing very gently yet thoroughly to combine. Let stand for 15 minutes at room temperature to allow the flavors to blend.

Serve at room temperature. Or cover and refrigerate for at least 1 hour and serve chilled. Sprinkle with the mint just before serving.

Advance Preparation The salad can be stored, covered, in the refrigerator for up to twelve hours. Serve chilled.

PER SERVING

Calories 150 · Protein 2g · Total Fat 7g · Saturated Fat 1g · Cholesterol 0mg · Carbohydrate 22g · Dietary Fiber 4g · Sodium 4mg

Roasted Red Pepper and Zucchini Salad

This is a popular end of the summer salad or antipasto throughout Italy, when red bell peppers—actually ripened green peppers containing lots more vitamin C—and zucchini are abundant. If you'd like, strips of roasted eggplant (see Catalan Grilled Vegetables, page 27) can also be added.

MAKES 4 SERVINGS

2 large red bell peppers (about 8 ounces each)
4 small zucchini (about 4 ounces each)
2 tablespoons extra-virgin olive oil
2 tablespoons balsamic vinegar
2 large cloves garlic, finely chopped
½ teaspoon dried oregano
Salt and freshly ground black pepper, to taste
2 tablespoons finely chopped fresh flat-leaf parsley or basil (optional)

Adjust the oven rack to 4 inches from the heating element and preheat the oven to broil.

Trim the top and bottom off each pepper and cut in half lengthwise. Remove the seeds and inner white membranes. Slice each half lengthwise into 3 even strips. Arrange the pepper strips, skin side up, on an ungreased baking sheet. Broil until partially charred, about 5 minutes. Place in a paper bag, twist tightly to close, and leave for 20 minutes. Peel off the skins with your fingers or a small paring knife. Slice lengthwise into ½-inch-wide strips. Place in a large shallow serving bowl and set aside.

Meanwhile, in a medium stockpot or saucepan large enough to accommodate a 9-inch steaming basket, put 1 inch of water. Place the steaming basket in the pot and add the whole zucchini. Bring to a boil over high heat. Cover tightly, reduce the heat to medium, and steam until barely tender, 5 to 7 minutes. Remove the zucchini with tongs and let cool to room temperature. Trim the ends of each zucchini and slice in half lengthwise. Slice each half lengthwise into ½-inch-wide strips. Add to the bowl with the red pepper strips.

In a small bowl or pitcher, whisk together the oil, vinegar, garlic, oregano, salt, and pepper. Pour the dressing over the peppers and zucchini, tossing well to combine. Season with additional salt and pepper as necessary. Let stand for 15 minutes at room temperature to allow the flavors to blend. Toss again.

Sprinkle with the parsley or basil, if using, and serve at room temperature. Or cover and refrigerate for at least 1 hour and serve chilled.

Advance Preparation The salad can be stored, covered, in the refrigerator for up to twenty-four hours. Serve chilled or return to room temperature before serving.

PER SERVING

Calories 111 · Protein 3g · Total Fat 7g · Saturated Fat 1g · Cholesterol 0mg · Carbohydrate 12g · Dietary Fiber 4g · Sodium 7mg

New Potato and Young Green Bean Salad

The pairing of new potatoes and the tiny green beans known as haricots verts is a popular salad combination throughout France, especially in the spring and early summer. In the north, the combo might be dressed with white wine vinegar, a light vegetable oil, and Dijon mustard. In this southern variation, the warm vegetables are tossed with paper-thin slices of shallots marinated in a simple vinaigrette of red wine vinegar and olive oil.

MAKES 6 SERVINGS

- 2 tablespoons red wine vinegar
- 1 tablespoon water
- Salt and freshly ground black pepper, to taste
- ¼ cup extra-virgin olive oil
- 2 shallots, peeled and cut crosswise into paper-thin slices
- ¾ pound small green beans (about ¼ inch in diameter and about 2 inches long), trimmed if necessary
- 1½ pounds small new potatoes (about 1½ inches in diameter), preferably red-skinned, unpeeled, scrubbed

In a large bowl, whisk the vinegar and water with salt and pepper. Add the oil in a thin stream, whisking constantly until well combined. Add the shallots, toss briefly, and set aside to marinate.

Prepare a large bowl of ice water and set aside. In a medium stockpot or saucepan large enough to accommodate a 9-inch steaming basket, put 1 inch of water. Place the steaming basket in the pot and add the green beans. Bring to a boil over high heat. Cover tightly, reduce the heat to medium, and steam until the beans are crisp-tender, 3 to 5 minutes, depending on size. Immediately refresh the green beans in the ice water for 5 minutes. Drain well and set aside.

Place the potatoes in a large saucepan or medium stockpot with salted water to cover; bring to a boil over high heat. Reduce the heat to a gentle boil and cook until the potatoes are just tender, 10 to 15 minutes, depending on size. Drain and set aside to cool slightly.

As soon as the potatoes are cool enough to handle, yet still quite warm, cut them in half. Stir the reserved dressing several times, and add the warm potato halves. Toss gently until the potatoes are

Cook's Tip

Large green beans cut into 2-inch lengths can be substituted for the young variety, but the cooking time will increase slightly. Medium boiling potatoes, quartered, can be used if the tiny new ones are unavailable. To avoid discoloring, toss the green beans with the dressed potatoes shortly before serving.

thoroughly coated. Gently toss in the beans. Adjust the seasonings as necessary. Serve warm or at room temperature.

Advance Preparation This salad can stand at room temperature for one hour before serving. It can also be covered and refrigerated for up to twenty-four hours. Bring to room temperature before serving. However, the acidity of the vinegar will cause red-skinned potatoes and the green beans to lose some pigment.

PER SERVING

Calories 171 · Protein 3g · Total Fat 9g · Saturated Fat 1g · Cholesterol 0mg · Carbohydrate 21g · Dietary Fiber 3g · Sodium 10mg

Moroccan Potato Salad

This is excellent potato salad, different from most in that it relies heavily on flat-leaf parsley for its distinctive flavor. To ensure its success, select new potatoes of relatively the same size and don't overcook them. To create an exotic medley, serve alongside the Moroccan Fresh Tomato Salad (page 82) and a bowl of Moroccan Carrot Soup (page 42).

MAKES 4 SERVINGS

- 1 pound new potatoes, unpeeled, scrubbed
- ¾ cup finely chopped fresh flat-leaf parsley
- 1 small red onion (about 4 ounces), finely chopped
- 1½ tablespoons extra-virgin olive oil
- ½ tablespoon distilled white vinegar
- 1 large clove garlic, finely chopped
- Salt and freshly ground black pepper, to taste

Place the potatoes in salted water to cover in a medium stockpot; bring to a boil over high heat. Reduce the heat to medium-high and cook until fork tender but not mushy, 10 to 18 minutes, depending on size. Drain and set aside to cool until slightly warm.

In a medium bowl, combine the parsley, onion, oil, vinegar, garlic, salt, and pepper. Peel and coarsely chop the potatoes. While still slightly warm, add to the parsley mixture, tossing gently yet thoroughly to combine. Let stand for 15 minutes at room temperature to allow the flavors to blend. Serve at room temperature. Or cover and refrigerate for at least 1 hour and serve chilled.

Advance Preparation The salad can be stored, covered, in the refrigerator for up to twenty-four hours. Serve chilled or return to room temperature before serving.

PER SERVING

Calories 128 · Protein 2g · Total Fat 5g · Saturated Fat 1g · Cholesterol 0mg · Carbohydrate 19g · Dietary Fiber 2g · Sodium 12mg

Radicchio and Butter Lettuce Salad with Toasted Walnuts

Bitter radicchio and sweet butter lettuce are frequent partners in Italian salads. Though the addition of Dijon mustard to the vinaigrette is not traditionally Italian, I love the extra piquancy it lends to this colorful salad. Pine nuts or almonds can be substituted for the walnuts, or omit the nuts altogether, if you prefer.

MAKES 4 SERVINGS

- 2 tablespoons extra-virgin olive oil
- 2 tablespoons fresh orange juice
- 1 tablespoon balsamic vinegar
- 1 teaspoon Dijon mustard
- ½ teaspoon sugar
- Salt and freshly ground black pepper
- 3 cups torn radicchio, washed and dried
- 3 cups torn butter lettuce, washed and dried
- 2 tablespoons coarsely chopped toasted walnuts (see Cook's Tip, page 121)

In a salad bowl, whisk together the oil, orange juice, vinegar, mustard, sugar, salt, and pepper. Add the radicchio and butter lettuce; toss well to combine. Sprinkle with the walnuts and serve at once.

PER SERVING

Calories 103 · Protein 2g · Total Fat 9g · Saturated Fat 1g · Cholesterol 0mg · Carbohydrate 4g · Dietary Fiber 1g · Sodium 24mg

Romaine Salad with Roasted Garlic Vinaigrette

Roasting garlic brings out its natural sweetness. In pureed form, its addition to this simple vinaigrette lends the following salad more depth and subtle garlic flavor.

MAKES 4 TO 6 SERVINGS

- 8 large cloves garlic, peeled, left whole
- ¼ cup extra-virgin olive oil
- 1 tablespoon vegetable broth, preferably Basic Vegetable Broth (page 38) or low-sodium canned
- 1 tablespoon fresh lemon juice
- 1 tablespoon red wine vinegar
- 1 teaspoon Dijon mustard
- Salt and freshly ground black pepper, to taste
- 8 cups torn Romaine lettuce leaves, washed and dried

Preheat the oven to 450F (230C). Finely chop 1 clove of the garlic and set aside. Rub the remaining garlic with ¼ teaspoon of the oil and place on an ungreased baking sheet. Roast for 10 minutes, turning once, or until the garlic is browned on the outside and soft on the inside. Transfer to a small bowl. Add the broth and mash well with a fork until a smooth puree is formed. Set aside briefly to cool.

In a large salad bowl, whisk together the remaining oil, lemon juice, vinegar, mustard, the finely chopped garlic, salt, and pepper. Whisk in the mashed garlic mixture until well blended. Add the romaine and toss well to thoroughly coat with the dressing. Serve at once.

PER SERVING

Calories 150 · Protein 2g · Total Fat 14g · Saturated Fat 2g · Cholesterol 0mg · Carbohydrate 5g · Dietary Fiber 3g · Sodium 34mg

Variation For a reduced-fat version, substitute up to 2 tablespoons of vegetable broth for 2 tablespoons of the oil. Use the Concentrated Vegetable Broth (page 37) if you can, or reduce 6 tablespoons low-sodium canned broth over high heat, until it measures 2 tablespoons, and cool.

Romaine, Red Onion, and Chickpea Salad with Orange Vinaigrette

This refreshing side salad from Provence easily becomes a satisfying lunch or light supper served with a bowl of soup and crusty French bread. Although red onions are already on the mild side, soaking them in cold water further reduces their bite.

MAKES 4 TO 6 SERVINGS

¼ cup fresh orange juice
4 teaspoons extra-virgin olive oil
1 tablespoon fresh lemon juice
1 clove garlic, finely chopped
Salt and freshly ground black pepper, to taste
2 cups cooked chickpeas (see Box, page 18) or 1 (19-ounce) can chickpeas, drained and rinsed
1 small red onion (about 4 ounces), peeled, quartered, and thinly sliced crosswise, soaked in cold water to cover for 10 minutes, drained
8 cups torn red and/or green romaine lettuce leaves, washed and dried

In a medium bowl, whisk together the orange juice, oil, lemon juice, garlic, salt, and pepper. Add the chickpeas and onion; toss well to combine. Let stand for 15 minutes at room temperature to allow the flavors to blend. Toss again.

Divide the lettuce leaves evenly among 4 to 6 salad plates. Spoon the chickpea mixture evenly over the lettuce and serve at room temperature.

Advance Preparation The chickpea mixture can be stored, covered, in the refrigerator for up to twelve hours. Bring to room temperature before serving with the greens.

PER SERVING

Calories 212 · Protein 10g · Total Fat 7g · Saturated Fat 1g · Cholesterol 0mg · Carbohydrates 30g · Dietary Fiber 3g · Sodium 16mg

Romaine Salad with Lemon-Date Dressing

This decidedly sweet Moroccan-inspired salad is an excellent foil for many of the book's hotter, spicier dishes, particularly the Couscous with Seven-Vegetable Tagine (page 100). If you prefer a tangier salad, reduce the amount of sugar to taste.

MAKES 4 TO 6 SERVINGS

¼ cup extra-virgin olive oil
Juice of 1 medium lemon (about 3 tablespoons)
1½ teaspoons sugar, or less to taste
¼ teaspoon ground cinnamon
⅛ teaspoon coriander seeds, crushed
Salt and freshly ground black pepper, to taste
¼ cup chopped pitted dates
8 cups torn romaine lettuce leaves, washed and dried

In a large salad bowl, whisk together the oil, lemon juice, sugar, cinnamon, coriander, salt, and pepper until well blended. Let rest for a few minutes to allow the sugar to dissolve.

Whisk the dressing again, and stir in the dates. Add the romaine and toss well to thoroughly coat with the dressing. Serve at once.

PER SERVING

Calories 177 · Protein 2g · Total Fat 14g · Saturated Fat 2g · Cholesterol 0mg · Carbohydrate 14g · Dietary Fiber 4g · Sodium 10mg

Variation For a reduced-fat version, substitute up to 2 tablespoons of vegetable broth for 2 tablespoons of the oil. Use the Concentrated Vegetable Broth (page 37) if you can, or reduce 6 tablespoons low-sodium canned broth over high heat, until it measures 2 tablespoons, and cool.

Sicilian Summer Salad of Roasted Red Onion, Potatoes, Green Beans, and Olives

A natural for picnics, versions of this salad appear throughout Sicily in the summer. What makes the following recipe particularly tasty is the whole roasted red onion that is given equal weight with the potatoes and green beans.

MAKES 4 SERVINGS

1 medium red onion (about 8 ounces), peeled
2 tablespoons plus ½ teaspoon extra-virgin olive oil
2 medium boiling potatoes (about 4 ounces each), preferably red-skinned, unpeeled
8 ounces green beans, trimmed
¼ cup kalamata olives, pitted and halved
¼ cup Italian-style green olives, pitted and halved
Salt, preferably the coarse variety, and freshly ground black pepper, to taste

Preheat the oven to 400F (205C). Rub the onion with the ½ teaspoon oil and place on an ungreased baking sheet. Roast for about 40 minutes or until charred and tender through the center. When cool enough to handle, peel the charred outer layer away and discard. Cut the remaining onion into 1½-inch chunks. Set aside.

Meanwhile, place the potatoes in a medium saucepan with salted water to cover; bring to a boil over high heat. Reduce the heat to medium-high and cook for about 20 minutes, or until tender through the center but still firm. Drain. When cool enough to handle, cut into 1½-inch chunks. Set aside.

Prepare a large bowl of ice water and set aside. Bring a medium stockpot filled with salted water to a boil over high heat. Add the green beans and cook until crisp-tender, about 5 minutes. Drain and immediately refresh in the ice water for 5 minutes. Drain well. Cut into 2-inch pieces and set aside.

Place the onion, potatoes, green beans, olives, and remaining oil in a medium bowl. Season with salt and pepper. Toss gently yet thoroughly to combine. Serve at room temperature.

Advance Preparation The salad can be covered and refrigerated for up to twenty-four hours. Bring to room temperature before serving.

PER SERVING

Calories 169 · Protein 2g · Total Fat 12g · Saturated Fat 1g · Cholesterol 0mg · Carbohydrate 14g · Dietary Fiber 2g · Sodium 314mg

Spinach and Orange Salad with Pine Nuts and Raisins

This is a classic Spanish combination of spinach, citrus, dried fruit, and nuts. For a tangier variation, omit the raisins and replace them with chopped kalamata or other good-quality black olives.

MAKES 4 TO 6 SERVINGS

- 8 cups torn spinach leaves, washed and dried
- 2 large navel oranges, peeled (all white pith removed), cut into thin rounds
- ¼ cup pine nuts, toasted (see Cook's Tip, page 121)
- ¼ cup raisins, soaked in warm water to cover for 10 minutes, drained
- ¼ cup extra-virgin olive oil
- 2 tablespoons fresh orange juice
- 2 tablespoons sherry vinegar
- Salt and freshly ground black pepper, to taste

In a large salad bowl, combine the spinach, oranges, pine nuts, and raisins. In a small bowl, whisk together the oil, juice, vinegar, salt, and pepper until well blended. Add to the spinach mixture and toss gently yet thoroughly to combine. Serve at once.

PER SERVING

Calories 259 · Protein 7g · Total Fat 19g · Saturated Fat 3g · Cholesterol 0mg · Carbohydrate 22g · Dietary fiber 5g · Sodium 91mg

Variation For a reduced-fat version, substitute up to 2 tablespoons of vegetable broth for 2 tablespoons of the oil. Use the Concentrated Vegetable Broth (page 37) if you can, or reduce 6 tablespoons low-sodium canned broth over high heat, until it measures 2 tablespoons, and cool.

Moroccan Fresh Tomato Salad

This spicy tomato salad can also be used to garnish anything from grilled eggplant to veggie burgers. **MAKES 4 SERVINGS**

3 medium ripe tomatoes (about 6 ounces each), cored and cut into small pieces
Salt, to taste
¼ cup chopped fresh flat-leaf parsley
¼ cup chopped fresh cilantro
1 small jalapeño chile pepper, seeded and finely chopped
1 tablespoon extra-virgin olive oil
1 tablespoon distilled white vinegar
½ teaspoon ground cumin
Freshly ground black pepper, to taste

Place the tomatoes in a colander. Sprinkle lightly with salt and toss gently; let drain for 30 minutes.

In a medium bowl, combine the parsley, cilantro, jalapeño chile, oil, vinegar, cumin, salt, and pepper. Add the drained tomatoes, mixing gently yet thoroughly to combine. Let stand for 15 minutes at room temperature to allow the flavors to blend. Toss gently again.

Serve at room temperature. Or cover and refrigerate for 1 hour and serve chilled.

Advance Preparation The salad can be stored, covered, in the refrigerator for up to twenty-four hours. Serve chilled or return to room temperature before serving.

PER SERVING

Calories 62 · Protein 1g · Total Fat 4g · Saturated Fat 1g · Cholesterol 0mg · Carbohydrate 7g · Dietary Fiber 2g · Sodium 14mg

Tunisian Roasted Vegetable Salad

I love this fiery salsalike salad, but be forewarned—it's not for those with tender palates. The heat, of course, can be toned down according to taste. For an appetizer, serve as a dip with plain pita bread or Garlic-Herb Pita Toasts (page 26). For an exotic main dish, toss with couscous and serve slightly warm or at room temperature, accompanied by the refreshing Romaine Salad with Lemon-Date Dressing (page 80).

MAKES 6 SERVINGS

1 medium green bell pepper (about 6 ounces)
1 medium red bell pepper (about 6 ounces)
3 medium ripe tomatoes, about 6 ounces each
3 small onions (about 4 ounces each), unpeeled
2 to 4 fresh jalapeño chile peppers, or to taste
¼ cup plus 1 tablespoon extra-virgin olive oil
Juice of 1 large lemon (about 4 tablespoons)
3 large cloves garlic, finely chopped
1 teaspoon ground caraway, or to taste
½ teaspoon coriander seeds, crushed
Salt and freshly ground black pepper, to taste
Pita bread

Preheat the oven to 450F (230C). Lightly oil a large baking sheet. Rub the bell peppers, tomatoes, onions, and jalapeño chiles with the 1 tablespoon oil and arrange on the baking sheet. Roast, turning frequently with tongs, until the skins are blackened and the insides are soft, removing the tomato and chiles after 10 to 20 minutes, bell peppers after 25 to 35 minutes, and onions after 40 to

50 minutes. As the chiles and bell peppers finish cooking, transfer to paper bags, twist closed, and set aside for 20 minutes.

When cool enough to handle, stem and peel the onions; finely chop. Peel and seed the tomatoes; coarsely chop. Using your fingers or a paring knife, slip the skins off the bell peppers and chiles (wash your hands immediately after handling the chiles, or if your skin is sensitive, wear rubber gloves). Cut each one lengthwise into halves, removing and discarding cores and seeds; finely chop. Place all the roasted vegetables in a large mixing bowl and add the remaining oil, lemon juice, garlic, caraway, coriander, salt, and pepper. Mix well to thoroughly combine. Cover with plastic wrap and let stand at room temperature for 1 hour to allow the flavors to blend. Stir well.

Serve at room temperature, or cover and refrigerate for at least 1 hour and serve chilled, accompanied by pita bread.

Advance Preparation The salad can be covered and refrigerated for up to two days. Serve chilled or return to room temperature before serving.

PER SERVING

Calories 165 · Protein 2g · Total Fat 12g · Saturated Fat 2g · Cholesterol 0mg · Carbohydrate 15g · Dietary Fiber 3g · Sodium 11mg

Main-Course Salads

Catalan Rice Salad with Sherry-Tomato Vinaigrette

Perfect for a quick weeknight supper, this is also an outstanding make-ahead winter buffet dish to prepare when company's coming. With the exception of the celery, all of the ingredients come straight from the pantry, and the finished salad holds up well on a buffet. The use of arborio rice, boiled pasta-style, ensures that the salad can be stored in the refrigerator a day in advance without the rice grains becoming too firm.

MAKES 4 TO 6 SERVINGS

1½ cups arborio rice
2 tablespoons sherry vinegar or balsamic vinegar
½ tablespoon tomato paste
¼ cup extra-virgin olive oil
¼ teaspoon sugar
Salt and freshly ground black pepper, to taste
3 stalks celery, strings removed, if desired, thinly sliced
1 (7¼-ounce) jar roasted red bell peppers, drained, cut into ½-inch-wide strips
½ cup drained diced canned tomatoes
¼ cup raisins, soaked in warm water to cover for 10 minutes, drained

Bring about 3 quarts salted water to a boil in a large pot over high heat; add the rice and boil until tender yet still firm to the bite, stirring a few times, 12 to 15 minutes. Drain and transfer to a large bowl. Set aside to cool slightly.

In a small bowl, combine the vinegar and tomato paste; slowly whisk in the oil. Add the sugar, salt, and pepper; whisk well to combine.

Add the celery, peppers, tomatoes, and raisins to the rice; toss well to combine. Add the vinaigrette, tossing well to combine. Serve warm or at room temperature.

PER SERVING

Calories 424 · Protein 6g · Total Fat 14g · Saturated Fat 2g · Cholesterol 0mg · Carbohydrate 69g · Dietary Fiber 2g · Sodium 59mg

Cook's Tip

Long-grain white rice can be substituted for the arborio, and cooked in the same manner, but serve the salad within a few hours of preparing. If you must refrigerate it, reheat, covered, on medium-low power in a microwave oven until barely warm, then toss well to restore the rice's fluffiness.

Lebanese Bread Salad (Fattoush)

This Middle Eastern salad, which evolved as an economical means for using up stale pita bread, is just one example among many that the simplest of Mediterranean dishes are often the most delicious. While the sumac berries that traditionally flavor fattoush are optional in this recipe, their exotic lemony flavor makes them worth seeking out in Middle Eastern markets and specialty shops.

MAKES 2 MAIN-COURSE SERVINGS OR 4 FIRST-COURSE SERVINGS

- 2 medium day-old pita breads, preferably whole wheat
- 1 large clove garlic, halved
- 2 tablespoons plus 1 teaspoon olive oil
- 2 ripe medium tomatoes (about 6 ounces each), cored and coarsely chopped
- 1 cup chopped red onion
- 1 medium cucumber (6 to 8 ounces), peeled and coarsely chopped
- ¼ cup finely chopped fresh flat-leaf parsley or cilantro or a combination
- 2 tablespoons finely chopped fresh mint
- Juice of ½ large lemon (about 2 tablespoons)
- 1 to 2 teaspoons coarsely ground sumac berries (optional)
- Salt and freshly ground black pepper, to taste
- 4 cups torn mixed greens or other lettuce, washed and dried

Preheat the oven to broil. Separate each pita into halves. Rub the flat side of one of the garlic halves evenly over the rough undersides of the bread. Arrange the bread halves, smooth sides up, on a large baking sheet. Brush the tops evenly with the 1 teaspoon oil. Broil 4 to 6 inches from the heating element for 1 to 2 minutes, or until tops are nicely toasted, taking care not to burn. Set aside.

Place the tomatoes, onion, cucumber, parsley, mint, lemon juice, sumac berries (if using), and remaining oil in a large bowl. Finely chop the remaining garlic and add to the bowl. Season with salt and pepper and toss to combine. Set aside for 15 minutes; toss again.

Using your fingers, break the toasted pita rounds into bite-size chips. Just before serving, combine the pita chips and greens in a large salad bowl. Add the tomato mixture and toss well to combine. Serve at once.

Advance Preparation The toasted pita can be prepared several hours before using in the recipe. The tomato mixture can be held an hour or so at room temperature before combining with the pita and greens and serving.

PER MAIN-COURSE SERVING

Calories 406 · Protein 12g · Total Fat 18g · Saturated Fat 3g · Cholesterol 0mg · Carbohydrate 56g · Dietary Fiber 11g · Sodium 354mg

Cook's Tips

This is one of those recipes where "serve at once" should be taken seriously; unless, that is, you don't mind soggy pita chips.

While the recipe easily doubles to serve four for dinner, you'll need quite a big salad bowl for tossing!

Tuscan Bread Salad
(Panzanella)

Panzanella, perhaps the best known of Italian bread salads, is also perhaps the simplest. The key to its success is the use of dense, slightly stale Italian or sourdough bread and a classic Italian vinaigrette. If desired, chopped cucumber, bell pepper, and olives can be added before tossing the bread with the listed ingredients.

MAKES 4 TO 6 SERVINGS

- 2 cloves garlic, finely chopped
- ½ teaspoon salt, plus additional, to taste
- ½ cup extra-virgin olive oil
- 2 tablespoons vegetable broth, preferably Basic Vegetable Broth (page 38) or low-sodium canned
- 2 tablespoons red wine vinegar
- 1 tablespoon fresh lemon juice
- Freshly ground black pepper, to taste
- 6 cups cubed dense, slightly stale Italian or sourdough bread
- 3 medium tomatoes (about 6 ounces each), coarsely chopped
- 1 medium red onion (about 6 ounces), chopped
- ½ cup chopped fresh basil
- ½ cup chopped fresh flat-leaf parsley
- Romaine lettuce leaves (optional)

In a mortar and pestle, or with the back of a teaspoon in a small bowl, mash together the garlic and salt until pastelike. Transfer to a large salad bowl. Whisk in the oil, broth, vinegar, lemon juice, and pepper until well blended. Reserve 2 tablespoons of the dressing and set aside.

Add the bread to the salad bowl and toss well to combine with the dressing. Let stand for 15 to 30 minutes to absorb the dressing, tossing a few times. Just before serving, add the tomatoes, onion, basil, parsley, and reserved dressing; toss well to combine. Season with additional salt and pepper as necessary. Serve at once, over the lettuce leaves, if desired.

PER SERVING

Calories 413 · Protein 6g · Total Fat 29g · Saturated Fat 4g · Cholesterol 0mg · Carbohydrate 35g · Dietary Fiber 5g · Sodium 573mg

Ligurian Bread Salad with Vegetables (Condigion)

Condigion is an old Ligurian layered bread salad that was originally made with leftover ship's biscuits brought home by returning seafarers, probably tired of fish and hungry for fresh vegetables. This version substitutes baguette rounds for the biscuits and dispenses with the communal salad bowl of tradition. However, if you don't own four relatively large salad bowls, prepare one big salad, creating four layers instead of two. Also, feel free to use your favorite ingredients.

MAKES 4 SERVINGS

- 24 (¼-inch-thick) baguette rounds (3 to 4 ounces total)
- 3 large cloves garlic, 1 halved, 2 finely chopped
- 1 tablespoon plus 4 teaspoons red wine vinegar
- 1 tablespoon water
- ¼ cup finely chopped fresh basil
- ¼ teaspoon dried oregano
- 1 cup frozen baby green peas, completely defrosted and drained
- 2 tablespoons drained capers
- 4 small vine-ripened tomatoes (about 4 ounces each), cored, halved lengthwise, then cut into thin wedges
- Salt and freshly ground black pepper, to taste
- 1 (6-ounce) jar marinated artichoke hearts, drained, thinly sliced
- 1 (7¼-ounce) jar roasted red bell peppers, drained, cut into thin strips
- 1 small red onion (about 4 ounces), peeled, quartered, and thinly sliced, soaked in cold water to cover 10 minutes, drained
- 1 medium cucumber (6 to 8 ounces), peeled and thinly sliced
- 8 teaspoons extra-virgin olive oil
- ½ cup kalamata olives, pitted and chopped

Preheat the oven to 350F (175C). Arrange the baguette rounds in a single layer on an ungreased baking sheet. Bake for 5 minutes, or until lightly toasted. Remove the baking sheet from the oven

Cook's Tip

To make dividing of the vegetables easy, keep each sliced tomato separate from the others. With the exceptions of the pea and basil mixtures, which are already approximated, arrange the other salad ingredients in four equal mounds on a large cutting board, then visually divide in half when assembling each individual salad.

and rub the top sides of the toasts with the halved garlic. Mix the 1 tablespoon of the vinegar with the water; sprinkle evenly over the toasts. Set aside.

In a small bowl, combine the basil, oregano, and the chopped garlic. In another small bowl, combine the peas and capers. Set aside.

To assemble the salads: Arrange 3 toasts on the bottom of each of 4 large salad bowls. Top each with one-eighth of the tomatoes. Season the tomatoes lightly with salt and pepper, then sprinkle with about 1¾ teaspoons of the basil mixture, followed by about 2 tablespoons of the pea mixture, one-eighth of the artichokes, one-eighth of the red peppers, one-eighth of the onion, and one-eighth of the cucumber. Drizzle the cucumber layer with 1 teaspoon of the oil, and ½ teaspoon of the remaining vinegar. Sprinkle the cucumber layer with one-eighth of the olives. Add another layer of toasts, and repeat the layering process one more time, ending with the olives. Season with salt and pepper. Let the salads rest for 15 to 30 minutes to let the flavors blend. Toss each salad individually and serve at once.

PER SERVING

Calories 343 · Protein 8g · Total Fat 19g · Saturated Fat 2g · Cholesterol 0mg · Carbohydrate 40g · Dietary Fiber 8g · Sodium 776mg

Variation Place all the ingredients in a large salad bowl without layering, season with salt and pepper to taste, and toss well to combine. Let stand for about 15 minutes to let the flavors blend. Season with additional salt and pepper as necessary, toss again, and serve.

Marinated Lentil Salad

Lentils are perhaps the best loved of all legumes in France, valued even more than the split pea because of their versatility in salads as well as soups. Their quick-cooking nature is especially appreciated by cooks during the sweltering summer months in Provence; they often marinate the lentils overnight and enjoy this refreshing salad for lunch the next day. **MAKES 4 SERVINGS**

- 3 tablespoons extra-virgin olive oil
- 1 cup chopped onion
- ½ cup chopped carrots
- 2 cups vegetable broth, preferably Basic Vegetable Broth (page 38) or low-sodium canned
- 2 cups water
- 1 cup lentils, picked over and rinsed
- 2 parsley sprigs
- ¼ teaspoon dried thyme leaves
- 1 bay leaf
- Salt and freshly ground black pepper, to taste
- 2 tablespoons red wine vinegar
- 1 teaspoon Dijon mustard
- 2 tablespoons chopped shallots (about 1 medium) or red onion
- 2 tablespoons finely chopped fresh flat-leaf parsley
- 8 butter lettuce leaves, rinsed and drained
- 8 small radicchio leaves, rinsed and drained

In a medium stockpot or a large saucepan, heat 1 tablespoon of the oil over medium heat. Add the onion and carrots; cook, stirring often, until softened, about 5 minutes. Add the broth, water, lentils, parsley sprigs, thyme, bay leaf, salt, and pepper; bring to a boil over medium-high heat. Reduce the heat and simmer gently, partially covered, until the lentils are tender but not mushy, stirring occasionally, 30 to 45 minutes, depending on the age of the lentils. Drain well, reserving ¼ cup of the cooking liquid. Transfer the lentil mixture to a medium bowl. Remove and discard the parsley sprigs and bay leaf.

In a small bowl, whisk together the remaining oil, reserved cooking liquid, vinegar, mustard, salt, and pepper. Add to the lentils, along with the shallot. Toss gently yet thoroughly to combine. Cover and refrigerate for at least 3 hours, stirring occasionally. Just before serving, stir in the chopped parsley.

To serve, arrange 2 butter lettuce leaves and 2 radicchio leaves on each of 4 serving plates. Mound equal portions of the marinated lentils in the center.

Advance Preparation The marinated lentils can be stored, covered, in the refrigerator for up to two days. Serve chilled.

PER SERVING

Calories 334 · Protein 22g · Total Fat 11g · Saturated Fat 2g · Cholesterol 0mg · Carbohydrate 40g · Dietary Fiber 21g · Sodium 337mg

Variation To serve as a pick-up appetizer, either fill the butter lettuce or radicchio leaves with the marinated lentils, or place some marinated lentils at the ends of large spinach or romaine lettuce leaves and roll up. For a quick sandwich, tuck a few spoonfuls into pita bread halves.

Italian-Style Brown Rice Salad

Brown rice is seldom used in Italian cooking, but in the Piedmont region, where rice, not pasta, rules, variations of this popular salad made with different forms of rice can be found. As with most of the grain-based salads in this book, the ingredients can be changed according to individual preference.

MAKES 4 TO 6 MAIN-COURSE OR 8 SIDE-DISH SERVINGS

- 3⅓ cups vegetable broth, preferably Basic Vegetable Broth (page 38) or low-sodium canned
- 1½ cups uncooked brown rice
- 1 cup thawed frozen baby green peas
- 1 (7¼-ounce) jar roasted red bell peppers, drained and chopped
- 1 (6-ounce) jar marinated artichoke hearts, drained and thinly sliced
- 1 bunch scallions (6 to 8), white and green parts, thinly sliced
- 2 stalks celery, finely chopped
- ½ cup green Italian-style olives, pitted and chopped
- ¼ cup chopped fresh flat-leaf parsley and/or basil
- 2 tablespoons drained capers
- 2 tablespoons extra-virgin olive oil
- 1 tablespoon white wine vinegar
- Salt and freshly ground black pepper, to taste
- Pine nuts or slivered almonds, toasted (optional; see Cook's Tip, page 121)

Combine the vegetable broth and rice in a medium saucepan; bring to a boil over high heat. Reduce the heat to low, cover, and cook until all of the broth has been absorbed, 30 to 35 minutes. Fluff with a fork and let stand, uncovered, for about 5 minutes.

Combine the peas, red peppers, artichokes, scallions, celery, olives, parsley, capers, oil, vinegar, salt, and pepper in a large salad bowl. Add the warm rice and toss well to combine. Sprinkle with the nuts if desired. Serve warm or at room temperature.

Advance Preparation The prepared salad can be held at room temperature for up to two hours. Refrigerate any leftovers; the rice kernels will become firm. To restore some of their softness, reheat the covered salad on medium-low power in a microwave oven until just warm throughout, then toss well before serving.

PER MAIN-COURSE SERVING

Calories 458 · Protein 19g · Total Fat 11g · Saturated Fat 2g · Cholesterol 0mg · Carbohydrate 74g · Dietary Fiber 11g · Sodium 727mg

Rice Salad with Saffron and Green Olives

Served with crusty bread and a green salad, this outstanding rice dish from the La Mancha region of central Spain easily becomes the main event. While saffron may be its defining ingredient, the secret to its success lies in the slow cooking of the onions, so don't rush this step. Arborio rice is used because the starchier grains of this Italian variety will retain their tenderness when refrigerated.

MAKES 4 TO 6 MAIN-COURSE OR 8 SIDE-DISH SERVINGS

- 1½ cups arborio rice
- ¼ cup extra-virgin olive oil
- 2 medium onions (about 6 ounces each), chopped
- 3 cloves garlic, thinly sliced lengthwise
- ¼ to ½ teaspoon saffron threads, steeped in ½ cup hot vegetable broth, preferably Basic Vegetable Broth (page 38) or low-sodium canned
- ½ cup Madeira, port, or medium-dry sherry
- ½ cup zante currants or dark raisins
- Salt and freshly ground black pepper, to taste
- ½ cup chopped fresh mint
- 1 cup pitted whole green olives
- ½ cup slivered almonds or pine nuts, toasted (optional; see Cook's Tip, page 121)

Bring about 3 quarts salted water to a boil in a large pot over high heat; add the rice and boil until tender yet still firm to the bite, stirring a few times, 12 to 15 minutes. Drain and transfer to a large bowl.

Heat the oil in a medium skillet over medium heat. Add the onions and garlic and cook for 1 minute, stirring constantly. Immediately reduce the heat to low and cook, stirring occasionally, until the onions are soft and slightly golden, about 20 minutes. Add the saffron-broth mixture and bring to a boil over medium-high heat; boil for 30 seconds, or until the liquid is almost completely evaporated. Remove from the heat and let cool for 1 minute. Add to the rice, stirring well to combine.

In a small saucepan, bring the Madeira and currants to a simmer over medium heat. Simmer for 10 minutes, or until the liquid is almost completely evaporated. Remove from the heat and let cool for 1 minute. Add the contents of the pan to the rice, stirring well to combine. Season with salt and pepper to taste. When the rice has cooled to room temperature, stir in the mint. Serve at room temperature, garnished with the olives and the nuts, if using.

Advance Preparation The salad, without the nuts, can be stored, covered, in the refrigerator for up to twenty-four hours. Bring to room temperature before serving.

PER MAIN-COURSE SERVING

Calories 536 · Protein 9g · Total Fat 17g · Saturated Fat 2g · Cholesterol 0mg · Carbohydrate 80g · Dietary Fiber 4g · Sodium 375mg

Provençal Couscous Tabbouleh Salad

In Provence and in Paris, as well, couscous is commonly substituted for the bulgur wheat of the traditional Middle Eastern salad. With the use of the instant variety, this classic dish is ready in a mere thirty minutes or so. Zucchini, peas, and artichoke hearts are the variables in the following rendition—feel free to use whatever other combination strikes your fancy, so long as the other ingredients remain about the same.

MAKES 5 TO 6 MAIN-COURSE OR 10 TO 12 APPETIZER SERVINGS

2 cups vegetable broth, preferably Basic Vegetable Broth (page 38) or low-sodium canned
⅓ cup plus 1 tablespoon extra-virgin olive oil
¼ teaspoon salt, plus additional, to taste
1½ cups instant couscous
8 ounces zucchini, preferably 1 green and 1 yellow, trimmed and chopped
Juice of 3 medium lemons (about 9 tablespoons)
1 pound plum tomatoes, diced
2 bunches scallions (12 to 16), mostly white parts, thinly sliced
1½ cups fresh mint leaves, finely chopped
1 cup fresh flat-leaf parsley, finely chopped
1 cup cooked fresh or frozen green peas (do not use canned)
4 canned whole artichoke hearts, drained, chopped, and squeezed dry between paper towels
Freshly ground black pepper, to taste
Swiss chard, spinach, or romaine or other large lettuce leaves

In a medium skillet with a tight-fitting lid, bring the broth, the 1 tablespoon oil, and the ¼ teaspoon salt to a boil. Working quickly, add the couscous and zucchini, stirring well to combine. Cover and remove from the heat. Let stand for 7 minutes. Uncover and fluff with a fork. Leave to cool for 15 minutes.

Meanwhile, in a large mixing bowl, whisk together the lemon juice and the remaining oil. Add the tomatoes, scallions, mint, parsley, peas, artichokes, salt, and pepper. Stir well to combine. Add the cooled couscous mixture and toss well to combine. Season with additional salt and pepper as necessary.

Cover and let stand for 20 minutes at room temperature to allow the flavors to blend, stirring occasionally. Or cover and refrigerate for at least 1 hour and serve chilled.

Serve directly from the bowl as a dip, surrounded with the chard or other whole leaves to use as scoops. Or arrange the leaves on a large serving platter or individual plates, and spoon the couscous salad over them.

Advance Preparation The salad may be stored, covered, in the refrigerator for up to twenty-four hours. Serve chilled or return to room temperature before serving.

PER MAIN-COURSE SERVING

Calories 487 · Protein 19g · Total Fat 18g · Saturated Fat 3g · Cholesterol 0mg · Carbohydrate 67g · Dietary Fiber 14g · Sodium 448mg

Tabbouleh Salad with Chickpeas

Bulgur is a nutritious and convenient ready-cooked wheat product that has been a staple in the eastern Mediterranean for thousands of years. Originally, it was prepared after the wheat harvest, predominately by women who boiled whole wheat kernels until they swelled, spread them on flat roofs to dry in the sun, then spent days cracking and sieving them to separate the grains according to size. Today, modern methods accomplish essentially the same thing. Although the coarse and large-grain varieties are further cooked in pilafs and soups, the fine-grain bulgur used in tabbouleh simply requires rehydrating in water. It's little wonder that this easy appetizer has such universal appeal. By adding a few cups of cooked chickpeas, the following recipe goes one step further to create a healthy main course. I like lots of lemon in this dish; add less if you prefer a little less tang in your tabbouleh. One medium-size lemon typically yields about three tablespoons of juice.

MAKES 6 MAIN-COURSE SERVINGS

- 1¼ cups fine-grain bulgur
- 1¼ cups warm water
- 8 to 9 tablespoons fresh lemon juice, or to taste
- ⅓ cup extra-virgin olive oil
- 2 cups cooked chickpeas (see Box, page 18) or 1 (19-ounce) can chickpeas, drained and rinsed
- 2 medium tomatoes (about 6 ounces each), cored and diced
- 1 bunch scallions (6 to 8), white and green parts, thinly sliced
- 1½ cups finely chopped fresh flat-leaf parsley
- ½ cup finely chopped fresh mint leaves
- Salt and freshly ground black pepper, to taste
- Romaine or other large lettuce leaves (optional)

Place the bulgur and water in a medium bowl. Stir well to combine. Let stand for about 30 minutes, stirring occasionally, or until the bulgur has absorbed all of the liquid and feels dry.

Meanwhile, in a large bowl, whisk together the lemon juice and oil. Add the chickpeas, tomatoes, scallions, parsley, mint, salt, and pepper; stir well to combine. Add the bulgur, tossing well to combine. Season with additional salt and pepper as necessary.

Cover and let stand at room temperature for 1 hour to allow the flavors to blend, stirring occasionally. Or cover and refrigerate for at least 1 hour and serve chilled. If desired, arrange the optional lettuce leaves on a large serving platter or individual plates and spoon the tabbouleh salad over them.

Advance Preparation The salad may be stored, covered, in the refrigerator for up to twenty-four hours. Serve chilled or return to room temperature before serving.

PER SERVING

Calories 344 · Protein 11g · Total Fat 15g · Saturated Fat 2g · Cholesterol 0mg · Carbohydrate 48g · Dietary Fiber 13g · Sodium 38mg

Variations If you don't have fine-grain bulgur, medium-grain can be substituted. Use three times the amount of water. Bring the water to a boil, combine well with the bulgur, and soak for a few hours until the bulgur is swelled and fluffy. Drain off the excess water, transfer to a sieve, and shake until the grains feel dry. Proceed as directed in the recipe.

For a classic tabbouleh salad, omit the chickpeas and reduce the amount of lemon juice to taste. Serve directly from the bowl as a dip, surrounded with romaine or other large lettuce leaves as scoops.

Mediterranean Wheat Berry Salad

Chewy wheat berries—whole-wheat kernels available at many health-food stores—are often served as refreshing salads, tabbouleh-style, throughout the Mediterranean. Aside from cooking the wheat berries, which can be done well in advance, this is basically an assembled salad, perfect to take to a picnic or potluck supper. You can vary the vegetables according to whim, as virtually anything goes. If wheat berries or the listed substitutes are unavailable, cooked whole-wheat couscous, cooked medium-grain bulgur, or soaked fine bulgur can be substituted. If you do use wheat berries, make sure they are a soft strain, not a hard variety like red spring wheat kernels.

MAKES 4 TO 6 SERVINGS

1 cup whole soft winter wheat berries, kamut, or spelt, soaked overnight in water to cover
2 medium tomatoes (about 6 ounces each), seeded and chopped
1 medium red bell pepper (about 6 ounces), chopped
1 medium green bell pepper (about 6 ounces), chopped
1 cup thawed frozen baby green peas
1 bunch scallions (6 to 8), both white and green parts, thinly sliced
½ cup pitted kalamata olives, chopped
½ cup drained marinated quartered artichoke hearts, thinly sliced lengthwise
½ cup finely chopped fresh flat-leaf parsley
2 tablespoons drained capers
2 cloves garlic, finely chopped
Salt and freshly ground black pepper, to taste
¼ cup extra-virgin olive oil

2 tablespoons fresh lemon juice
2 tablespoons white wine vinegar
Romaine or Bibb lettuce leaves (optional)

Drain the wheat berries. In a large saucepan, bring the drained wheat berries and enough salted water to cover by 2 inches to a boil over high heat. Reduce the heat, cover, and simmer 1½ to 2 hours, or until the wheat berries are cooked through but still chewy. Drain well and set aside to cool.

Place the wheat berries, tomatoes, bell peppers, peas, scallions, olives, artichokes, parsley, capers, garlic, salt, and pepper in a large salad bowl. Toss well to combine.

In a small bowl, whisk together the oil, lemon juice, and vinegar. Add to the salad bowl, tossing well to combine. Season with additional salt and pepper as necessary. Let stand at room temperature for 30 minutes to allow the flavors to blend, stirring a few times.

Serve at room temperature, arranged over lettuce leaves, if using, or cover and refrigerate for at least 1 hour and serve chilled.

Advance Preparation The cooked wheat berries can be stored, covered, in the refrigerator for two to three days before using in the salad. The tossed salad can be stored, covered, in the refrigerator for up to twenty-four hours. Serve chilled or return to room temperature before serving.

PER SERVING

Calories 447 · Protein 9g · Total Fat 23g · Saturated Fat 2g · Cholesterol 0mg · Carbohydrate 57g · Dietary Fiber 13g · Sodium 593mg

Pasta, Rice, and Other Grains

Main Courses, First Courses, and Side Dishes from Easy Spaghetti to Exotic Couscous

Grains are the rock, the foundation, or the backbone, if you'd rather, of the Mediterranean diet. In fact, absent these complex carbohydrates, a cuisine almost as old as time would basically collapse. Wheat, whether in the form of bread, pasta, couscous, bulgur, or wheat berries, is the most important of these grains. Second in importance is rice, classified into two types—short grain, used in risotto and paella, and long grain, used in pilaf. Corn is used to make polenta, which is nothing more than coarsely ground cornmeal, or corn grits; it is also used in certain breads, such as pizza. Barley, usually in hulled or pearled form, finds its way into soups, stews, pilafs, and occasionally bread. To be sure, while all of these staples are rather bland on their own, you simply can't make the bulk of the Mediterranean's most delicious—and nutritious—dishes without them. Indeed, picture paella without rice, primavera without pasta, or tabbouleh without bulgur, and picture a still life of orphaned vegetables left behind on a cutting board.

Curiously enough, a few Americans of late, in the hopes of losing weight, are succumbing to the trend of essentially wiping out most carbohydrates from their daily diets. They are swapping them for added protein, typically in the form of beef, bacon, eggs, and cheese, most of which are high in cholesterol and saturated fat. The jury's still out on whether such diets promote weight loss by drastically cutting carbohydrates, or by cleverly cutting calories through depression of the dieter's appetite via excessive protein intake. However, one thing is certain: there is virtually no place on this planet where people normally eat a very low carbohydrate diet. On the contrary, in the Mediterranean and in countries like Japan with the thinnest, and generally healthiest, people, the diets consist overwhelmingly of carbohydrates.

That said, fiber-rich whole-grain products are the healthiest. Unfortunately, refined pasta and white rice predominate in Mediterranean cooking, but understandably so—they typically taste better (in the case of pasta, considerably so). Unless the sauce with which it's tossed is highly spicy or on the rustic side, whole-wheat pasta is too heavy or mealy for many people's tastes—not light and just firm to the bite, like its refined counterpart cooked al dente. A happy compromise that many seem to be making these days is to cook equal parts whole wheat and refined together. If you choose this alternative, be sure to check the cooking times on the respective packages, as they are usually different. On the other hand, whole-wheat couscous is in no need of such a compromise. Many actually prefer its slightly nutty taste to the refined type, and I highly recommend its use throughout this book. In either case, for practical purposes, all the recipes in this book use the instant variety. As for brown rice, it is seldom used in Mediterranean cooking except by macrobiotics. Fortunately, in several instances it can be used quite successfully in lieu of white rice, namely in long-simmering soups, salads that are eaten shortly after preparing, and stuffed vegetable dishes that call for precooked rice. It is definitely not recommended, however, as a substitute for arborio rice in risotto. While you could use it as an interesting, and healthful, substitute for long-grain white rice in pilaf, you will have to increase the cooking time. But if you are really looking to add bulk to your diet, seek out any of the bulgur, wheat berry, polenta, or barley recipes throughout this book. As sources of fiber, they are unsurpassed in the indispensable grain department.

Pasta and Other Wheat Products

Bulgur Pilaf with Dried Fruits

Bulgur pilaf is a delightful change from the usual rice, and provides significantly more protein and fiber. In Turkey, where they are a major export, dried apricots and figs are typically included with the standard currants or raisins of a basic rice pilaf. Try to use medium-grain bulgur for this dish—the fine grain used in tabbouleh is not really suited for this type of cooking.

MAKES 4 TO 6 MAIN-COURSE
OR 8 SIDE-DISH SERVINGS

¼ cup dried apricots, coarsely chopped
¼ cup dried figs, coarsely chopped
2 tablespoons zante currants or dark raisins
2½ cups vegetable broth, preferably Basic Vegetable Broth (page 38) or low-sodium canned
3 tablespoons extra-virgin olive oil
2 cups chopped onions (about 2 medium)
1½ cups medium-grain bulgur
1 cinnamon stick or ¼ teaspoon ground cinnamon
Pinch ground allspice
Salt and freshly ground black pepper, to taste
¼ cup pine nuts or slivered almonds, toasted (see Cook's Tip, page 121)
¼ chopped fresh flat-leaf parsley
¼ cup chopped fresh mint

Place the apricots, figs, and currants in a small bowl with enough warm water to cover; let stand for 10 minutes. Drain well and set aside.

Meanwhile, in a small saucepan, bring the broth to a simmer over medium-high heat. Cover, remove from the heat, and set aside.

In a large wide saucepan or medium deep-sided skillet with a lid, heat the oil over medium-low heat. Add the onions and cook, stirring, until very soft but not browned, 10 to 15 minutes. Increase the heat to medium and add the bulgur; cook, stirring, for 1 minute. Add the hot broth, cinnamon, allspice, salt, and pepper. Bring to a brisk simmer. Reduce the heat to low, cover, and simmer until all the liquid has been absorbed, 15 to 20 minutes. Remove from the heat and let stand, covered, for 5 minutes.

Uncover the saucepan and remove the cinnamon stick, if used. Fluff the pilaf with a fork. Add the fruits, nuts, parsley, and mint, tossing with the fork to combine. Serve warm or at room temperature.

PER MAIN-COURSE SERVING

Calories 459 · Protein 18g · Total Fat 16g · Saturated Fat 2g · Cholesterol 0mg · Carbohydrate 69g · Dietary Fiber 21g · Sodium 342mg

Capellini with Fondue de Tomatoes

Save your juiciest vine-ripened tomatoes for this classic Provençal dish, in which tomatoes are literally melted in a pan with hot olive oil for a few minutes, then tossed with thin noodles. A naturally chunky sauce with lots of flavorful brothlike tomato juice, the fondue can be tossed with any pasta of your choice and is also good spooned over rice, couscous, polenta, fresh vegetables, or beans. Lots of crusty French bread will ensure that none of the delicious juices are left behind on the plate.

MAKES 4 MAIN-COURSE OR 6 TO 8 PASTA-COURSE SERVINGS

2 tablespoons extra-virgin olive oil
3 cloves garlic, thinly sliced lengthwise
2 pounds very ripe vine-ripened tomatoes, coarsely chopped, all the juices included
Salt, preferably the coarse variety, to taste
1 to 2 tablespoons finely chopped fresh basil
1 to 2 tablespoons finely chopped fresh flat-leaf parsley
1 to 2 tablespoons thinly sliced scallion greens
Freshly ground black pepper, to taste
12 ounces capellini, spaghettini, or other thin pasta

In a large nonstick skillet, heat the oil over medium heat. Add the garlic and cook, stirring, until golden, 2 to 3 minutes. Add the tomatoes and bring to a boil over high heat. Immediately remove the skillet from the heat and season with salt, stirring well to combine.

Let the tomatoes soften in the skillet, uncovered, for 5 to 10 minutes, or until the tomatoes feel warm to the touch. Stir in the basil, parsley, scallion greens, and pepper.

Meanwhile, in a large stockpot, cook the pasta in boiling salted water according to package directions until al dente. Drain and transfer to a large bowl. Add the tomato sauce and toss well to thoroughly combine. Serve at once.

PER MAIN-COURSE SERVING

Calories 423 · Protein 13g · Total Fat 9g · Saturated Fat 1g · Cholesterol 0mg · Carbohydrate 74g · Dietary Fiber 4g · Sodium 26mg

Conchiglie with Green and Black-Eyed Peas, Pearl Onions, and Basil

This mild-tasting dish is usually a hit with children, who like the idea of discovering tiny green and black-eyed peas and pearl onions hidden inside conch shells. Ready in under thirty minutes, it's a gift for working parents. While the black-eyed pea is typically associated with American southern cooking, it is also a popular legume enjoyed by many throughout the Mediterranean. Any firm precooked bean, however, can be substituted.

MAKES 4 TO 6 MAIN-COURSE OR 8 PASTA-COURSE SERVINGS

2 tablespoons extra-virgin olive oil
2 large cloves garlic, finely chopped
1½ cups frozen baby green peas and pearl onions, thoroughly thawed and drained

¾ cup vegetable broth, preferably Basic Vegetable Broth (page 38) or low-sodium canned
¼ teaspoon dried thyme leaves
Salt and freshly ground black pepper, to taste
1½ cups cooked black-eyed peas (see Box, page 18) or 1 (15-ounce) can black-eyed peas, rinsed and drained
12 ounces medium pasta shells (conchiglie)
¼ cup finely chopped fresh basil

In a medium skillet with a lid, heat the oil over medium-low heat. Add the garlic and cook, stirring, until just softened, about 2 minutes. Add the peas and pearl onions, broth, thyme, salt, and pepper. Cook, covered, until the vegetables are just tender, about 3 minutes. Add the black-eyed peas and cook, covered, until the black-eyed peas are heated through, about 2 minutes. Remove from the heat and keep covered.

Meanwhile, cook the pasta in boiling salted water according to package directions until just al dente. Drain well and return to the pot. Stir in the pea mixture. Cover and place over low heat until the pasta is tender and has absorbed most of the broth, 5 minutes, stirring once. Stir in the basil and serve at once.

PER MAIN-COURSE SERVING

Calories 547 · Protein 24g · Total Fat 9g · Saturated Fat 1g · Cholesterol 0mg · Carbohydrate 93g · Dietary Fiber 14g · Sodium 148mg

Variation To create a classic Italian springtime pasta course, use orecchiette instead of the shell pasta and omit the black-eyed peas and basil.

Couscous with Peas, Lettuce, and Mint

Peas and mint are such a refreshing combination; the addition of shredded butter lettuce and lemon only enhances this quality. Ready in just about fifteen minutes, the following couscous dish makes a quick-cooking and pleasant warm-weather meal.

MAKES 4 TO 6 MAIN-COURSE OR 8 SIDE-DISH SERVINGS

2 tablespoons extra-virgin olive oil
1 bunch scallions (6 to 8), white and some green parts, thinly sliced
2¼ cups vegetable broth, preferably Basic Vegetable Broth (page 38) or low-sodium canned
2 tablespoons fresh lemon juice
2 cups frozen baby green peas, thawed and well drained
¼ medium head butter lettuce, shredded
¼ teaspoon dried lemon peel
Salt and freshly ground black pepper, to taste
1½ cups instant couscous, preferably whole wheat
2 tablespoons finely chopped fresh mint
Lemon wedges (optional)

In a large deep-sided skillet with a lid, heat the oil over medium heat. Add the scallions and

Cook's Tip

To easily shred the lettuce, cut the lettuce into quarters, then in half lengthwise, tightly roll up each half, then thinly slice crosswise.

cook, stirring constantly, for 1 minute. Add the broth and lemon juice; cover and bring to a boil over high heat. Uncover and add the peas, lettuce, lemon peel, salt, and pepper. When the mixture returns to a boil, quickly stir in the couscous. As soon as the mixture returns to a boil, cover, remove from the heat, and let stand until all the broth is absorbed, 7 minutes.

Uncover and fluff with a fork. Add the mint and toss well with the fork to combine. Serve warm or at room temperature, accompanied with lemon wedges for squeezing over each portion, if desired.

Advance Preparation Preferably without the mint, the dish can be stored, covered, in the refrigerator for up to twenty-four hours. Return to room temperature or reheat in a low oven, and toss with the mint just before serving.

PER MAIN-COURSE SERVING

Calories 402 · Protein 19g · Total Fat 8g · Saturated Fat 1g · Cholesterol 0mg · Carbohydrate 65g · Dietary Fiber 10g · Sodium 385mg

Couscous with Seven-Vegetable Tagine

Moroccans consider it lucky to combine seven vegetables in one dish. By prepping all the vegetables first, this rich and colorful tagine, or stew, served atop instant couscous, is ready in less than one hour. In the fall and winter, cabbage, turnips, and butternut squash can replace some of the vegetables—so long as the total remains seven!

MAKES 5 OR 6 MAIN-COURSE SERVINGS

- 2½ tablespoons extra-virgin olive oil
- 1 large onion (10 to 12 ounces), chopped
- 2 cloves garlic, slivered
- 5 cups vegetable broth, preferably Microwave Vegetable Broth (page 37) or low-sodium canned
- 2 medium tomatoes (about 6 ounces each), peeled, seeded, and chopped
- 1 boiling potato (about 4 ounces), cut into 8 pieces
- Salt and freshly ground black pepper, to taste
- 1 small carrot (about 2 ounces), peeled and sliced into thin rounds
- 1 cup fresh or frozen green peas (see Cook's Tip, page 101)
- 4 medium asparagus stalks (about 4 ounces) or 8 thin asparagus stalks, trimmed, scaled if necessary, and cut into 2-inch lengths
- 2 ounces fresh large green beans, trimmed, cut into 2-inch pieces, or 2 ounces fresh small green beans, trimmed, left whole
- 2 cups cooked chickpeas (see Box, page 18) or 1 (19-ounce) can chickpeas, drained and rinsed
- 1 medium red bell pepper (about 6 ounces), coarsely chopped
- 1 small zucchini (about 4 ounces), preferably yellow, thinly sliced
- 1 tablespoon harissa sauce or Chinese chile paste (or crushed red pepper flakes, to taste) (see Tunisian Chickpea Soup, page 52, for information about harissa)
- 2 cups instant couscous, preferably whole wheat
- ½ cup chopped fresh cilantro
- 1½ tablespoons fresh lemon juice

In a medium stockpot, heat 2 tablespoons of the oil over medium heat. Add the onion and garlic and cook until softened and lightly golden, stirring often, about 5 minutes. Stir in 2 cups of the broth, tomatoes, potato, salt, and pepper; bring to a boil over high heat. Add the carrots and the fresh peas, medium asparagus, and large green beans, if using; return to a boil. Cover, reduce the heat, and simmer for 10 minutes. (If using the frozen peas, thin asparagus, and small green beans, just add the carrots and cook for 10 minutes, then add these vegetables in the next step with the chickpeas.) Add the chickpeas, red bell pepper, zucchini, and crushed red pepper flakes, if using; bring to a boil over medium-high heat. Cover, reduce the heat, and simmer gently until all the vegetables are tender, 7 to 10 minutes.

Meanwhile, in a large saucepan, bring the remaining 3 cups of broth to a boil. Stir in the couscous and the remaining ½ tablespoon oil. Cover and remove from the heat. Let stand until all the broth is absorbed, 7 minutes. Uncover and fluff with a fork.

Just before serving, add the cilantro, lemon juice, and the harissa or chile paste, if using, to the stewed vegetables, stirring well to combine. Season with additional salt and pepper as necessary. Serve over the hot couscous.

PER SERVING

Calories 585 · Protein 31g · Total Fat 10g · Saturated Fat 1g · Cholesterol 0mg · Carbohydrate 97g · Dietary Fiber 15g · Sodium 564mg

Cook's Tip

The cooking time for fresh peas is largely dependent upon their age and freshness. If using very young fresh peas, add them at the time indicated for the frozen variety.

Zucchini-Lemon Couscous

With versatile zucchini available year-round, this is one of the simplest and most delicious ways to enjoy couscous any season. To turn it into a colorful hot meal, serve warm tossed with the Sautéed Cherry Tomatoes with Mediterranean Herbs (page 157) and sprinkle with toasted pine nuts. For an easy picnic entree, serve at room temperature garnished with fancy on-the-vine cherry tomatoes and black olives.

MAKES 6 TO 8 SIDE-DISH OR 4 MAIN-COURSE SERVINGS

- 1½ tablespoons extra-virgin olive oil
- 1 bunch scallions (6 to 8), white parts chopped, ½ cup thinly sliced green tops reserved
- ½ pound zucchini (about 1 medium), finely diced
- 2 cups vegetable broth, preferably Basic Vegetable Broth (page 38) or low-sodium canned
- Juice of ½ large lemon (about 2 tablespoons)
- ¼ teaspoon chopped dried lemon peel
- Salt and freshly ground black pepper, to taste
- 1½ cups instant couscous, preferably whole wheat

In a medium saucepan, heat the oil over medium heat. Add the white part of the scallions and cook, stirring, until softened, about 2 minutes. Add the zucchini and cook, stirring, for 2 minutes. Add the broth, lemon juice, lemon peel, salt, and pepper; bring to a boil over high heat. Stir in the couscous; cover and remove from the heat. Let stand until all the liquids are absorbed, 7 minutes.

Uncover and fluff the couscous with a fork. Add the reserved scallion greens and toss well with the fork to combine. Serve warm or at room temperature.

PER SIDE-DISH SERVING

Calories 223 · Protein 10g · Total Fat 4g · Saturated Fat 1g · Cholesterol 0mg · Carbohydrate 37g · Dietary Fiber 4g · Sodium 182mg

Ditali with Cauliflower

This unusual and tasty dish is a specialty of Sicily, where it is typically made with a strongly flavored green cauliflower native to the region. Any type of cauliflower, whether white or purple, can be used with success in this recipe.

MAKES 6 MAIN-COURSE OR 8 PASTA-COURSE SERVINGS

- 4 tablespoons extra-virgin olive oil
- 1 cup soft white bread crumbs
- 1 large head cauliflower (2 to 2¼ pounds), cut into florets, then finely chopped
- 4 large cloves garlic, finely chopped
- ⅛ teaspoon crushed red pepper flakes
- 1 (14-ounce) can whole tomatoes, drained and chopped, juices reserved
- ¼ cup drained capers, slightly crushed in a mortar and pestle or in a small bowl with the back of a spoon
- ¼ cup vegetable broth, preferably Basic Vegetable Broth (page 38) or low-sodium canned
- 2 tablespoons tomato paste
- Salt and freshly ground black pepper, to taste
- ⅛ to ¼ teaspoon saffron threads, steeped in ¼ cup hot vegetable broth 10 minutes
- 16 ounces ditali or other small tubular pasta such as tubetti
- ¼ cup chopped fresh basil

In a large deep-sided nonstick skillet with a lid, heat 1 tablespoon of the oil over medium-low heat. Add the bread crumbs and cook, stirring often, until golden, 15 to 20 minutes. Transfer to a small bowl and set aside.

Add the remaining oil to the skillet and heat over medium heat. Add the cauliflower and cook, stirring, until the cauliflower is just softened, about 5 minutes. Add the garlic and red pepper and cook, stirring, for 3 minutes. Add the tomatoes and their juices, capers, broth, tomato paste, salt, and pepper; bring to a brisk simmer over medium-high heat. Reduce the heat, cover, and simmer for 15 minutes, stirring occasionally, or until the cauliflower is very tender. Stir in the saffron mixture and increase the heat to medium. Cook, uncovered, stirring occasionally, until the liquids are greatly reduced, 10 minutes. Keep warm.

Meanwhile, cook the pasta in boiling salted water according to package directions until al dente. Drain well. Add to the cauliflower mixture,

Cook's Tip

To save about 15 minutes, toast the bread crumbs in a separate skillet or in a preheated 350F (175C) oven while you prepare the cauliflower sauce. To toast in the oven, spread the bread crumbs in a single layer on a light-colored baking sheet (a dark surface tends to overbrown them). Drizzle with the oil. Bake until golden, stirring a few times, 3 to 4 minutes.

stirring well to combine. Add the basil, stirring well to combine. Serve at once, with the reserved bread crumbs passed separately.

Advance Preparation The cauliflower sauce can be kept warm over low heat for about one hour. Toss with the pasta and serve. It can also be covered and refrigerated for up to one day. Reheat over low heat. Prepare the bread crumbs separately.

PER MAIN-COURSE SERVING

Calories 444 · Protein 15g · Total Fat 11g · Saturated Fat 2g · Cholesterol 0mg · Carbohydrate 73g · Dietary Fiber 7g · Sodium 368mg

Farfalle with Sautéed Radicchio, Fennel, and Toasted Walnuts

With radicchio and fennel wearing bow ties for dinner, this festive pasta dish is perfect for the holidays or other special occasions. Sautéing curbs the radicchio's natural bitterness, which is further offset by the hint of sweet licorice in the fennel. Aromatic toasted walnuts provide a crunchy crowning touch.

MAKES 4 TO 6 MAIN-COURSE OR 8 PASTA-COURSE SERVINGS

¼ cup extra-virgin olive oil
3 large cloves garlic, finely chopped
1 bunch scallions (6 to 8), white parts chopped, ½ cup thinly sliced green tops reserved
2 medium heads radicchio (about 12 ounces total), cored, rinsed, and drained, cut lengthwise into ½-inch-thick strips
1 medium fennel bulb (about 12 ounces), trimmed, cut crosswise into ¼-inch-thick slices, 2 tablespoons chopped feathery green leaves reserved
Salt and freshly ground black pepper, to taste
12 ounces farfalle (bow tie or butterfly pasta), fusilli, or penne
4 tablespoons coarsely chopped walnuts, toasted (see Cook's Tip, page 121)

In a large deep-sided nonstick skillet with a lid, heat the oil over medium heat. Add the garlic and the white parts of the scallions; cook, stirring, until just softened, about 2 minutes. Add the radicchio, fennel, salt, and pepper; reduce the heat to low. Cover and cook, stirring often, until the radicchio is slightly wilted and beginning to turn brown and the fennel is crisp-tender, 10 to 15 minutes.

Meanwhile, cook the pasta in boiling salted water according to package directions. Drain well and return to the cooking pot. Add the radicchio-fennel mixture and the reserved scallion greens and fennel leaves; toss well to combine. Serve at once, sprinkled with the walnuts.

PER MAIN-COURSE SERVING

Calories 541 · Protein 16g · Total Fat 20g · Saturated Fat 2g · Cholesterol 0mg · Carbohydrate 78g · Dietary Fiber 6g · Sodium 73mg

Fettuccine with Green Beans and Tomatoes

No crisp-tender vegetables here—the idea behind the long, slow cooking of this delicious pasta sauce is to create green beans flexible enough to be twirled easily with the pasta strands. The cooking time is largely dependent upon the thickness and freshness of the beans. As the sauce can be made a few days ahead of serving, this is a great dish for company.

MAKES 4 MAIN-COURSE OR 6 TO 8 PASTA-COURSE SERVINGS

- 2 tablespoons extra-virgin olive oil
- 4 large cloves garlic, finely chopped
- 2¼ pounds tomatoes, peeled, seeded, and chopped
- ½ teaspoon dried oregano
- ⅛ teaspoon cayenne pepper, or to taste
- ¾ pound long green beans, trimmed, left whole
- ½ cup vegetable broth, preferably Basic Vegetable Broth (page 38) or low-sodium canned
- Salt and freshly ground black pepper, to taste
- 12 ounces egg-free fettuccine
- ½ teaspoon coarse salt, or to taste

In a large deep-sided skillet with a lid, heat the oil over medium-low heat. Add the garlic and cook, stirring, until fragrant, 2 to 3 minutes. Add the tomatoes, oregano, and cayenne. Bring to a brisk simmer over medium-high heat. Reduce the heat to medium and cook, uncovered, stirring occasionally, until the mixture begins to form a sauce, about 10 minutes.

Add the green beans, broth, salt, and pepper; stir well to coat the beans. Cover, reduce the heat, and simmer gently until the beans are very tender, 1½ to 2 hours, stirring occasionally.

Cook the pasta in boiling salted water according to package directions until al dente. Drain well and transfer to a large serving bowl. Add the sauce and coarse salt, tossing well to combine. Serve at once.

Advance Preparation The sauce can be stored, covered, in the refrigerator for up to two days. Reheat over low heat and toss with freshly cooked pasta.

PER MAIN-COURSE SERVING

Calories 462 · Protein 16g · Total Fat 9g · Saturated Fat 1g · Cholesterol 0mg · Carbohydrate 82g · Dietary Fiber 8g · Sodium 332mg

Fettuccine with Spicy Raw Tomato, Herb, and Caper Sauce

This fiery raw tomato sauce is incredibly easy to make in a food processor. The optional walnuts, though not traditional, have been included because they provide a nice counterpoint to the dish's spiciness, as well as extra protein.

MAKES 6 MAIN-COURSE OR 8 PASTA-COURSE SERVINGS

- 1 pound plum tomatoes, seeded and coarsely chopped
- ½ cup packed fresh flat-leaf parsley
- ½ cup packed fresh mint leaves
- ½ cup packed fresh basil leaves
- ¼ cup drained capers

3 cloves garlic, chopped
½ teaspoon crushed red pepper flakes, or to taste
Pinch sugar, or more to taste
Salt and freshly ground black pepper, to taste
6 tablespoons extra-virgin olive oil
1 pound egg-free fettucine
½ cup coarsely chopped walnuts, toasted (optional; see Cook's Tip, page 121)
Freshly chopped parsley (optional)

Reserve about one-third of the chopped tomatoes. Combine the remaining tomatoes, parsley, mint, basil, capers, garlic, red pepper flakes, sugar, salt, and black pepper in a food processor fitted with the metal blade; process until a smooth paste is formed. With the motor running, add the oil in a thin, steady stream. Transfer the mixture to a large serving bowl.

Meanwhile, cook the fettuccine in boiling salted water according to package directions until al dente. Drain well and add to the bowl with the tomato mixture. Add the reserved tomatoes and toss like a salad until well combined. Serve immediately, garnished with the optional walnuts and parsley, if using.

PER MAIN-COURSE SERVING

Calories 435 · Protein 12g · Total Fat 15g · Saturated Fat 2g · Cholesterol 0mg · Carbohydrate 63g · Dietary Fiber 5g · Sodium 78mg

Potato Gnocchi with Pesto

Although they've become fashionable in recent years, gnocchi are unpretentious Italian dumplings that are made with the humblest of ingredients, with potatoes being the most basic. They are also very easy to prepare and can be made in separate stages well ahead of serving. Gnocchi are usually eaten as a first course or side dish, but sauced with pesto and served with green beans or asparagus, they become the stuff of a simple yet very satisfying meal. In a pinch, serve with your favorite pasta sauce.

MAKES 6 MAIN-COURSE OR 8 SIDE-DISH SERVINGS

2 pounds russet potatoes (about 4 large)
1 tablespoon extra-virgin olive oil, plus extra for cooking
½ teaspoon salt, or to taste
¼ teaspoon freshly ground black pepper, or to taste
1½ to 1¾ cups all-purpose unbleached flour
1 recipe Poor Man's Pesto (page 107)

Preheat the oven to 450F (230C). Pierce the potatoes in a few places with the tines of a fork. Bake 50 minutes, or until soft. (Or bake in a microwave oven according to manufacturer's instructions.) Set aside to cool slightly. Reduce the oven to 350F (175C).

Bring a large stockpot of salted water and a few drops of the oil to a boil over medium-high heat. Lightly oil a large gratin or shallow baking dish and set aside.

When the potatoes are still hot but cool enough to safely handle, scoop the insides out into a medium bowl, discarding the skins. Add the salt and pepper and mash well with a fork. Gradually add 1½ cups of the flour. When a sticky mass forms, mash in the 1 tablespoon oil. Turn the dough out onto a lightly floured work surface and gently knead for 3 minutes, adding more flour if the mixture feels too sticky to be shaped.

Shape the dough into a rectangle and, using a sharp knife, divide into 8 equal sections, then cut each in half. Take each piece between floured palms and gently roll into ¾-inch-thick cylinders. Cut each cylinder crosswise into ½-inch-thick pieces. With a floured thumb, press each piece gently against the inside curve of a floured fork, so that the centers are slightly indented and decorative rib marks appear on the dough. (Or flatten each piece gently with your thumb into an indented disk.)

Working in batches so as not to crowd the pot, drop the gnocchi into the boiling water. As soon as they have all risen to the surface, 1 to 2 minutes, immediately reduce the heat to medium and simmer gently for 4 to 5 minutes. Transfer the gnocchi with a slotted spoon to a colander to drain. Return the water to a boil over medium-high heat and repeat with the next batch. When all the gnocchi have been cooked, reserve ⅓ cup of the cooking liquid.

Arrange the gnocchi in a single layer in the prepared baking dish. In a small bowl, combine the pesto with the reserved cooking liquid. Brush the gnocchi evenly with the pesto sauce and bake for about 10 minutes, or until just hot. Serve at once.

Advance Preparation After forming into cylinders, the uncooked gnocchi dough can be wrapped in kitchen towels or a few layers of paper towels, placed on a baking sheet, and refrigerated for up to twelve hours. If the cylinders have become too sticky, you will need to lightly roll them in more flour before cutting and shaping into the gnocchi. (Storing the dough in mass form is not recommended, as it grows far too sticky and requires too much additional flour.) Shaped gnocchi from a freshly made batch of dough can be covered with a kitchen towel and left at room temperature or refrigerated for one hour before boiling. But if the dough has previously been refrigerated, it's best to cook them shortly after forming, as they can quickly lose their shape. The cooked and drained gnocchi, without the pesto, can be held in the prepared baking dish, covered with plastic wrap, at room temperature for one hour before baking, or covered and refrigerated, with the pesto if desired, overnight before baking.

PER MAIN-COURSE SERVING

Calories 427 · Protein 10g · Total Fat 22g · Saturated Fat 3g · Cholesterol 0mg · Carbohydrate 52g · Dietary Fiber 3g · Sodium 424mg

Cook's Tip

The less flour you add to the dough, the lighter the gnocchi will be. The longer the dough rests, the stickier it becomes—inevitably, you'll need to add more flour.

Whenever practical, it's best to shape and cook the gnocchi shortly after kneading. When you must, always cover with porous materials such as kitchen towels, paper towels, or double layers of cheesecloth. Avoid plastic containers or plastic wrap unless the gnocchi have been cooked.

Poor Man's Pesto

The name *pesto* derives from the thousand-year-old Ligurian tradition of making this sauce in a mortar with a pestle. Traditional pesto Genovese almost always includes a combination of Parmesan and pecorino Romano cheeses with the following exceptions: when the pesto is to be stirred into soups or when the household can't afford the cheese—expensive for some, even in Italy. No matter. The following cheese-free recipe, adapted for a food processor or blender, proves yet again that fruity green olive oil is the heart and garden-fresh basil the soul of good pesto. It produces a thick, rather creamy sauce, which is thinned in most pasta recipes with a little pasta cooking liquid or vegetable broth. MAKES ABOUT 1 CUP

3 cups loosely packed fresh basil leaves
6 tablespoons pine nuts
2 to 4 large cloves garlic
¾ teaspoon coarse salt, or to taste
6 tablespoons fruity extra-virgin olive oil

Combine the basil, pine nuts, garlic, and salt in a food processor fitted with the metal blade or in a blender. Process or blend until the ingredients are finely chopped, scraping down the sides of the work bowl as necessary. Add the oil and process until smooth and creamy. If not using immediately, store tightly covered in the refrigerator for up to 2 days, or place in ice cube trays, cover tightly with plastic wrap, and store in the freezer no longer than 1 month for the best flavor.

Cook's Tip

Because pesto freezes well, you might want to make more if you have lots of basil on hand. For every extra cup of loosely packed basil leaves, add the following to the above recipe: 2 tablespoons pine nuts, 1 clove garlic (or to taste), ¼ teaspoon coarse salt (or to taste), and 2 tablespoons olive oil.

PER ABOUT 1 TABLESPOON

Calories 73 · Protein 2g · Total Fat 7g · Saturated Fat 1g · Cholesterol 0mg · Carbohydrate 2g · Dietary Fiber 0g · Sodium 90mg

Squash Gnocchi with Walnut Sauce

This variety is a bit lighter than the Potato Gnocchi (page 105) and is prepared in the same fashion, except that here both the squash and the potatoes are steamed. These are also good with Poor Man's Pesto (page 107), but only use about ¾ cup.

MAKES 4 MAIN-COURSE OR 6 TO 8 FIRST-COURSE SERVINGS

10 ounces russet potatoes (about 2 small or 1 extra large), peeled and cubed
6 ounces peeled, seeded, and cubed butternut squash (about ¼ of a small 2-pound squash)
½ tablespoon extra-virgin olive oil, plus extra for cooking
⅛ teaspoon freshly grated nutmeg
Salt and freshly ground black pepper, to taste
1 to 1¼ cups unbleached all-purpose flour
1 recipe Walnut Sauce (page 108)

In a medium stockpot or saucepan large enough to hold a 9-inch steaming basket, put 1 inch of water. Place the steaming basket in the pot and add the potatoes and squash. Bring to a boil over high heat. Cover tightly, reduce the heat to medium, and steam until both are very tender, about 15 minutes. Carefully transfer to a medium bowl and let cool slightly.

Meanwhile, preheat the oven to 350F (175C). Bring a large stockpot of salted water and a few drops of the oil to a boil over medium-high heat. Lightly oil a large gratin or shallow baking dish and set aside.

Add the nutmeg, salt, and pepper to the potatoes and squash; mash well with a fork. Gradually add 1 cup of the flour. When a sticky mass forms, mash in the ½ tablespoon oil. Turn the dough out onto a lightly floured work surface and gently knead for 3 minutes, adding more flour if the mixture feels too sticky to be shaped.

Shape the dough into a rectangle and, using a sharp knife, divide into 6 equal sections, then cut each section in half. Take each piece between floured palms and gently roll into ¾-inch-thick cylinders. Cut each cylinder crosswise into ½-inch-thick pieces. With a floured thumb, press each piece gently against the inside curve of a floured fork, so that the centers are slightly indented and decorative rib marks appear on the dough. (Or flatten each piece gently with your thumb into an indented disk.)

Working in batches so as not to crowd the pot, drop the gnocchi into the boiling water. As soon as they have all risen to the surface, 1 to 2 minutes, immediately reduce the heat to medium and simmer gently for 4 to 5 minutes. Transfer with a slotted spoon to a colander to drain. Return the heat to medium-high and repeat with the next batch. When all the gnocchi have been cooked, reserve ¼ cup of the cooking liquid.

Arrange the gnocchi in a single layer in the prepared baking dish. In a small bowl, combine the walnut sauce with the reserved cooking liquid. Spoon evenly over the gnocchi. Bake about 10 minutes, or until just hot. Serve at once.

PER MAIN-COURSE SERVING

Calories 377 · Protein 10g · Total Fat 18g · Saturated Fat 2g · Cholesterol 0mg · Carbohydrate 47g · Dietary Fiber 5g · Sodium 297mg

Walnut Sauce

More paste than sauce, this is meant to be thinned with the cooking liquid from the gnocchi or other pasta, steamed or blanched vegetables, or vegetable broth. It is especially delicious tossed with blanched or steamed fresh green beans. **MAKES ABOUT ¾ CUP**

½ cup chopped walnuts
1 cup packed flat-leaf parsley
2 tablespoons extra-virgin olive oil
1 tablespoon tomato paste
2 to 3 large cloves garlic
½ teaspoon coarse salt, or to taste

Place the nuts, parsley, oil, tomato paste, garlic, and salt in a food processor fitted with the metal blade or in a blender. Process or blend until a smooth paste is formed.

PER ABOUT 1 TABLESPOON

Calories 59 · Protein 2g · Total Fat 5g · Saturated Fat 1g · Cholesterol 0mg · Carbohydrate 2g · Dietary Fiber 1g · Sodium 97mg

Linguine with Asparagus and Tomato Coulis

Tomato coulis is a fundamental ingredient in Provençal cooking, used to dress pasta, polenta, green beans, and pizza and added to soups and stews, as well as other sauces. Unlike most tomato-based sauces, the seeds are typically included—indeed, no tomato sauce could be less trouble to make. The secret to its success is impeccably fresh, vine-ripened tomatoes, so canned substitutes are not recommended. The following recipe, ideal to serve in early spring when pencil-thin asparagus is in season, is meant to be a starting point—feel free to use the coulis as you would any pasta sauce. If pencil asparagus is unavailable, use medium asparagus—trim the tips and halve the stalks lengthwise, then cut as directed.

MAKES 6 MAIN-COURSE OR 8 PASTA-COURSE SERVINGS

- 2 tablespoons extra-virgin olive oil
- 3 large cloves garlic, finely chopped
- 3 pounds vine-ripened tomatoes, peeled and chopped, all the juices included (see Cook's Tip, below)
- 1½ tablespoons fresh thyme leaves or 1½ teaspoons dried
- ½ teaspoon sugar, or to taste
- Salt and freshly ground black pepper, to taste
- 12 ounces pencil-thin asparagus, tough ends trimmed and discarded, tips trimmed from stalks, stalks cut diagonally into 2-inch lengths
- 16 ounces dry linguine (do not use fresh)
- ¼ cup Niçoise or other good-quality black olives, pitted and chopped (optional)

In a large nonstick skillet, heat the oil over medium heat. Add the garlic and cook, stirring, until just golden, 2 to 3 minutes. Add the tomatoes and their juices, thyme, sugar, salt, and pepper; bring to a brisk simmer over medium-high heat. Reduce the heat and simmer gently, uncovered, stirring occasionally, until the mixture is reduced by about one-third and the sauce has thickened, 20 to 30 minutes. Correct the seasonings, adding additional sugar to taste if the sauce tastes too acidic.

Meanwhile, bring a large stockpot filled with salted water to a boil over high heat. Add the pasta and cook until almost al dente (al dente is typically 9 to 11 minutes for most brands of dry linguine), about 7 minutes. Add the asparagus and cook until the asparagus is tender and the pasta is al dente, 2 to 3 minutes. Drain well and transfer to a large warm bowl. Add the tomato coulis and the olives, if using, and toss well to combine. Serve at once.

Advance Preparation The tomato coulis can be cooled and stored, covered, in the refrigerator for up to three days. Or it can be transferred to a plastic freezer storage bag and frozen for up to one month.

PER MAIN-COURSE SERVING

Calories 375 · Protein 12g · Total Fat 7g · Saturated Fat 1g · Cholesterol 0mg · Carbohydrate 68g · Dietary Fiber 5g · Sodium 25mg

Cook's Tip

To peel the tomatoes, bring a medium stockpot filled with water to a boil over high heat; drop in the tomatoes and boil for 20 seconds. Drain and rinse under cold running water. Peel off the skins.

Linguine with Pesto, Potatoes, and Green Beans

This Ligurian dish is a specialty of Genoa, where heady pesto has been infusing pasta, potatoes, and green beans with basil and garlic for centuries. Originally a peasant dish, cheese was typically added when available and just as typically omitted when not. In either case, tossed with the garlicky Poor Man's Pesto, it simply isn't necessary here. Although the skins of red potatoes contrast nicely with the green pigment of the beans, any type of boiling potato can be used. If they're much larger than two inches in diameter, quarter them.

MAKES 5 OR 6 MAIN-COURSE OR 8 PASTA-COURSE SERVINGS

- 8 ounces small new potatoes (about 1½ inches in diameter), preferably red skinned, halved
- 4 ounces large green beans, trimmed
- 12 ounces dry linguine (do not use fresh)
- ⅔ cup Poor Man's Pesto (page 107)

Bring a large stockpot filled with salted water to a boil over high heat. Add the potatoes and green beans. When the water returns to a boil, reduce the heat to medium-high and boil gently for 3 minutes. Add the pasta and return the heat to high. When the water returns to a boil, reduce the heat slightly and boil gently until the pasta is al dente, 8 to 10 minutes. Reserve ½ cup of the cooking liquid, then drain the pasta and vegetables in a colander.

Transfer the pasta and vegetables to a large shallow serving bowl. Add the pesto and the reserved cooking liquid; toss well to combine. Serve at once.

PER MAIN-COURSE SERVING

Calories 442 · Protein 13g · Total Fat 16g · Saturated Fat 2g · Cholesterol 0mg · Carbohydrate 63g · Dietary Fiber 3g · Sodium 199mg

Variation

Pesto, Potatoes, and Green Beans

To create a delicious vegetable side dish to serve six, omit the pasta altogether and reduce the pesto to ½ cup. Increase the amount of potatoes to 1½ pounds and the green beans to ¾ pound. Boil them gently in a large stockpot of salted water until the potatoes are cooked through but not mushy and the beans are tender, 10 to 12 minutes. Drain, reserving about 3 tablespoons of the cooking liquid. Toss with the pesto and reserved cooking liquid. Serve at once.

Linguine with Tomato-Pesto Sauce

Unlike the original pesto from Liguria, Sicilian basil sauce is typically tossed with fresh tomatoes—perhaps because Sicilian cooks can't bear to see these soul mates far apart. To liven up the union, a pinch of cayenne is often added, as well. As this is virtually an uncooked sauce, impeccably fresh ingredients are a must.

MAKES 4 TO 6 MAIN-COURSE OR 8 PASTA-COURSE SERVINGS

- 2 cups packed fresh basil leaves
- ¼ cup pine nuts, toasted (see Cook's Tip, page 121)
- ¼ cup extra-virgin olive oil
- 4 large cloves garlic, finely chopped

½ teaspoon coarse salt
Pinch cayenne, or to taste (optional)
Freshly ground black pepper, to taste
12 ounces linguine
1 pound vine-ripened tomatoes, peeled, seeded, and chopped

Place the basil, pine nuts, oil, garlic, salt, cayenne (if using), and pepper in a food processor fitted with the metal blade or in a blender. Process or blend until smooth and well combined. Set aside.

Meanwhile, cook the pasta according to package directions until al dente; drain well. Transfer to a large bowl and immediately add the basil mixture and tomatoes; toss well to combine. Serve at once.

PER MAIN-COURSE SERVING

Calories 533 · Protein 16g · Total Fat 21g · Saturated Fat 3g · Cholesterol 0mg · Carbohydrate 74g · Dietary Fiber 4g · Sodium 254mg

Gratin of Macaroni, Tomatoes, Basil, and Olives

This hearty gratin from Provence seems to borrow a bit of technique from southwestern France, where the crust of the famous bean and meat casserole known as cassoulet is similarly broken into the dish, then "crusted over" again. Indeed, for extra protein, I often add a can of drained and rinsed red kidney beans before baking.

MAKES 4 TO 6 MAIN-COURSE OR 8 SIDE-DISH SERVINGS

10 ounces elbow macaroni
1 pound fresh plum tomatoes, coarsely chopped
1 (15-ounce) can red kidney beans, drained and rinsed, or 1½ cups cooked (see Box, page 18) (optional)
¾ cup kalamata, gaeta, or other good-quality black olives, pitted, coarsely chopped
3 tablespoons extra-virgin olive oil
½ cup shredded fresh basil
3 large cloves garlic, finely chopped
Salt and freshly ground black pepper, to taste
1 cup vegetable broth, preferably Basic Vegetable Broth (page 38) or low-sodium canned
¾ cup plain dry bread crumbs
Fresh basil leaves, for garnish (optional)
Black olives, for garnish (optional)

Preheat the oven to 400F (205C). In a medium stockpot filled with boiling salted water, slightly undercook the macaroni according to package directions. Drain in a colander.

Transfer the drained macaroni to a medium bowl. Add the tomatoes, beans (if using), olives, half the oil, shredded basil, garlic, salt, and pepper; toss well to combine.

Lightly oil a 12-inch gratin or 11 × 8-inch flameproof baking dish. Arrange the macaroni mixture in the dish. Pour in the broth and sprinkle ½ cup of the bread crumbs evenly over the top. Drizzle with the remaining oil. Bake for 20 to 25 minutes, or until the top is golden brown and crusty. Remove the gratin from the oven. Set the oven to broil.

With a large spoon, break through the crust and toss the mixture gently several times to combine. Flatten the top slightly with the back of the spoon, then sprinkle with the remaining bread crumbs. Place on a rack so that the top of the gratin is 4 to 6 inches from the heating element. Broil until the top is lightly browned, 2 to 3 minutes. Serve hot, garnished with fresh basil leaves and olives, if desired.

Advance Preparation The finished gratin can be refrigerated for up to twenty-four hours, but the bread crumb topping will have lost much of its crunch. Reheat in a low oven.

PER MAIN-COURSE SERVING

Calories 592 · Protein 15g · Total Fat 25g · Saturated Fat 2g · Cholesterol 0mg · Carbohydrate 77g · Dietary Fiber 5g · Sodium 992mg

Orecchiette with Broccoli Rabe

Apulia is both home to orecchiette, a wonderfully imaginative pasta shaped like little ears, and crazy for broccoli rabe, or rapini, a decidedly more aggressive green than its close cousin broccoli. Little wonder that this quick and easy recipe is a great favorite among Apulian home cooks and chefs alike. As with other strongly flavored dishes, it would never be served with cheese. If you can't locate orecchiette, use farfalle (bow ties), fusilli (corkscrews), or medium conchiglie (shells) instead.

MAKES 6 MAIN-COURSE OR 8 PASTA-COURSE SERVINGS

- 2 large bunches broccoli rabe (about 2 pounds), rinsed and drained, trimmed of any discolored leaves and tough bottom stems
- 1/4 cup extra-virgin olive oil
- 4 large cloves garlic, finely chopped
- 1/4 teaspoon crushed red pepper flakes, or to taste
- Salt, to taste
- 16 ounces orecchiette or other small-to-medium pasta

Bring a large stockpot filled with salted water to a boil over high heat. Working in two batches, add the broccoli rabe and blanch until barely tender, about 3 minutes. Using tongs or a pasta server, transfer to a colander. Rinse under cold running water and drain well. Transfer to a cutting board and coarsely chop. Set aside. (Either save the cooking liquid in the stockpot to cook the pasta, or discard and fill with fresh water.)

In a large deep-sided skillet with a lid, heat the oil over medium-low heat. Add the garlic and cook, stirring, until just softened, 2 to 3 minutes. Add the red pepper flakes and cook, stirring, for

Cook's Tip

When shopping for broccoli rabe (also known as broccoli di rape, broccoletti, or rapini), select only bunches with firm small stems and bright green leaves and buds. Unlike broccoli, whose leaves and most of the stems are discarded before cooking, broccoli rabe is essentially cooked in its entirety, with only discolored leaves and tough stem ends thrown away. Any stem much thicker than a pencil should be discarded when trimming the broccoli rabe.

about 30 seconds. Add the broccoli rabe and salt, stirring well to combine. Cover and cook, stirring a few times, until the stems of the broccoli rabe are tender, 5 to 7 minutes. Keep warm until needed.

Meanwhile, bring either the reserved cooking liquid or fresh salted water in the stockpot to a boil. Cook the pasta according to the package directions until al dente. Drain well and return to the stockpot. Add the broccoli rabe mixture and toss well to combine. Serve at once.

Advance Preparation The blanched and chopped broccoli rabe can be held at room temperature for about one hour, or covered and refrigerated for three to four hours, before completing the recipe. The cooked broccoli rabe sauce can be kept warm over very low heat for one hour before tossing with the pasta and serving.

PER MAIN-COURSE SERVING

Calories 406 · Protein 14g · Total Fat 11g, Saturated Fat 2g · Cholesterol 0mg · Carbohydrate 65g · Dietary Fiber 6g · Sodium 47mg

Variations

Orecchiette with Broccoli Rabe and Chickpeas Add about 1½ cups cooked chickpeas to the pasta just before draining.

Serve sprinkled with toasted bread crumbs, as for the Ditali with Cauliflower (page 102), or with toasted pine nuts.

Orzo Pilaf with Peas, Pearl Onions, and Roasted Red Peppers

This pretty dish is actually much closer to a risotto than a pilaf because of its creamy texture. Its mild taste makes it especially appealing to younger taste buds.

MAKES 4 TO 6 MAIN-COURSE OR 8 PASTA-COURSE SERVINGS

- 2 tablespoons extra-virgin olive oil
- 2 cloves garlic, finely chopped
- 12 ounces (about 1½ cups) orzo
- 3 cups vegetable broth, preferably Basic Vegetable Broth (page 38) or low-sodium canned
- 1½ cups frozen baby green peas and pearl onions, partially thawed
- 1 (7½-ounce) jar roasted red bell peppers, drained and chopped
- Salt and freshly ground black pepper, to taste

In a large deep-sided skillet with a lid, heat the oil over medium heat. Add the garlic and cook, stirring, for 2 minutes. Add the orzo and cook, stirring, for 2 minutes. Add the broth, peas and pearl onions, red peppers, salt, and black pepper. Bring to a boil over high heat. Reduce the heat, cover, and simmer, stirring a few times, until the orzo is tender yet still firm to the bite and has absorbed the liquids, about 15 minutes. Serve at once.

PER MAIN-COURSE SERVING

Calories 463 · Protein 22g · Total Fat 8g · Saturated Fat 1g · Cholesterol 0mg · Carbohydrate 75g · Dietary Fiber 8g · Sodium 438mg

Pasta Primavera with Roasted Vegetables, Basil, and Olives

Everyone loves pasta primavera, but the following recipe using roasted vegetables seems to get especially rave reviews. Delicious at room temperature, this is the recipe that probably comes closest to a pasta salad, as Americans know them, in this cookbook. It's ideal buffet or picnic fare.

MAKES 6 MAIN-COURSE OR 8 PASTA-COURSE OR SIDE-DISH SERVINGS

- ¼ cup extra-virgin olive oil
- 4 cloves garlic, finely chopped
- 1 medium red bell pepper (about 6 ounces), cut into ⅜-inch-thick strips
- 1 small yellow zucchini (about 4 ounces), cut in half crosswise, then cut lengthwise into ⅜-inch-thick strips
- 12 baby carrots (about 4 ounces), trimmed, peeled if necessary, cut lengthwise in half
- 8 thin stalks asparagus (about 3 ounces), trimmed and cut into 2-inch lengths
- 1 pound fresh plum tomatoes, seeded and cut into small pieces
- Salt and freshly ground black pepper, to taste
- ½ cup vegetable broth, preferably Basic Vegetable Broth (page 38) or low-sodium canned
- 16 ounces fusilli, rotelle, or other twisted pasta
- 1 bunch scallions (6 to 8), white and green parts, chopped
- 1 cup packed fresh basil leaves, chopped
- 12 black olives, preferably kalamata, pitted and chopped
- 12 green olives, preferably Greek or Italian, pitted and chopped

Preheat the oven to 400F (205C). In a large ovenproof skillet, heat the oil over medium heat. Add the garlic and cook until slightly golden, stirring, about 2 minutes. Add the bell pepper, zucchini, and carrots; cook for 1 minute, stirring and tossing constantly. Add the asparagus; cook for 1 minute, stirring and tossing constantly. Remove the skillet from the heat and add the tomatoes, salt, and pepper; toss well to combine.

Transfer the skillet to the oven and roast, uncovered, for 15 to 20 minutes, stirring halfway through, or until the vegetables are just tender and beginning to brown. Remove from the oven and stir in the broth; cover and keep warm until needed.

Meanwhile, cook the pasta in boiling salted water according to package directions until al dente; drain well. Transfer directly to the skillet and add the scallions, basil, and olives; toss well to combine. Serve warm or at room temperature.

Advance Preparation The dish can be held for one hour at room temperature. Or it can be stored, covered, in the refrigerator for up to twenty-four hours. Bring to room temperature or reheat slightly in a low oven before serving.

PER MAIN-COURSE SERVING

Calories 445 · Protein 13g · Total Fat 14g · Saturated Fat 2g · Cholesterol 0mg · Carbohydrate 69g · Dietary Fiber 5g · Sodium 264mg

Cook's Tip

Medium asparagus can be used if the thin ones are unavailable, but remove the tips and split the stalks lengthwise in half before cutting as directed in the recipe.

Penne with Porcini Mushroom Sauce

Dried porcini mushrooms, gathered wild from the hillsides of northern Italy, combine with locally cultivated fresh ones to give this pasta a subtly enticing, smoky flavor. A perfect fall or winter dish, this is that rare recipe whose flavor isn't compromised with the use of preserved ingredients.

MAKES 4 MAIN-COURSE OR 6 TO 8 PASTA-COURSE SERVINGS

1 ounce dried porcini or other dried wild mushrooms
2 tablespoons extra-virgin olive oil
1 medium onion (6 to 8 ounces), chopped
½ teaspoon dried oregano
¼ teaspoon dried basil
¼ teaspoon dried rubbed sage
8 ounces fresh white button mushrooms, cleaned, trimmed, and thinly sliced
2 large cloves garlic, finely chopped
1 (14½-ounce) can stewed tomatoes, juices reserved
2 tablespoons tomato paste
¼ teaspoon sugar
⅛ teaspoon freshly grated nutmeg
Salt and freshly ground black pepper, to taste
2 to 3 tablespoons chopped fresh parsley
12 ounces penne or other short tubular pasta

Soak the dried mushrooms in 1 cup hot water for 15 minutes; drain, reserving the soaking liquid. Strain the soaking liquid through a coffee filter or paper towel–lined strainer and set aside. Rinse the mushrooms thoroughly; chop coarsely and set aside.

In a large nonstick skillet, heat the oil over medium heat. Add the onion, oregano, basil, and sage and cook, stirring, until the onion is softened but not browned, 3 to 4 minutes. Increase the heat to medium-high; add the fresh mushrooms, reserved dried mushrooms, and the garlic. Cook, stirring constantly, until the mushrooms soften, 3 to 4 minutes. Stir in the reserved soaking liquid, tomatoes and their juices, tomato paste, sugar, nutmeg, salt, and pepper. Bring to a boil, breaking the tomatoes apart as necessary with a wooden spoon. Reduce the heat to medium-low and simmer, uncovered, for 10 minutes, or until the juices have slightly thickened. Remove from the heat and season with additional salt and pepper as needed. Stir in the parsley, cover, and keep warm until needed.

Meanwhile, cook the pasta in boiling salted water according to package directions until al dente. Drain and transfer to a large warmed pasta bowl or individual warmed serving plates; ladle the sauce over the top. Serve at once.

Advance Preparation The cooled mushroom sauce, without the parsley, can be stored, covered, in the refrigerator for up to two days. Reheat over low heat and serve with freshly cooked pasta.

PER MAIN-COURSE SERVING

Calories 470 · Protein 15g · Total Fat 9g · Saturated Fat 1g · Cholesterol 0mg · Carbohydrate 86g · Dietary Fiber 6g · Sodium 338mg

Penne with Sweet Pepper and Tomato Sauce

This sweet pepper and tomato sauce derives its sweetness not from sugar, but from slightly caramelized onions and the red bell pepper, whose natural sugars are more concentrated than the green variety. If red bell peppers are not available, substitute with yellow.

MAKES 4 TO 6 MAIN-COURSE OR 8 PASTA-COURSE SERVINGS

- 2½ tablespoons extra-virgin olive oil
- 1 medium onion (about 6 ounces), finely chopped
- 2 large cloves garlic, finely chopped
- 1 pound ripe tomatoes, peeled, seeded, and chopped
- 1 large red bell pepper (about 8 ounces), chopped
- ⅛ teaspoon crushed red pepper flakes, or to taste
- Salt and freshly ground black pepper, to taste
- 2 tablespoons finely chopped fresh basil
- 2 to 3 tablespoons vegetable broth, preferably Basic Vegetable Broth (page 38) or low-sodium canned or water
- 1 pound penne or other short tubular pasta
- ½ teaspoon coarse salt

In a large nonstick skillet with a lid, heat the oil over medium-low heat. Add the onion and cook, stirring occasionally, until very tender, about 15 minutes. Add the garlic and increase the heat to medium; cook, stirring constantly, until the onion begins to caramelize, about 5 minutes. Add the tomatoes, bell pepper, red pepper flakes, salt, and black pepper; bring to a boil over medium-high heat. Reduce the heat to medium-low, cover, and simmer, stirring occasionally, until the bell pepper is very soft, 15 to 20 minutes.

Transfer the mixture to a food processor fitted with the metal blade or to a blender; process or blend until smooth and pureed. Return the mixture to the skillet and stir in the basil. Reheat over low heat, stirring occasionally, adding vegetable broth or water as needed to make a smooth sauce. Cover and keep warm until needed.

Meanwhile, cook the penne in boiling salted water according to package directions until al dente; drain well. Transfer to a large bowl and toss with the sauce and coarse salt. Serve at once.

Advance Preparation The sauce can be stored, covered, in the refrigerator for up to two days. Reheat over low heat and serve with freshly cooked pasta.

PER MAIN-COURSE SERVING

Calories 553 · Protein 17g · Total Fat 11g · Saturated Fat 2g · Cholesterol 0mg · Carbohydrate 98g · Dietary Fiber 6g · Sodium 271mg

"Enraged" Penne

As the name implies, this is a hot, peppery dish whose heat can be toned down according to taste. Using the ½ teaspoon of crushed red pepper flakes will yield the traditionally hot arrabiata sauce, but if serving to the more tender-palated, you might want to start with ¼ teaspoon and go from there. Due to its decidedly spicy character, this recipe is an excellent example of a pasta preparation that would never be offered with cheese in Italy.

MAKES 4 MAIN-COURSE OR
6 TO 8 PASTA-COURSE SERVINGS

- 2 tablespoons extra-virgin olive oil
- 2 large cloves garlic, finely chopped
- 1 (28-ounce) can whole plum tomatoes, juices reserved
- 2 to 3 pepperoncini (small pickled Italian peppers), seeded and chopped (optional)
- ½ teaspoon crushed red pepper flakes, or to taste
- Pinch of sugar, or to taste
- Salt, to taste
- 12 ounces penne or other short tubular pasta

In a large nonstick skillet, heat the oil over medium-high heat. Add the garlic and cook, stirring constantly, until just golden, about 2 minutes. Add the tomatoes and their juices, pepperoncini (if using), red pepper flakes, sugar, and salt. Bring to a boil, crushing the tomatoes with the back of a wooden spoon. Reduce the heat to medium-low and simmer, uncovered, until the sauce is thickened but still chunky, about 20 minutes, stirring and breaking up the tomatoes occasionally.

Meanwhile, cook the pasta according to package directions until al dente; drain well. Transfer to a large bowl and toss with the sauce. Serve at once.

Advance Preparation The sauce can be stored, covered, in the refrigerator for up to three days. Reheat over low heat and serve with freshly cooked pasta.

PER MAIN-COURSE SERVING

Calories 418 · Protein 13g · Total Fat 9g · Saturated Fat 1g · Cholesterol 0mg · Carbohydrate 73g · Dietary Fiber 4g · Sodium 429mg

Spaghettini with Green Sauce

Made with just five main ingredients in barely five minutes, this simple green sauce will fast become part of your recipe file for super-quick weeknight suppers.

MAKES 4 MAIN-COURSE OR
6 TO 8 PASTA-COURSE SERVINGS

- ¼ cup extra-virgin olive oil
- 8 cloves garlic, finely chopped
- 2 cups packed fresh flat-leaf parsley, finely chopped
- ¼ cup vegetable broth, preferably Basic Vegetable Broth (page 38) or low-sodium canned
- Salt, preferably the coarse variety, and freshly ground black pepper, to taste
- 12 ounces spaghettini or other thin pasta

In a medium nonstick skillet, heat the oil over medium-low heat. Add the garlic and cook, stirring frequently, until lightly browned, about 5 minutes. Add the parsley and broth and stir until just combined. Immediately remove from the heat and season with coarse salt and pepper.

Meanwhile, cook the pasta in boiling salted water according to package directions until al dente. Drain well and transfer to a warm serving bowl. Add the parsley-garlic mixture and toss well to combine. Season with additional coarse salt, if necessary. Serve at once.

PER MAIN-COURSE SERVING

Calories 476 · Protein 14g · Total Fat 15g · Saturated Fat 2g · Cholesterol 0mg · Carbohydrate 71g · Dietary Fiber 6g · Sodium 86mg

Variation Substitute fresh cilantro for half of the parsley. Although Italian cooks in Italy seldom use the leaf (they use the dried seed, which is known as coriander), many are using it here and acquiring a taste for it.

Radiatore with Herbed Oven-Roasted Tomatoes

Oven-roasted tomatoes are a real taste treat, so meltingly delicious that you might want to double the following recipe and use the extra batch later in the week to spoon over polenta or smear on toasted bread, bruschetta-style.

MAKES 6 MAIN-COURSE OR 8 PASTA-COURSE SERVINGS

- 5 tablespoons extra-virgin olive oil
- 2 (28-ounce) cans whole tomatoes, drained, halved lengthwise, and seeded
- ¼ cup chopped fresh flat-leaf parsley
- 6 large cloves garlic, coarsely chopped
- ½ teaspoon dried rosemary leaves
- ½ teaspoon dried thyme leaves
- ½ teaspoon dried oregano
- Salt and freshly ground black pepper, to taste
- 1 pound radiatore, preferably tricolored, or rotini, fusilli, or other corkscrew-shaped pasta
- ¼ to ½ cup heated vegetable broth, preferably Basic Vegetable Broth (page 38) or low-sodium canned

Preheat the oven to 300F (150C). Oil the bottom and sides of a 10-inch pie plate with 1 tablespoon of the oil. Place the tomatoes, parsley, garlic, rosemary, thyme, oregano, and remaining oil in a large mixing bowl. Season with salt and pepper, and toss gently yet thoroughly to combine. Arrange in the prepared pie plate.

Bake for 1 hour, uncovered, turning and basting every 15 to 20 minutes. Bake for 1 to 1½ hours more, turning every 15 to 20 minutes (this is important, so that the mixture doesn't stick and brown), or until the tomatoes are a deep red and meltingly tender. Break apart with a large wooden spoon and set aside.

Cook the pasta in boiling salted water according to the package directions until al dente; drain well. Transfer to a large bowl and toss with the roasted tomato mixture, adding vegetable broth as needed to make a thinner sauce. Serve at once.

Advance Preparation The roasted tomatoes can be stored, covered, in the refrigerator for up to four days. Reheat over low heat and serve with freshly cooked pasta.

PER MAIN-COURSE SERVING

Calories 443 · Protein 13g · Total Fat 13g · Saturated Fat 2g · Cholesterol 0mg · Carbohydrate 69g · Dietary Fiber 5g · Sodium 614mg

Rotelle with Mixed Summer-Vegetable Sauce

This dish is a wonderful way to combine fresh eggplant, zucchini, bell peppers, and tomatoes. Indeed, if you are a home gardener, you will have considered your months of effort well spent after the first mouthful. Because the amount of eggplant used here is relatively small and is incorporated with so many other flavors, salting it first isn't necessary.

MAKES 4 TO 6 MAIN-COURSE OR 8 PASTA-COURSE SERVINGS

2 tablespoons extra-virgin olive oil
1 large onion (about 10 ounces), finely chopped
3 large cloves garlic, finely chopped
8 ounces eggplant (about ½ medium) cut into ¼-inch cubes
8 ounces zucchini (about 1 medium), chopped
1 medium red bell pepper (about 6 ounces), chopped
2 pounds ripe plum tomatoes, peeled, seeded, and coarsely chopped, or 1 (28-ounce) can peeled plum tomatoes, drained, seeded, and coarsely chopped
½ teaspoon sugar, or to taste
¼ teaspoon crushed red pepper flakes, or to taste
Salt and freshly ground black pepper, to taste
About 1 cup vegetable broth, preferably Basic Vegetable Broth (page 38) or low-sodium canned
1 teaspoon tomato paste
12 ounces rotelle, fusilli, or other spiral-shaped pasta

In a large nonstick skillet with a lid, heat the oil over medium-low heat. Add the onion and garlic and cook, stirring, until softened, about 10 minutes. Add the eggplant, zucchini, and bell pepper. Cook, stirring, until the vegetables begin to soften, about 3 minutes. Add the tomatoes, sugar, red pepper flakes, salt, and black pepper. Increase the heat to medium-high and cook, stirring frequently, until the tomatoes break down and begin to form a sauce, about 10 minutes.

Add the 1 cup broth and tomato paste, stirring well to combine. Cover and reduce the heat to maintain a gentle simmer, stirring occasionally, until all the vegetables are tender and a sauce has formed, about 10 minutes. (If a thinner sauce is desired, stir in additional broth as necessary.) Cover and keep warm until needed.

Meanwhile, cook the pasta in boiling salted water according to package directions until al dente; drain well. Transfer to the skillet and toss well. Serve at once.

Advance Preparation The sauce can be held, covered, over very low heat for one hour before tossing with the pasta. Or it can be stored, covered, in the refrigerator for up to two days. Reheat over low heat and serve with freshly cooked pasta.

PER MAIN-COURSE SERVING

Calories 496 · Protein 18g · Total Fat 9g · Saturated Fat 1g · Cholesterol 0mg · Carbohydrate 89g · Dietary Fiber 9g · Sodium 171mg

"Golden" Spaghetti Pie with Olives and Raisins

This unusual pasta entree is more a spaghetti pie when served on a pizza pan, as it is here. The decidedly Sicilian sweet-and-sour combination of olives and raisins is an unexpected delight. It is also one of the few pasta dishes in this book without a hint of garlic.

MAKES 6 MAIN-COURSE OR 8 PASTA-COURSE SERVINGS

- 1¼ cups kalamata, gaeta, or other good-quality black olives, pitted and coarsely chopped
- ¾ cup golden raisins, soaked in warm water to cover for 10 minutes, drained
- ½ cup unseasoned dry bread crumbs
- 3 tablespoons extra-virgin olive oil
- ¼ cup pine nuts, lightly toasted (see Cook's Tip, page 121)
- 2 tablespoons drained capers
- Freshly ground black pepper, to taste
- 16 ounces spaghetti

Preheat the oven to broil. In a medium bowl, mix together the olives, raisins, bread crumbs, half of the oil, pine nuts, and capers; season with pepper. Set aside.

Meanwhile, cook the pasta in boiling salted water according to package directions until al dente. Drain well, return to the pot, and add the remaining olive oil, tossing well to combine. Add the olive-raisin mixture; toss to combine.

Pour the spaghetti mixture into an ungreased large pizza pan or large flameproof shallow casserole. Press firmly with the back of a large spoon or spatula until packed down. Broil 4 to 6 inches from the heating element until lightly golden, 2 to 3 minutes. Cut into wedges and serve at once.

PER MAIN-DISH SERVING

Calories 605 · Protein 13g · Total Fat 25g · Saturated Fat 2g · Cholesterol 0mg · Carbohydrate 84g · Dietary Fiber 3g · Sodium 882mg

Variation Substitute chopped dried apricots, also plumped in warm water, for the golden raisins.

Spaghettini with Walnut-Garlic Sauce

This variation on *salsa di noce,* or walnut sauce, is heavier on the garlic because it lacks the cheese, and sometimes milk, that is often stirred in at the end. I love its more pungent flavor yet lighter consistency.

MAKES 6 MAIN-COURSE OR 8 PASTA-COURSE SERVINGS

- ½ cup chopped walnuts, toasted (see Cook's Tip, page 121)
- ¼ cup extra-virgin olive oil
- 1 cup packed fresh flat-leaf parsley
- ¼ cup vegetable broth, preferably Basic Vegetable Broth (page 38) or low-sodium canned, plus ¼ cup additional broth (optional)
- 6 cloves garlic, peeled
- 1 tablespoon unseasoned dry bread crumbs
- ½ teaspoon coarse salt, or to taste
- 16 ounces spaghettini or other thin pasta

Place the walnuts, oil, parsley, ¼ cup broth, garlic, bread crumbs, and salt in a food processor

Cook's Tip

Toasting Nuts *To toast chopped walnuts, slivered almonds, pine nuts, or other small nut shapes or pieces in the oven:* Preheat the oven to 350F (175C). Spread the nuts in a single layer on an ungreased light-colored baking sheet. Bake until lightly golden, about 5 minutes, stirring halfway through the cooking time. Immediately remove from the baking sheet and set aside to cool.

To toast on the stovetop: Heat a small skillet over medium heat. Add the nuts and cook, stirring constantly, until lightly golden, 3 to 5 minutes. Immediately remove from the skillet and set aside to cool. For larger whole nuts and nut pieces, increase the cooking time by a few minutes.

fitted with the metal blade or in a blender. Process or blend until smooth.

Meanwhile, cook the pasta in boiling salted water according to package directions until al dente. If not using the additional vegetable broth, reserve ¼ cup of the cooking liquid, then drain the pasta in a colander.

Transfer the pasta to a large serving bowl. Add the walnut sauce and either the additional broth, if using, or the reserved cooking liquid; toss well to combine. Serve at once.

PER MAIN-COURSE SERVING

Calories 446 · Protein 14g · Total Fat 16g · Saturated Fat 2g · Cholesterol 0mg · Carbohydrate 62g · Dietary Fiber 4g · Sodium 229mg

Vermicelli Nests with Chickpeas, Spinach, and Tomato

This version of the whimsical French *palourdes en nids*, or "clams in nests," is equally delicious prepared with Swiss chard or dandelion greens. The barely cooked sauce can be spooned over other pasta, rice, couscous, polenta, or steamed vegetables.

MAKES 4 TO 6 MAIN-COURSE OR 8 PASTA-COURSE SERVINGS

- 2 tablespoons extra-virgin olive oil
- 2 large cloves garlic, finely chopped
- 1½ cups cooked chickpeas (see Box, page 18) or 1 (15-ounce) can chickpeas, rinsed and drained
- 1 cup dry white wine
- 2 to 3 teaspoons fresh thyme leaves or 1 teaspoon dried
- 1 pound fresh plum tomatoes, seeded and chopped
- 8 ounces fresh spinach, stemmed, cut crosswise into ½-inch-wide strips
- Pinch sugar
- Salt and freshly ground black pepper, to taste
- 12 ounces vermicelli, capellini, or spaghettini

In a large nonstick skillet, heat the oil over medium heat. Add the garlic and cook, stirring, for 2 minutes. Add the chickpeas and toss to coat with the garlic and oil. Add the wine and thyme. Bring to a boil over high heat. Add the tomatoes, spinach, sugar, salt, and pepper. Toss well to thoroughly combine and remove the skillet from the heat. Set aside until the tomatoes are just warm to the touch, about 5 minutes.

Meanwhile, in a large stockpot, cook the pasta in boiling salted water according to package directions until al dente; drain well. Arrange equal amounts of the pasta in small circular piles resembling birds' nests in the bottoms of pasta or soup bowls. Divide the chickpea and tomato mixture evenly among the bowls. Pour the remaining liquids in the skillet evenly over all and serve at once.

PER MAIN-COURSE SERVING

Calories 540 · Protein 16g · Total Fat 9g · Saturated Fat 1g · Cholesterol 0mg · Carbohydrate 91g · Dietary Fiber 5g · Sodium 62mg

Rice

Arborio Rice with Roasted Peppers, Basil, Pine Nuts, and Olives

This delicious medley of rice, vegetables, herbs, nuts, and olives could almost be classified a salad, especially since it's quite good served at room temperature. An assortment of different-hued peppers, if you can find them, makes it quite colorful, as well.

MAKES 4 TO 6 MAIN-COURSE OR 8 SIDE-DISH SERVINGS

3 large bell peppers (about 8 ounces each), preferably a mixture of red, yellow, and green
1½ cups arborio rice
1 tablespoon chopped dried orange peel
3 tablespoons extra-virgin olive oil
4 large cloves garlic, finely chopped
½ cup pine nuts
½ cup pitted green black olives, preferably kalamata
½ cup pitted green olives, preferably Italian-style
½ cup packed shredded fresh basil leaves
Salt and freshly ground black pepper, to taste
Cherry tomatoes, for garnish (optional)

Adjust the oven rack to 4 inches from the heating element and preheat the oven to broil. Trim the top and bottom off each pepper and cut in half lengthwise. Remove the seeds and inner white membranes, or ribs. Slice each half lengthwise into 3 even strips. Arrange the pepper strips, cut side down, on an ungreased baking sheet. Broil until partially charred, about 5 minutes. Place in a paper bag, twist tightly to close, and leave for 20 minutes. Peel off the skins with your fingers or with a small pairing knife. Slice lengthwise into ½-inch-wide strips and set aside.

Meanwhile, bring 3 quarts salted water to a boil in a large pot over high heat. Add the rice and orange peel; boil until the rice is tender but still firm to the bite, stirring a few times, 12 to 15 minutes. Drain well and set aside.

Heat the oil in a large deep-sided skillet over medium heat. Add the garlic and cook, stirring constantly, for 2 minutes. Add the pine nuts and cook, stirring constantly, for 2 minutes. Add the reserved peppers and olives and cook, stirring constantly, for 2 minutes. Add the reserved cooked rice, basil, salt, and pepper; cook, tossing and stirring constantly to thoroughly combine, for 2 minutes. Remove from the heat.

Season with additional salt and pepper, if necessary. Serve warm or at room temperature, garnished with the cherry tomatoes, if desired.

Advance Preparation The dish can be stored, covered, in the refrigerator for up to two days, but the nuts will have lost some of their crunch. Bring to room temperature or reheat over low heat.

PER MAIN-COURSE SERVING

Calories 491 · Protein 7g · Total Fat 21g · Saturated Fat 2g · Cholesterol 0mg · Carbohydrate 69g · Dietary Fiber 2g · Sodium 635mg

Variations To make a delicious pasta salad, substitute 12 ounces ziti, cooked according to the package directions, for the arborio rice, and serve at room temperature.

If you prefer, substitute orzo pasta, cooked according to the package directions until al dente, for the arborio rice. While both long-grain white rice and brown rice will work in a pinch, unlike the arborio and orzo, the grains will begin to harden after a few hours at room temperature, and don't store well in the refrigerator.

Green Rice

Green rice is typically made in the spring with young sorrel or dandelion greens, but can be enjoyed throughout the year with spinach, Swiss chard, escarole, or other similar greens. As the natural sweetness of the grains masks the bitterness of the greens, this rather creamy rice dish is a great way to get children to eat these iron-rich foods.

MAKES 8 TO 10 SIDE-DISH OR 4 TO 6 MAIN-COURSE SERVINGS

- ¼ cup extra-virgin olive oil
- 2 cups long-grain rice
- 1 large onion (10 to 12 ounces), finely chopped
- 4 cloves garlic, finely chopped
- 4½ cups vegetable broth, preferably Basic Vegetable Broth (page 38) or low-sodium canned
- 4 ounces sorrel, dandelion, spinach, Swiss chard, or escarole, finely chopped
- Salt and freshly ground black pepper, to taste

In a large deep-sided skillet with a lid, heat the oil over medium-high heat. Add the rice, onion, and garlic and cook, stirring constantly, until beginning to brown, 2 to 3 minutes.

Add the broth, greens, salt, and pepper; bring to a brisk simmer. Reduce the heat to low, cover, and simmer until all the liquid has been absorbed but the mixture is slightly creamy, about 20 minutes. Serve hot.

PER SIDE-DISH SERVING

Calories 279 · Protein 10g · Total Fat 7g · Saturated Fat 1g · Cholesterol 0mg · Carbohydrate 43g · Dietary Fiber 3g · Sodium 305mg

Variation For a main course to serve six, add 1 cup raisins along with the broth and greens, and toss with ½ cup toasted pine nuts or slivered almonds just before serving. There are about 513 calories, 17 grams of fat (2 saturated), 18 grams of protein, 411 milligrams sodium, and no cholesterol per serving. If you use dandelion greens, you can also count on receiving 100 percent of the daily recommended dose of vitamin A, 25 percent of vitamin C, 10 percent of calcium, and 40 percent of iron. Not bad for a meal ready in a mere 30 minutes!

Quick Farmer's Paella

Paella is the national dish of Spain, a saffron-seasoned, rice-based meal-in-itself whose other ingredients vary from region to region. In the coastal provinces, namely Valencia, where it originated, seafood predominates. In the landlocked provinces, chicken, rabbit, and ham outweigh the shellfish. In the province of Murcia, blessed with a bounty of vegetables, paella is virtually meatless, consisting of peas, carrots, artichokes, bell peppers, and tomatoes, with lima beans and almonds added as rich sources of protein. The following recipe is a quick-cooking rendition of the latter and produces delicious paella almost too pretty to eat. If using very young fresh peas, add them at the same time indicated for the frozen variety.

MAKES 4 TO 6 MAIN-COURSE SERVINGS

2 cups vegetable broth, preferably Basic Vegetable Broth (page 38) or low-sodium canned
¼ teaspoon saffron threads
3 tablespoons extra-virgin olive oil
1 medium onion (about 6 ounces), finely chopped
2 cloves garlic, finely chopped
1 small red bell pepper (about 4 ounces), and finely chopped
1 pound tomatoes, peeled and chopped, all the juices included, or 1 (14½-ounce) can whole tomatoes, chopped, juices included
⅛ teaspoon crushed red pepper flakes, or to taste
Salt and freshly ground black pepper, to taste
1 cup arborio rice
1 (10-ounce) package frozen baby lima beans, completely thawed

1 (8-ounce) package frozen artichoke hearts, completely thawed
4 ounces young carrots (12 to 16), trimmed, peeled, and halved lengthwise, or
4 ounces mature carrots, sliced into thin rounds
1 cup fresh or frozen green peas, completely thawed if frozen
¼ cup slivered almonds or pine nuts, toasted (see Cook's Tip, page 121)

In a small saucepan, combine the broth and saffron; bring to a simmer over medium-high heat. Remove from the heat, cover, and set aside.

In a large deep-sided nonstick skillet with a lid, heat the oil over medium heat. Add the onion and garlic and cook, stirring, for 2 minutes. Add the bell pepper and cook, stirring, for 3 minutes. Add the tomatoes and their juice, red pepper flakes, salt, and pepper; stir well to combine. Bring to a brisk simmer over medium-high heat. Reduce the heat and simmer, uncovered, for 3 minutes.

Add the rice and stir well to combine. Add the lima beans, artichokes, and reserved broth; bring to a brisk simmer over medium-high heat. Reduce the heat, cover, and simmer gently for 10 minutes. Add the carrots and fresh peas, if using; cover and simmer gently for 10 minutes. Add the frozen peas, if using. Simmer, covered, until the rice is tender and the mixture is creamy, not runny, 5 to 10 minutes, stirring occasionally. Stir in the almonds and season with additional salt and pepper as necessary. Serve at once.

PER SERVING

Calories 527 · Protein 21g · Total Fat 15g · Saturated Fat 2g · Cholesterol 0mg · Carbohydrate 80g · Dietary Fiber 12g · Sodium 354mg

Rice and Lima Beans with Sofregit

A fundamental sauce in Catalan cooking, sofregit consists primarily of onions and tomatoes that are cooked down together into a sweet mass. Here garlic, cumin, and a jalapeño chile (omit, if you prefer) are added, and the sofregit is tossed with rice and lima beans. If you aren't a fan of lima beans, substitute your favorite cooked bean (black-eyed peas are nice here) and add to the sauce for the last few minutes of cooking to heat through.

MAKES 4 TO 6 MAIN-COURSE OR 8 SIDE-DISH SERVINGS

4 tablespoons extra-virgin olive oil
1 pound onions, chopped
1½ pounds fresh tomatoes, peeled, seeded, and chopped
1 jalapeño chile pepper, seeded and finely chopped
4 cloves garlic, finely chopped
½ teaspoon whole cumin seeds
Salt and freshly ground black pepper, to taste
1½ cups arborio rice
1 (10-ounce) package frozen baby lima beans, completely thawed

In a large deep-sided skillet, heat 3 tablespoons of the oil over medium-low heat. Add the onions and cook, stirring occasionally, until very tender and lightly golden, about 30 minutes. Add the tomatoes, jalapeño chile (if using), garlic, cumin, salt, and pepper; bring to a brisk simmer over medium-high heat. Reduce the heat to medium-low and simmer, uncovered, for about 20 minutes, stirring occasionally, or until the sauce is thickened and most of the liquids have evapo-

Cook's Tip

If the lima beans are completely defrosted, they will cook through at the same rate as the rice.

rated. Cover and keep warm over low heat until needed.

Meanwhile, bring 3 quarts of salted water to a boil in a large pot over high heat. Add the rice and lima beans and return to a boil. Boil until the rice and lima beans are tender, stirring a few times, 12 to 15 minutes. Drain well in a colander, then return to the pot. Add the remaining oil, tossing well to evenly coat. Add the contents to the skillet, tossing well to combine with the sauce. Season with additional salt and pepper as necessary. Serve warm.

Advance Preparation The cooled sauce can be stored, covered, in the refrigerator for two to three days before completing the recipe. The finished dish can be stored, covered, in the refrigerator for two days. Reheat in a low oven.

PER MAIN-COURSE SERVING

Calories 549 · Protein 14g · Total Fat 15g · Saturated Fat 2g · Cholesterol 0mg · Carbohydrate 92g · Dietary Fiber 7g · Sodium 68mg

Variation Instead of the rice and lima beans, add chopped roasted red peppers, sliced cooked artichoke hearts, and/or pitted chopped black olives to the tomato mixture, and toss with penne or other short tubular pasta.

Provençal Lemon-Herb Rice

It's hard to imagine life without lemons on the Mediterranean. Indeed, they lend a definitive, refreshing touch to so many dishes, as evidenced in the following one from Provence—perhaps the most delicious long-grain white rice recipe of all. The addition of toasted pine nuts or almonds and steamed broccoli turns this popular side dish into a fine meal serving two or three.

MAKES 4 TO 5 SIDE-DISH OR 2 TO 3 MAIN-COURSE SERVINGS

- 1½ tablespoons extra-virgin olive oil
- 2 tablespoons finely chopped onion
- 1 cup long-grain rice
- 2 cups vegetable broth, preferably Basic Vegetable Broth (page 38) or low-sodium canned
- 2 tablespoons fresh lemon juice
- ½ teaspoon grated fresh lemon peel or ¼ teaspoon dried
- ¼ teaspoon dried thyme leaves
- Salt and freshly ground black pepper, to taste
- 2 tablespoons finely chopped fresh basil, flat-leaf parsley, or mint

In a medium saucepan, heat the oil over medium-low heat. Add the onion and cook, stirring, until translucent, about 3 minutes. Add the rice and increase the heat to medium; cook, stirring, for 1 minute. Add the broth, lemon juice, lemon peel, thyme, salt, and pepper. Bring to a boil over high heat. Reduce the heat to low, cover, and simmer until all the liquids have been absorbed and the rice is tender and slightly creamy, 17 to 20 minutes.

Add the fresh herbs, stirring well to combine. Let stand, uncovered, for 1 minute. Fluff with a fork and serve at once.

PER SIDE-DISH SERVING

Calories 243 · Protein 9g · Total Fat 5g · Saturated Fat 1g · Cholesterol 0mg · Carbohydrate 39g · Dietary Fiber 2g · Sodium 261mg

Rice Pilaf with Currants, Golden Raisins, and Pine Nuts

Originating in the Middle East, rice pilaf is perhaps the most basic of all rice dishes. While there are various ingredients that can be added to it, the following recipe is a fairly standard one, substantial enough for dinner. Other dried fruits, such as apricots, figs, or dates, can be used in lieu of the currants or raisins. To make plain rice pilaf suitable as a bed for vegetables or a simple side dish, omit the fruits, nuts, and cinnamon, as well as the garlic and turmeric, if desired.

MAKES 4 TO 6 MAIN-COURSE OR 8 SIDE-DISH SERVINGS

- 2 tablespoons zante currants or dark raisins
- 2 tablespoons golden raisins
- 2¼ cups vegetable broth, preferably Basic Vegetable Broth (page 38) or low-sodium canned
- 3 tablespoons extra-virgin olive oil
- ½ cup finely chopped onion
- 2 large cloves garlic, crushed
- 1½ cups long-grain white rice, rinsed well and drained
- ½ teaspoon ground turmeric
- 1 cinnamon stick or ¼ teaspoon ground cinnamon
- Salt and freshly ground black pepper, to taste
- ¼ cup pine nuts or slivered almonds, toasted (see Cooks Tip, page 121)

Place the currants and golden raisins in a small bowl with enough warm water to cover for 10 minutes. Drain well and set aside.

Meanwhile, in a small saucepan, bring the broth to a simmer over medium-high heat. Cover, remove from the heat, and set aside.

In a large wide saucepan, heat the oil over medium heat. Add the onion and cook, stirring, for 2 minutes. Add the garlic and cook, stirring, until the garlic is fragrant and onion is softened but not browned, 2 minutes. Add the rice and cook, stirring, until the rice begins to turn a very pale brown, about 3 minutes. Immediately add the hot broth, turmeric, cinnamon, salt, and pepper; stir well to combine. Bring to a brisk simmer. Reduce the heat to low, cover, and simmer until all the liquids have been absorbed, 16 to 18 minutes. Remove from the heat and let stand, covered, for 5 minutes.

Uncover the saucepan and remove the cinnamon stick, if used. Fluff the pilaf with a fork. Add the fruits and nuts, tossing with the fork to combine. Serve at once.

PER MAIN-COURSE SERVING

Calories 470 · Protein 14g · Total Fat 16g · Saturated Fat 2g · Cholesterol 0mg · Carbohydrate 71g · Dietary Fiber 6g · Sodium 298mg

Herbed Risotto with Tomato and Basil, Provençal Style

In Provence, a type of risotto using long-grain rice that is both steamed and stirred in broth is frequently made. While not as creamy as a traditional Italian risotto, the resulting dish is quite delicious. Use the following recipe's basic method as a model for preparing other risotto with long-grain white rice when arborio rice is not available. Broth or water can replace the wine, if desired.

MAKES 4 TO 6 MAIN-COURSE OR 8 SIDE-DISH SERVINGS

- 4 tablespoons extra-virgin olive oil
- 2 large cloves garlic, finely chopped
- 2 cups long-grain white rice
- ¼ cup dry white wine
- 3¾ cups vegetable broth, preferably Basic Vegetable Broth (page 38) or low-sodium canned
- 2 bay leaves, crumbled
- ¼ teaspoon dried thyme leaves
- 1 pound fresh plum tomatoes, seeded and cut into small chunks
- ½ cup packed fresh basil leaves, coarsely chopped
- ½ cup pine nuts, toasted (optional; see Cook's Tip, page 121)
- Salt, preferably the coarse variety, and freshly ground black pepper, to taste

In a large deep-sided skillet with a tight-fitting lid, heat half the oil over medium-low heat. Add the garlic and cook, stirring, for 2 minutes. Add the rice and stir to coat the grains. Add the wine and cook, stirring frequently, until the liquid evaporates. Stir in 1¾ cups of the broth, the bay leaves, and thyme; bring to a brisk simmer over high heat. Decrease heat to medium-low, cover, and cook for 10 minutes. Without stirring, add 1 cup of the broth; cover and cook for 10 minutes. Without stirring, add the remaining 1 cup broth; cover and cook for another 10 minutes. Uncover and check rice. If rice appears runny, decrease heat to low and cook, stirring constantly, until the rice has absorbed all the liquid but is still moist, 1 to 2 minutes.

Remove the skillet from the heat and add the remaining oil, stirring well to combine. Add the tomatoes, basil, pine nuts (if using), salt, and pepper. Toss well and serve at once.

PER MAIN-COURSE SERVING

Calories 546 · Protein 18g · Total Fat 15g · Saturated Fat 2g · Cholesterol 0mg · Carbohydrate 83g · Dietary Fiber 5g · Sodium 501mg

Oven-Baked Spanish Saffron Rice with Pimiento

Saffron-scented rice flecked with pimiento is a classic Spanish side dish. Tossed with toasted pine nuts and olives or raisins, the following recipe easily becomes a delicious dinner for two or three. You can substitute long-grain rice for the short-grain Valencia-style or arborio, but the dish, though still quite tasty, will not be quite as creamy.

MAKES 4 TO 5 SIDE-DISH OR 2 TO 3 MAIN-COURSE SERVINGS

2 tablespoons extra-virgin olive oil
2 tablespoons finely chopped onion
1 cup Valencia-style or arborio short-grain rice
1¾ cups vegetable broth, preferably Basic Vegetable Broth (page 38) or low-sodium canned
¼ teaspoon saffron threads, steeped in ¼ cup hot vegetable broth for 10 minutes
¼ cup diced pimiento, drained
¼ teaspoon dried thyme leaves
Salt and freshly ground black pepper, to taste

Preheat the oven to 350F (175C).

In a medium ovenproof deep-sided skillet with a lid, heat the oil over medium-low heat. Add the onion and cook, stirring, until translucent, about 5 minutes. Add the rice and increase the heat to medium; cook, stirring, for 1 minute. Add the broth, saffron mixture, pimiento, thyme, salt, and pepper, stirring well to combine. Bring to a boil over medium-high heat. Cover and immediately transfer the skillet to the oven. Bake for 15 minutes.

Remove the skillet from the oven and let stand, covered, for 10 minutes. Uncover and stir with a wooden spoon to evenly distribute the ingredients. Let stand, uncovered, for 1 minute before fluffing with a fork. Serve at once.

PER SIDE-DISH SERVING

Calories 256 · Protein 9g · Total Fat 7g · Saturated Fat 1g · Cholesterol 0mg · Carbohydrate 39g · Dietary Fiber 2g · Sodium 269mg

Saffron-Scented Risotto alla Milanese

Perhaps the most misunderstood of all Italian dishes, risotto is actually a straightforward technique for cooking arborio rice to chewy, creamy perfection. By gradually adding hot broth to the plump, high-starch kernels, the idea is to cause the rice to slowly absorb enough hot liquid until it swells and forms a luscious union of tender, yet firm grains. So long as you wait until the rice has absorbed each addition of liquid, stir constantly, and begin to taste-test after about fifteen minutes, you can't go wrong. The total cooking time from the first addition of broth to the completion of this dish is typically eighteen to twenty minutes.

MAKES 4 OR 5 SIDE-DISH, 4 FIRST-COURSE, OR 2 OR 3 MAIN-COURSE SERVINGS

2¾ cups vegetable broth, preferably Basic Vegetable Broth (page 38) or low-sodium canned, plus ¼ cup hot broth, if necessary
¼ cup dry white wine
⅛ teaspoon saffron threads
1 tablespoon extra-virgin olive oil
1 shallot, finely chopped
1 cup arborio rice
Salt and freshly ground black pepper, to taste

Combine the 2¾ cups of broth and the wine in a small saucepan; bring to a simmer over medium-high heat. Remove from the heat and stir in the saffron. Cover and barely simmer over low heat.

In a medium skillet, heat the oil over medium heat. Add the shallot and cook, stirring, until softened but not browned, 2 to 3 minutes. Add the rice and cook, stirring, for 2 minutes.

Reduce the heat to medium-low and add ¼ cup of the simmering broth mixture to the skillet. Cook, stirring constantly, until almost all of the liquid has been absorbed. Continue adding ¼ cup of the broth mixture at a time and cooking and stirring until it is almost absorbed and all the broth mixture has been used, seasoning with salt and pepper after the last broth addition. The mixture should be creamy, not runny, and the rice should be tender yet still firm to the bite. (At this point, taste the rice. If the rice tastes too hard, add the ¼ cup additional hot broth and cook, stirring, until it is absorbed.) Serve at once.

PER SIDE-DISH SERVING

Calories 246 · Protein 11g · Total Fat 3g · Saturated Fat 1g · Cholesterol 0mg · Carbohydrate 39g · Dietary Fiber 2g · Sodium 366mg

Variation The recipe can easily be doubled, but select a larger skillet, add the broth and saffron mixture in ½ cup, versus ¼ cup, increments, and allow for a few minutes additional cooking time.

Spring Vegetable Risotto

An assortment of blanched tender young vegetables combines with plump and creamy risotto to create a colorful springtime main course, as easy to make as it is elegant. Although optional, a garnish of tiny pear tomatoes, if you can find them, provides the perfect golden touch. Use this recipe as a model for many of your favorite vegetables, so long as those on the sturdy side—bell peppers, artichoke hearts, broccoli, beets—are precooked until not quite tender, either by blanching, steaming, or roasting. Thinly sliced mushrooms and chopped greens such as spinach or escarole can be added to the rice along with the first addition of liquid. As a general rule, for every one cup of rice, you will need about three cups of simmering broth. The total cooking time from the first addition of liquid to the rice to the completion of a risotto containing vegetables is typically about twenty-five minutes. But let your taste buds be the guide.

MAKES 4 TO 6 MAIN-COURSE OR 8 FIRST-COURSE SERVINGS

5½ cups vegetable broth plus additional, if necessary, preferably Basic Vegetable Broth (page 38) or low-sodium canned

½ cup dry white wine

6 ounces baby carrots, trimmed and peeled if large, halved lengthwise

8 ounces pencil-thin asparagus, tough stem ends trimmed, tips trimmed from stalks, stalks cut into 2-inch lengths

4 ounces small green beans (about ¼ inch in diameter and about 2 inches long), trimmed if necessary

2 tablespoons extra-virgin olive oil

2 bunches scallions (12 to 16), white parts chopped, 1/4 cup thinly sliced green tops reserved
1½ cups arborio rice
1 cup frozen baby green peas, completely thawed
Salt and freshly ground black pepper, to taste
Yellow pear tomatoes, for garnish (optional)

In a medium stockpot, bring the 5½ cups of broth and the wine to a boil over medium heat. Add the carrots, return to a boil, and blanch for 3 minutes. Add the asparagus stalks and green beans, return to a boil, and blanch for 1 minute. Add the asparagus tips, return to a boil, and blanch for 1 minute, or until all the vegetables are almost crisp-tender. With a slotted spoon, transfer to a bowl and set aside until needed. Reduce the heat under the broth mixture until it barely simmers. (You will typically need to use between 4½ and 5 cups liquid in all to complete the risotto. Add additional broth to the liquids to equal at least 5 cups, if necessary.)

In a large deep-sided skillet, heat the oil over medium heat. Add the white parts of the scallions and cook, stirring, until softened but not browned, 2 to 3 minutes. Add the rice and cook, stirring, for 2 minutes.

Reduce the heat to medium-low and add ½ cup of the simmering broth mixture to the skillet. Cook, stirring constantly, until almost all of the liquid has been absorbed. Continue adding the broth mixture ½ cup at a time, cooking and stirring until it is almost completely absorbed and the rice begins to soften, about 15 minutes. Stir in the peas and another ½ cup of the broth mixture. Continue to stir constantly until the liquid has almost all been absorbed. Stir in the reserved vegetables, adding more of the broth mixture as needed, until the mixture is creamy, not runny, the rice is tender yet firm to the bite, and the vegetables are heated through, about 5 more minutes. Remove from the heat and stir in the reserved scallion greens. Serve at once, garnished with the pear tomatoes, if using.

PER MAIN-COURSE SERVING

Calories 481 · Protein 25g · Total Fat 7g · Saturated Fat 1g · Cholesterol 0mg · Carbohydrate 75g · Dietary Fiber 11g · Sodium 793mg

Cook's Tip

Medium asparagus can be used if the pencil-thin ones are unavailable, but split the stalks lengthwise in half and cook the tips a bit longer. Large green beans cut into 2-inch lengths can be substituted for the young variety, but cook them as long as the carrots.

Other Grains

Polenta with Stewed Peppers and Tomatoes

Polenta becomes the perfect bed for this tasty topping of stewed garden-fresh bell peppers and juicy plum tomatoes, otherwise know as peperonata in Italy. The stewed vegetables are equally delicious served over rice or tossed with penne, ziti, or other tubular-shaped pasta. They also make a fine topping for crostini, bruschetta, pizza, or focaccia.

MAKES 4 MAIN-COURSE SERVINGS

- 3 cups water
- 1 cup polenta (coarse-ground yellow cornmeal), regular or instant variety
- 3 tablespoons extra-virgin olive oil
- 3 cloves garlic, finely chopped
- Salt, to taste
- 1 medium onion (about 6 ounces), cut lengthwise in half, thinly sliced crosswise
- 1 large red bell pepper (about 8 ounces), cut lengthwise into thin strips
- 1 large yellow or green bell pepper (about 8 ounces), cut lengthwise into thin strips
- 1 pound fresh plum tomatoes, coarsely chopped
- ¼ teaspoon dried oregano, or more to taste
- Freshly ground black pepper, to taste
- ½ teaspoon red wine vinegar
- ½ teaspoon sugar
- 2 tablespoons finely chopped fresh flat-leaf parsley (optional)
- Pitted black olives, preferably kalamata (optional)

Lightly oil a 9½- or 10-inch pie plate; set aside.

If using regular polenta: In a large deep-sided saucepan, preferably on a back burner (the polenta tends to sputter), bring the water to a boil over high heat. Slowly add the polenta, stirring constantly with a long-handled wooden spoon. Reduce the heat to low and stir in 1 tablespoon of the oil, one-third of the chopped garlic, and salt. Cover and cook, stirring occasionally, until the corn particles are tender, about 15 minutes. Remove from the heat and let stand, covered, for 5 minutes.

If using instant polenta: In a medium deep-sided saucepan, preferably on a back burner, combine the water, polenta, 1 tablespoon of the oil, and one-third of the garlic, and salt. Bring to a boil over high heat; immediately reduce the heat to medium and cook, stirring often with a long-handled wooden spoon, for 5 minutes.

Immediately spoon the polenta into the prepared pie plate, pressing down with the back of a large spoon to form a smooth surface. Let stand for 20 minutes to become firm. Cover with foil and keep warm.

Meanwhile, in a medium stockpot, heat the remaining oil over medium heat. Add the onion and cook, stirring often, until softened but not browned, about 5 minutes. Add the bell peppers and remaining garlic; cook, stirring often, until the peppers are softened but still somewhat firm, 5 to 8 minutes. Add the tomatoes, oregano, salt, and pepper; bring to a boil over medium-high heat. Reduce the heat to medium-low, cover, and simmer for 20 minutes, stirring occasionally, or until the vegetables are tender but not mushy. Add the vinegar and sugar, stirring well to combine. Cook, uncovered, stirring occasionally, until the mixture is slightly thickened, about 5 minutes.

Spoon the tomato mixture on top of the firm polenta. Garnish with the parsley and olives, if using. Cut into wedges and serve warm.

Advance Preparation The cooled stewed vegetables can be covered and refrigerated for up to two days. The finished dish can be covered and refrigerated for up to twenty-four hours. Reheat, covered, in a low oven.

PER SERVING

Calories 306 · Protein 6g · Total Fat 11g · Saturated Fat 2g · Cholesterol 0mg · Carbohydrate 48g · Dietary Fiber 8g · Sodium 13mg

Barley Pilaf with Mushrooms

This is a melt-in-your-mouth pilaf, much more similar to a creamy risotto than the characteristically dry pilaf. Despite the 1½ hours–plus cooking time, it's virtually a labor-free dish, perfect for preparing on weekends when you're busy with other chores. Though optional, flecks of green parsley and red pimiento lend this dish a pretty, festive look.

MAKES 4 MAIN-COURSE OR 6 TO 8 SIDE-DISH SERVINGS

- ¼ cup extra-virgin olive oil
- 1 small onion (about 4 ounces), chopped
- 2 ounces carrots (about 1 small) chopped
- 1 stalk celery, chopped
- 1 cup pearl barley
- 8 ounces white button mushrooms, quartered
- 3¾ cups vegetable broth, preferably Basic Vegetable Broth (page 38) or low-sodium canned
- Salt and freshly ground black pepper, to taste
- ¼ cup chopped fresh parsley (optional)
- ¼ cup diced pimiento (optional)

Preheat the oven to 350F (175C). Lightly oil a 2-quart baking dish with a lid and set aside.

In a large nonstick skillet, heat the oil over medium heat. Add the onion, carrots, and celery and cook, stirring, for 3 minutes. Add the barley and cook, stirring, for 2 minutes. Add the mushrooms and cook, stirring, for 2 minutes. Remove from the heat and stir in 1½ cups of the broth. Season with salt and pepper. Transfer contents to the prepared dish.

Cover the dish and bake for 30 minutes. Stir in another 1½ cups of broth and bake, covered, for 30 minutes more. Stir in the remaining broth and, if using, the parsley and/or pimiento. Bake, uncovered, for 20 to 30 minutes, or until most of the liquid has been absorbed by the barley but the mixture is creamy. Serve warm.

Advance Preparation The cooled dish can be stored, covered, in the refrigerator for up to two days. Reheat in a low oven.

PER MAIN-COURSE SERVING

Calories 369 · Protein 17g · Total Fat 14g · Saturated Fat 2g · Cholesterol 0mg · Carbohydrate 46g · Dietary Fiber 12g · Sodium 501mg

Variation For an earthier dish, substitute half of the cultivated mushrooms with fresh wild mushrooms or cultivated brown cremini.

Vegetables and Legumes

Main Courses and Side Dishes from Simple Gratins to Sumptuous Ragouts

If grains are the foundation of Mediterranean cuisine, then vegetables are its framework, the fabric of fabulous food from Barcelona to Beirut. Indeed, while the Spanish depend heavily on rice, the Italians on pasta, and the Lebanese on bulgur wheat, the common thread that has bound these creative cooks together through the ages is their reliance on vegetables to bring these staples to life. What, after all, would Spanish rice be without the saffron scents and flecks of red pimiento, Italian spaghetti without a fresh tomato and basil sauce, or Lebanese tabbouleh without the parsley and lemon? Rather boring, I'm afraid. It is the vegetables, herbs, and spices that give many otherwise dreary dishes their defining color and spark.

In many Mediterranean households, vegetables alone are the predominant part of a meal—a soup of broccoli and parsnips in Italy, a salad of cucumber, tomatoes, and onion in the Middle East, a stew of potatoes and green beans in Greece, a gratin of spinach and lots of garlic in Provence. Not surprisingly, fresh vegetables are a highly prized commodity, and cooking is largely a seasonal affair. To keep themselves well stocked, many families tend their own vegetable gardens or plots year-round. For those who don't have the space, time, or inclination, it hardly matters—from small villages to big cities, in June or January, gorgeous vegetables that glisten like gems are in ample supply in both open-air and supermarkets. But don't expect to see fresh peas in February or cauliflower in July; from family kitchens to four-star restaurants, seasonal vegetables dictate what's for dinner.

Frequently paired with fresh vegetables is a panoply of protein-packed beans and legumes—lentils, chickpeas, fava beans, lima beans, kidney beans, split peas, to name a few—both dried and fresh. Indeed, since biblical times, long before the concept of protein was ever evolved, it seems that Mediterranean cooks have instinctively always known that lentils, chickpeas, and fava beans—all Old World beans—provided a duly amount of nourishment akin to the meat that was often scarce in their largely vegetarian diet. When the kidney bean in all its various forms was introduced from the New World sometime after 1492, it was quickly embraced as yet another source of sustenance. To make these fresh vegetable and bean combinations healthier still, thrifty cooks further combine them with a multitude of grains, from rice to bulgur wheat. Not that beans and legumes never appear on the table alone—on the contrary, they are often savored on their own, seasoned with nothing more than garlic, salt, pepper, and a good olive oil.

As with the salads, the success of the recipes in this chapter depends largely on impeccably fresh vegetables. The rules are different, however, for beans and legumes, as the large majority of the recipes throughout this book rely on either freshly cooked dried beans or thoroughly rinsed and drained canned beans. This is largely a practical matter, as beans such as fresh favas, for example, are virtually impossible to purchase in most parts of the United States, and beans such as fresh limas, which are available at limited times in certain markets—namely, farmers' markets—take too long to shell for the average American cook to be bothered. Indeed, for many busy cooks, nothing beats the convenience of canned beans—in all but a handful of recipes, they are an option. If you do opt to cook your beans from the dried state, remember that while dried beans store well, the older they are the longer it will take to cook them. But if you haven't a clue as to how long that package of dried chickpeas has been sitting on your pantry shelf, don't fret—soak them twice as long.

Vegetable Side Dishes

Artichoke Hearts, Mushrooms, and Peas in a Lemon Sauce

This sophisticated mélange from Provence makes an elegant vegetable side dish. If you aren't using the optional butter lettuce leaves as "cups," serve it in little bowls or over rice to contain the delicious sauce. MAKES 4 SERVINGS

- 3 tablespoons fresh lemon juice (juice from 1 medium lemon)
- 4 globe artichokes (about 8 ounces each)
- 1½ tablespoons extra-virgin olive oil
- 4 ounces white button mushrooms, thinly sliced
- 1 cup fresh or frozen green peas, completely thawed if frozen
- ¼ cup vegetable broth, preferably Concentrated Vegetable Broth (page 38), or ¾ cup low-sodium canned reduced over high heat to ¼ cup
- Salt, if necessary, and freshly ground black pepper, to taste
- Butter lettuce leaves (optional)

Fill a medium bowl with water and add 2 tablespoons of the lemon juice; set aside.

Pull off the dark green outer leaves of each artichoke until the pale green part, or heart, is revealed. With a sharp, serrated knife, cut about 1 inch off the top of each artichoke and trim the stem end down to the pale green heart. Spread the top leaves apart and pull out the inner core of yellow leaves. With a small spoon or your fingers, scrape out the hairy choke inside. Cut each artichoke into quarters and add to the lemon water to prevent browning. When ready to cook, drain the artichokes. Meanwhile, bring a medium stockpot filled with salted water to a boil over high heat.

Drop the artichokes into the boiling water and return to a boil. Reduce the heat to a brisk simmer and cook, uncovered, until the artichokes are tender, 12 to 15 minutes. Drain and set aside.

In a medium nonstick skillet with a lid, heat the oil over medium heat. Add the mushrooms and cook, stirring, until they begin to release their juices, about 2 minutes. Add the peas, broth, and remaining lemon juice; bring to a simmer over medium-high heat. Cover, reduce the heat, and simmer gently until the peas are just tender, 10 to 15 minutes for fresh peas, depending upon their age and freshness, 3 to 5 minutes for frozen. Uncover and add the reserved artichoke quarters. Cook over low heat, stirring gently, until all is heated through.

Season with salt, if necessary, and pepper. Spoon into butter lettuce leaf cups, if desired. Serve at once.

PER SERVING

Calories 135 · Protein 8g · Total Fat 5g · Saturated Fat 1g · Cholesterol 0mg · Carbohydrate 17g · Dietary Fiber 7g · Sodium 180mg

Grilled Asparagus

Many think asparagus too elegant for the grill, but not on the Mediterranean, where all but the pencil-thin are rolled in olive oil, than grilled over hot coals to juicy perfection. The secret is a moderate fire, frequent turning, a careful eye, and a vegetable grid. But if you'd rather, directions for broiling and grilling on the stovetop have been provided, as well.

MAKES 4 SERVINGS

1¼ pounds medium asparagus, tough stem ends trimmed
1½ tablespoons extra-virgin olive oil
½ teaspoon coarse salt
Freshly ground black pepper, to taste
1 to 2 tablespoons fresh lemon juice

Prepare a medium charcoal or gas grill. Or preheat a broiler or place a stovetop grilling pan with grids over medium heat.

Place the asparagus in a long shallow bowl and drizzle with the oil, turning the stalks to coat on all sides. Sprinkle with the coarse salt and a generous grinding of pepper, turning the stalks to coat on all sides. If grilling, arrange the asparagus in a single layer on a vegetable grid. If broiling, arrange in a single layer on a baking sheet. Position the charcoal grill rack or oven rack 6 to 8 inches from the heat source. If using a stovetop grill pan, arrange the asparagus in a single layer in the pan; cook in two batches to avoid overcrowding.

Grill or broil the asparagus until nicely browned but not charred on the outsides, turning frequently, 7 to 10 minutes. Transfer to a serving platter and sprinkle with the lemon juice, turning gently to coat on all sides. Serve warm or at room temperature.

PER SERVING

Calories 60 · Protein 1g · Total Fat 5g · Saturated Fat 1g · Cholesterol 0mg · Carbohydrate 3g · Dietary Fiber 1g · Sodium 236mg

Roasted Asparagus with Mushrooms

Asparagus and mushrooms are a subtle pair, perfect when a touch of understated elegance is called for at the table. Roasting in the oven intensifies their taste, while the balsamic vinegar sharpens it.

MAKES 4 SERVINGS

1¼ pounds medium asparagus, tough stem ends trimmed
½ pound medium white button mushrooms, stemmed and quartered
2 tablespoons extra-virgin olive oil
Salt, preferably the coarse variety, and freshly ground black pepper, to taste
2 to 3 teaspoons balsamic or sherry vinegar

Preheat the oven to 425F (220C). In a nonstick baking sheet with sides, toss the asparagus and mushrooms with the oil and season with salt and pepper. Spread the vegetables in a single layer.

Roast for 10 to 15 minutes, or until the vegetables are tender and browned, turning once or twice. Transfer the vegetables to a serving platter. Sprinkle with the vinegar, tossing gently to combine. Season with additional salt and pepper as necessary. Serve warm or at room temperature.

PER SERVING

Calories 88 · Protein 3g · Total Fat 7g · Saturated Fat 1g · Cholesterol 0mg · Carbohydrate 6g · Dietary Fiber 2g · Sodium 3mg

Variation For a slightly earthier flavor, substitute fresh wild mushrooms, cultivated brown cremini, or thin slices of portobello for the button variety.

Asparagus with Black Olives and Orange Vinaigrette

Asparagus are often dressed in citrus vinaigrettes across the Mediterranean. Bits of juicy kalamata olives provide the crowning touch in this elegant first course or refreshing side dish.

MAKES 4 TO 6 SIDE-DISH OR FIRST-COURSE SERVINGS

- 1½ pounds medium asparagus, tough stem ends trimmed
- 2 tablespoons extra-virgin olive oil
- 2 tablespoons fresh orange juice
- 1 tablespoon white wine vinegar
- ½ tablespoon fresh lemon juice
- ½ teaspoon sugar
- Salt and freshly ground black pepper, to taste
- 2 tablespoons chopped black kalamata olives

Bring a large stockpot filled with salted water to a boil over high heat. Fill a large bowl with ice water and set aside.

Add the asparagus to the boiling water and cook until crisp-tender, about 5 minutes, depending on thickness. Drain and immediately refresh in the ice water for 5 minutes. Drain well and set aside.

In a small bowl, whisk together the oil, orange juice, vinegar, lemon juice, sugar, salt, and pepper. Arrange the asparagus in a shallow rectangular serving bowl. Drizzle with the dressing, turning the asparagus with tongs to evenly coat. Sprinkle with the olives and serve at room temperature. Or cover and refrigerate for at least one hour and serve chilled.

Advance Preparation The dish can be covered and refrigerated for up to twenty-four hours, but the asparagus will lose the bright green color.

PER SERVING

Calories 98 · Protein 2g · Total Fat 8g · Saturated Fat 1g · Cholesterol 0mg · Carbohydrate 6g · Dietary Fiber 2g · Sodium 91mg

Asparagus in Orange Sauce

This Provençal-style combination of the season's first asparagus with the season's last oranges is at once a fitting farewell to winter and a harbinger of spring. When out of season, substitute green beans for the asparagus and frozen concentrate for the fresh orange juice.

MAKES 4 TO 6 SERVINGS

- 1½ pounds pencil-thin asparagus, tough stem ends trimmed
- ½ cup fresh orange juice
- ½ cup dry white wine
- ½ cup vegetable broth, preferably Basic Vegetable Broth (page 38) or low-sodium canned
- ½ tablespoon extra-virgin olive oil
- Salt and freshly ground black pepper, to taste

Bring a large pot of salted water to a boil; add the asparagus and cook until just tender, 3 to 4 minutes, depending on thickness. Drain into a colander and immediately refresh under cold running water; drain and return to pot.

Meanwhile, in a small saucepan, bring the orange juice, wine, and broth to a boil over medium heat. Reduce until about ¼ cup remains. Whisk in the oil. Pour over the asparagus, tossing well to coat; season with salt and pepper. Heat over low heat until the asparagus are hot. Serve warm.

Advance Preparation The refreshed asparagus and reduced sauce can be held separately at room temperature for up to one hour before completing the dish. The sauce can be made a day in advance and refrigerated.

PER SERVING

Calories 73 · Protein 3g · Total Fat 2g · Saturated Fat 0g · Cholesterol 0mg · Carbohydrate 7g · Dietary Fiber 2g · Sodium 68mg

Sicilian-Style Broccoli

This quick-cooking method of cooking broccoli in just a little liquid until it evaporates can be used with cauliflower, as well.

MAKES 4 TO 6 SERVINGS

- 1 head broccoli (about 1¼ pounds)
- 2 tablespoons extra-virgin olive oil
- 2 large cloves garlic, finely chopped
- ½ cup vegetable broth, preferably Basic Vegetable Broth (page 38) or low-sodium canned
- 2 tablespoons drained capers, slightly crushed in a mortar and pestle or with the back of a spoon in a small bowl
- ⅛ teaspoon crushed red pepper flakes, or to taste (optional)
- Salt and freshly ground black pepper, to taste

Cut off and separate the broccoli florets. Trim the tough ends of the stalks; peel, if necessary, and cut crosswise into ⅜-inch-thick slices.

In a large skillet with a lid, heat the oil over medium heat. Add the garlic and cook, stirring, until golden, 1 to 2 minutes. Add the broccoli florets and stalks, vegetable broth, capers, and red pepper flakes, if using. Bring to a simmer over medium-high heat. Reduce the heat to medium-low, cover, and cook until the broccoli is tender but still firm, 5 to 7 minutes. Uncover, increase the heat to high, and cook, tossing and stirring constantly, until any remaining broth evaporates, 1 to 2 minutes. Season with salt and pepper. Serve warm or at room temperature.

PER SERVING

Calories 109 · Protein 6g · Total Fat 7g · Saturated Fat 1g · Cholesterol 0mg · Carbohydrate 8g · Dietary Fiber 5g · Sodium 142mg

Variation Instead of the capers, add 2 tablespoons of dark raisins or zante currants that have been plumped in warm water for 10 minutes, then drained. Sprinkle with toasted pine nuts just before serving.

Braised Broccoli Rabe with Prunes, Golden Raisins, and Pine Nuts

Like broccoli, its more mildly flavored cousin and fellow cruciferous vegetable, broccoli rabe (or broccoli di rape, broccoletti, or rapini) is a nutritional powerhouse rich in cancer-fighting antioxidants, which strongly merits its inclusion in a healthy diet. That said, it's an aggressive green widely popular in southern Italy whose taste needs taming to suit most American palates. The addition of dried fruits and toasted pine nuts in this particular recipe accomplishes the task beautifully. Broccoli rabe is available at Italian grocers, health-food stores, gourmet markets, and, increasingly, major supermarkets, but if you can't locate it, broccoli can be substituted. Serve over rice or small pasta for a complete meal.

MAKES 4 SERVINGS

1 large bunch broccoli rabe (about 1 pound), rinsed and drained
½ tablespoon extra-virgin olive oil
¼ cup finely chopped onion
4 pitted prunes, cut into ¼-inch-thick strips, soaked in warm water to cover for 10 minutes, drained
2 tablespoons golden or dark raisins, soaked in warm water to cover for 10 minutes, drained
¼ cup vegetable broth, preferably Concentrated Vegetable Broth (page 38), or ¾ cup low-sodium canned vegetable broth reduced over high heat to ¼ cup
Salt, if necessary, and freshly ground black pepper, to taste
2 tablespoons pine nuts or slivered almonds, toasted (see Cook's Tip, page 121)

Bring a large stockpot of salted water to a boil. Meanwhile, remove any discolored leaves from the broccoli rabe and discard. Cut off about ½ inch of the tough bottom stems and discard. Chop the remaining broccoli rabe into 1½- or 2-inch pieces. Add the broccoli rabe to the boiling water and boil for 3 minutes. Drain in a colander and immediately rinse under cold running water. Drain well, pressing on the broccoli rabe with the back of a spoon to remove excess water.

In a large nonstick skillet with a lid, heat the oil over medium heat. Add the onion and cook, stirring, until lightly colored, about 3 minutes. Reduce the heat to medium-low and add the broccoli rabe, prunes, raisins, and broth; toss well to combine. Cover and cook until the broccoli rabe is tender, 3 minutes. Uncover and increase the heat to medium-high. Cook, stirring constantly, until the liquids are greatly reduced, 1 to 2 minutes. Remove from the heat and season with salt, if necessary, and pepper. Add the pine nuts or almonds, tossing well to combine. Serve warm.

PER SERVING

Calories 121 · Protein 7g · Total Fat 5g · Saturated Fat 1g · Cholesterol 0mg · Carbohydrate 17g · Dietary Fiber 5g · Sodium 129mg

Baked Cabbage with Garlic

These hearty wedges of cabbage are delicious served with crusty Italian bread or over rice to sop up their flavorful juices. For a colorful vegetable medley, present them on a platter interspersed with boiled whole new red potatoes and steamed baby carrots.

MAKES 4 SERVINGS

- 1 small firm cabbage (about 1½ pounds), outer leaves removed, cored, and quartered
- 1½ tablespoons extra-virgin olive oil
- 2 cloves garlic, finely chopped
- ¼ cup vegetable broth, preferably Concentrated Vegetable Broth (page 37), or ¾ cup low-sodium canned vegetable broth reduced over high heat to ¼ cup
- Salt and freshly ground black pepper, to taste

Preheat the oven to 425F (220C). Lightly oil a deep-sided baking dish.

Fill a medium stockpot or saucepan large enough to hold a 9-inch steaming basket with 1 inch of water. Place the steaming basket in the pot and add the cabbage. Bring to a boil over high heat. Cover tightly, reduce the heat to medium, and steam until softened but not limp, 7 to 10 minutes. Carefully transfer the cabbage to prepared dish; set aside.

In a small saucepan, heat the oil over medium-low heat. Add the garlic and cook, stirring, for 2 minutes. Spoon the oil mixture evenly over the cabbage quarters. Add the broth to the dish and season the cabbage with salt and pepper. Cover the dish tightly with a lid or foil. Bake for about 20 minutes, or until the cabbage is tender through the center when pierced with the tip of a sharp knife. Serve hot, with the cooking liquid spooned over each portion.

PER SERVING

Calories 101 · Protein 5g · Total Fat 6g · Saturated Fat 1g · Cholesterol 0mg · Carbohydrate 10g · Dietary Fiber 5g · Sodium 128mg

Carrots with Fennel, Provençal Style

The carrot is a remarkably versatile vegetable, one whose inherent sweetness is a pleasant contrast in both sweet-and-sour combinations and spicy dishes. The following recipe from Provence, however, unabashedly plays up its sweetness. It's so yummy, you might not want dessert.

MAKES 4 SERVINGS

- 1 pound sturdy young carrots, about 2 inches long and ¾ inches wide, peeled if necessary
- 1 cup vegetable broth, preferably Basic Vegetable Broth (page 38) or low-sodium canned
- 2 tablespoons Marsala, port, or sherry
- ½ teaspoon whole fennel seeds or aniseeds
- Salt, to taste
- 1 tablespoon extra-virgin olive oil
- 2 teaspoons sugar
- Freshly ground black pepper, to taste
- 1 tablespoon finely chopped fresh fennel leaves (optional)

Combine the carrots, broth, Marsala, and fennel seeds in a medium deep-sided skillet with a lid; add enough water to just cover the carrots. Season with salt and bring to a boil over high heat. Reduce the heat, cover, and simmer until the carrots are tender yet still firm, about 20 minutes.

Uncover the skillet and cook over high heat, stirring occasionally, until most of the liquids have evaporated, 5 to 8 minutes. Remove the skillet from the heat and add the oil and sugar, tossing and stirring to combine. Return to high heat and cook, shaking the pan constantly, until the carrots are lightly glazed, about 1 minute. Season with pepper and sprinkle with the chopped fennel, if using. Serve at once.

Advance Preparation After the initial simmering, the carrots can be held at room temperature for one hour before completing the dish. Or they can be stored, covered, in the refrigerator for up to twenty-four hours.

Cook's Tip

Fennel leaves are the feathery fronds found on the stalks of fennel bulbs. If you ask the produce department staff of your local supermarket nicely, they will probably let you leave with some free of charge, as, sadly, the purchaser discards most of this pretty garnish anyway.

PER SERVING

Calories 99 · Protein 4g · Total Fat 4g · Saturated Fat 0g · Cholesterol 0mg · Carbohydrate 13g · Dietary Fiber 4g · Sodium 165mg

Cauliflower with Capers in Herbed Vinaigrette

Cauliflower and capers are frequently coupled in a variety of dishes throughout the Mediterranean. They certainly bring out the best in each other in this tangy first course or side dish.

MAKES 4 TO 6 SERVINGS

- 1 large head cauliflower (2 to 2¼ pounds), cut into florets
- ¼ cup drained capers, lightly crushed in a mortar and pestle, or with the back of a spoon in a small bowl
- ¼ cup vegetable broth, preferably Concentrated Vegetable Broth (page 37), or ¾ cup low-sodium canned reduced over high heat to ¼ cup
- 2 tablespoons extra-virgin olive oil
- 2 tablespoons white wine vinegar
- 2 tablespoons finely chopped fresh basil
- 2 tablespoons finely chopped fresh flat-leaf parsley
- 2 tablespoons chopped fresh chives or green tops of scallions.
- 2 cloves garlic, finely chopped
- Salt and freshly ground black pepper, to taste

Cut the cauliflower florets into 1-inch pieces. In a medium stockpot or saucepan large enough to accommodate a 9-inch steaming basket, put 1 inch of water. Place the steaming basket in the pot and add the cauliflower florets. Bring to a boil over high heat. Cover tightly, reduce the heat to medium, and steam for 5 to 7 minutes, or until tender. Carefully remove the steaming basket and let the cauliflower cool slightly.

Place the warm cauliflower in a large shallow bowl and add the capers, tossing well to combine. In a small bowl, whisk together the broth, oil, vinegar, basil, parsley, chives, garlic, salt, and pepper. Add to the cauliflower mixture, tossing well to combine. Serve slightly warm or at room temperature. Or cover and refrigerate for at least one hour and serve chilled.

Advance Preparation The dish can be stored, covered, in the refrigerator for up to twenty-four hours before serving.

PER SERVING

Calories 104 · Protein 5g · Total Fat 7g · Saturated Fat 1g · Cholesterol 0mg · Carbohydrate 8g · Dietary Fiber 4g · Sodium 213mg

Braised Belgian Endives with Clementines

Although Belgian endive is a relative newcomer to French kitchens, having moved from Brussels to France at the end of the nineteenth century, the north of France is the world's largest producer of endives today. Throughout France during wintertime, particularly in the south where clementines grow in abundance, the rather bitter and pale vegetable is frequently paired with the decidedly sweet and vivid fruit in various salads and side dishes for a delightful contrast of taste and color. The use of olive oil, not butter, renders this particular recipe Provençal.

MAKES 4 SERVINGS

- 4 small Belgian endives (about 1 pound)
- 4 clementines or tangerines
- Juice of ½ medium lemon (about 1½ tablespoons)

2 teaspoons extra-virgin olive oil
Salt and freshly ground black pepper, to taste
½ tablespoon confectioners' sugar

Preheat the oven to 375F (190C). Lightly oil a shallow baking dish just large enough to hold the endives in a single layer; set aside. With a sharp pairing knife, remove the stems of the endives by removing cone-shaped pieces from the root ends and discard them; rinse the endives well.

In a medium saucepan, bring 4 cups of salted water to a boil; add the endives and boil for 5 minutes. Drain well and pat dry with paper towels. Arrange the endives in the prepared dish. Slice 2 of the clementines in half and squeeze their juice over the endives, using a strainer to catch any seeds. Repeat with the lemon half. Brush the oil evenly over the tops of the endives; sprinkle with salt and pepper, then dust with the sugar.

Cover the baking dish tightly with foil. Bake for 15 minutes. Meanwhile, peel the remaining clementines and separate into segments; cut each segment in half crosswise, removing any seeds. Set aside.

Remove the endives from the oven. Arrange the halved clementine segments between and around the endives. Return to the oven and cook, uncovered, for 10 minutes more, or until the endives are lightly glazed and tender when pierced with a sharp knife. Serve warm.

PER SERVING

Calories 79 · Protein 2g · Total Fat 3g · Saturated Fat 0g · Cholesterol 0mg · Carbohydrate 14g · Dietary Fiber 4g · Sodium 22mg

Variation In a pinch, an 11-ounce can mandarin orange segments, drained, and ⅓ cup fresh orange juice can be substituted for the clementines or tangerines.

Baked Onions, Italian Style

Don't be inclined to overlook this simple recipe. Seasoned with salt and pepper, sprinkled with plain bread crumbs, drizzled with olive oil, then stashed in the oven for about seventy-five minutes, these caramelized onions literally melt in your mouth.

MAKES 4 SERVINGS

4 small yellow onions (4 to 5 ounces each), peeled
6 teaspoons extra-virgin olive oil
Salt, preferably the coarse variety, and freshly ground black pepper, to taste
4 teaspoons unseasoned dry bread crumbs

Preheat the oven to 350F (175C). Bring a large saucepan or medium stockpot of water to a boil over high heat. Add the onions, reduce the heat slightly, and simmer briskly for 5 minutes. Drain and let cool slightly.

When the onions are cool enough to handle, cut them in half crosswise. Lightly oil a shallow baking dish or pie plate just large enough to hold the halved onions in a single layer. Rub the rounded outsides of the onion halves evenly with 2 teaspoons of the oil. Arrange in the prepared dish.

Season each onion half with salt and pepper. Sprinkle each half with ½ teaspoon of the bread crumbs. Drizzle ½ teaspoon of the remaining oil on top of each half. Bake for 1 hour and 15 minutes, or until the tops are browned and caramelized. Serve warm.

PER SERVING

Calories 123 · Protein 2g · Total Fat 7g · Saturated Fat 1g · Cholesterol 0mg · Carbohydrate 14g · Dietary Fiber 3g · Sodium 20mg

Provençal Eggplant Gratin with Orange-Tomato Sauce

Orange peel, both fresh and dried, is a significant ingredient in many Provençal dishes, lending a delightful piquancy to various soups, stews, and sauces. Like many Provençal gratins, this one is thin, consisting of only two layers of eggplant, to promote fast cooking. Prebaking the eggplant while the sauce cooks also saves time and ensures that the eggplant will be meltingly tender. This is another good make-ahead dish, as the flavor of the reheated gratin is even better after a day in the refrigerator.

MAKES 6 TO 8 SERVINGS

4 tablespoons extra-virgin olive oil
1 large onion (about 10 ounces), chopped
1 cup chopped carrots
1 stalk celery, chopped
3 large cloves garlic, finely chopped
1 (28-ounce) can peeled whole tomatoes, drained, seeded, and chopped, juices reserved
1 teaspoon dried chopped orange peel
1 bay leaf
½ teaspoon sugar
Salt, preferably the coarse variety, and freshly ground black pepper, to taste
2 medium eggplants (about 12 ounces each), cut into ½-inch-thick rounds, sprinkled with salt, and set in a colander to drain for 30 minutes (see Cook's Tip, page 147)
¼ cup chopped fresh basil leaves
¼ cup unseasoned dry bread crumbs
Fresh basil leaves and/or black olives (optional)

Preheat the oven to 475F (245C). In a large nonstick skillet, heat half the oil over medium heat. Add the onion, carrots, celery, and garlic and cook, stirring, until softened, about 5 minutes. Add the tomatoes, orange peel, bay leaf, sugar, salt, and pepper; bring to a boil over medium-high heat. Reduce the heat and simmer gently, uncovered, stirring occasionally, until the mixture is thickened and the liquids greatly reduced, about 20 minutes.

While the sauce is simmering, lightly oil 2 medium baking sheets. Rinse the eggplant slices under cold running water and thoroughly dry with paper towels. Arrange the eggplant slices in a single layer on the prepared sheets. Brush the tops evenly with 1 tablespoon of the remaining oil. Cover tightly with foil and bake for 25 minutes. Uncover and set aside to cool slightly. Reduce the oven temperature to 425F (220C).

Remove the bay leaf from the sauce and discard. Transfer the sauce to a food processor fitted with the metal blade or to a blender. Process or blend until pureed. Stir in the basil and set aside until needed.

Lightly oil a gratin or flameproof shallow baking dish just large enough to hold half the egg-

Cook's Tip

If time doesn't permit, omit salting and draining eggplant that is to be stewed or baked with several ingredients, as any bitterness is typically masked by the other flavors.

plant slices in a single layer. Spread one-third of the tomato-orange sauce over the bottom. Arrange half the eggplant slices over the sauce, then top with another one-third of the sauce. Arrange the remaining eggplant slices over the sauce, then cover with the remaining sauce. Sprinkle the top evenly with the bread crumbs, then season with additional salt and pepper to taste. Drizzle with the remaining oil. Bake for 20 to 25 minutes, or until the top is lightly browned. Serve hot, garnished with fresh basil leaves and olives, if desired.

Advance Preparation The sauce, without the addition of the basil, can be made up to two days ahead and refrigerated. Stir in the basil just before assembling the gratin. Up until adding the bread crumbs, the gratin can be assembled and stored, covered, in the refrigerator overnight. Sprinkle with the bread crumbs, drizzle with oil, and bake. The baked gratin can be stored, covered, in the refrigerator for up to two days. Reheat, covered, in a low oven.

PER SERVING

Calories 180 · Protein 4g · Total Fat 10g · Saturated Fat 1g · Cholesterol 0mg · Carbohydrate 22g · Dietary Fiber 5g · Sodium 329mg

Roasted Green Beans with Slivered Almonds

In the Mediterranean, roasting green beans to their wrinkled state is a common method of concentrating this vegetable's natural sweetness. In the south of France, where almond trees abound, the pairing of green beans and the slivered nut is a classic combination. MAKES 4 SERVINGS

- 2 tablespoons vegetable broth, preferably Basic Vegetable Broth (page 38) or low-sodium canned
- 1 tablespoon fresh lemon juice
- 1 tablespoon extra-virgin olive oil
- 1¼ pounds green beans, trimmed
- Salt and freshly ground black pepper, to taste
- 2 tablespoons slivered almonds

Preheat the oven to 425F (220C). Lightly oil a baking sheet and set aside.

Combine the broth, lemon juice, and oil in a glass measuring cup. Place the beans on the prepared baking sheet and drizzle with the broth mixture. Spread the beans out into a single layer. Roast for 8 minutes.

Remove the baking sheet from the oven. Season the beans with salt and pepper, then stir and turn. Sprinkle with the almonds. Roast for 5 to 7 minutes, or until the beans are wrinkled and tender and the nuts are fragrant and browned. Serve at once.

PER SERVING

Calories 89 · Protein 3g · Total Fat 5g · Saturated Fat 1g · Cholesterol 0mg · Carbohydrate 9g · Dietary Fiber 4g · Sodium 23mg

Variation Substitute chopped hazelnuts for the almonds.

Green Beans, Spanish Style

Simplicity rules in this garlicky green bean dish from Andalusia. Medium asparagus can be cooked in the same easy fashion.

MAKES 4 SERVINGS

1½ pounds green beans, trimmed and halved
1½ tablespoons extra-virgin olive oil
3 to 4 large cloves garlic, finely chopped
Salt and freshly ground black pepper, to taste

Bring a large stockpot filled with salted water to a boil over high heat. Add the beans and cook until crisp-tender, about 5 minutes. Drain well.

In a large nonstick skillet, heat the oil over medium heat. Add the garlic and cook, stirring constantly, 1 minute. Add the drained green beans and season with salt and pepper. Cook, tossing and stirring constantly, until hot, 2 to 3 minutes. Serve at once.

Advance Preparation After blanching in the boiling water and draining, the beans may be refreshed under cold running water, drained again, and refrigerated, covered, for up to twenty-four hours. Bring to room temperature before completing the recipe.

PER SERVING

Calories 92 · Protein 3g · Total Fat 5g · Saturated Fat 1g · Cholesterol 0mg · Carbohydrate 11g · Dietary Fiber 5g · Sodium 9mg

Variation

Spicy Green Beans
Add 1 small dried hot red chile pepper (left whole) to the skillet along with the garlic, and remove it after cooking.

Green Beans with Sun-Dried Tomato and Black Olive Sauce

Piquant sun-dried tomatoes and tangy kalamata olives give green beans a welcome lift in this delicious side dish, perfect for serving on a dreary winter's day. The versatile sauce is more of an uncooked paste, and it can be used to perk up other vegetables such as asparagus, zucchini, and boiled new potatoes, as well as pasta, rice, and couscous.

MAKES 6 SERVINGS

¼ cup oil-packed sun-dried tomatoes, drained and 1 tablespoon oil reserved, finely chopped
¼ cup pitted black olives, preferably kalamata, finely chopped
½ tablespoon extra-virgin olive oil
2 large cloves garlic, finely chopped
¼ teaspoon dried oregano
Salt and freshly ground black pepper, to taste
1¾ pounds green beans, trimmed
¼ cup toasted slivered almonds or pine nuts (optional; see Cook's Tip, page 121)

Place the tomatoes and reserved oil, olives, olive oil, garlic, oregano, salt, and pepper in a small bowl; stir well to combine. Set aside.

Bring a large stockpot filled with salted water to a boil over high heat. Add the beans and cook until tender but still slightly crisp, about 7 minutes. Drain well and transfer to a warm shallow serving bowl. Add the olive mixture, tossing well to combine. Serve warm or at room temperature, garnished with the almonds or pine nuts, if desired.

Advance Preparation The sun-dried tomato-olive sauce can be stored, covered, in the refrigerator for several days before using.

PER SERVING

Calories 77 · Protein 2g · Total Fat 4g · Saturated Fat 1g · Cholesterol 0mg · Carbohydrate 10g · Dietary Fiber 4g · Sodium 19mg

Lima Beans with Lettuce, Scallions, and Mint

This refreshing side dish from the south of France will likely disarm even those who typically take a stand against lima beans. Tossed with rice or couscous, or tucked into a pita pocket, it also makes a fine meal. **MAKES 4 SERVINGS**

½ cup vegetable broth, preferably Basic Vegetable Broth (page 38) or low-sodium canned
1 (10-ounce) package frozen baby lima beans, partially thawed in package for 2 hours at room temperature, or 3 pounds fresh lima beans, shelled (see Cook's Tip, opposite)
4 scallions, white and green parts, finely chopped
½ teaspoon dried thyme leaves
Salt, to taste
1 large head butter or Bibb lettuce, shredded (see Cook's Tip, page 99)
1 tablespoon extra-virgin olive oil
Freshly ground black pepper, to taste
1 tablespoon finely chopped fresh mint

In a medium saucepan, bring the broth to a boil over high heat and add the beans, scallions, thyme, and salt; top with the lettuce. Cover the pan and bring back to a boil. Uncover, reduce the heat to medium, and cook, stirring, until the lettuce is wilted and well combined. Cook, uncovered, stirring occasionally, for about 20 minutes, or until the beans are tender and most of the liquid has evaporated. (Depending on the size, fresh beans may require longer cooking time; if the mixture becomes too dry before the beans are tender, add more broth or water as necessary).

Remove the pan from the heat and stir in the oil; season with pepper to taste. Just before serving, stir in the mint. Serve warm or at room temperature.

PER SERVING

Calories 139 · Protein 7g · Total Fat 4g · Saturated Fat 1g · Cholesterol 0mg · Carbohydrate 20g · Dietary Fiber 4g · Sodium 106mg

Cook's Tip

To shell fresh lima beans, remove the thin outer edge of each pod with a sharp knife or scissors; the beans will slip out.

Peas Braised with Lettuce and Mint

Cooking vegetables with lettuce is a time-honored French method of preserving the moisture of braised vegetables. This is the refreshing Provençal rendition of petits pois à la Française, with olive oil and mint replacing the butter and parsley of the Parisian classic. Some versions use less liquid and require a longer cooking time, thus directing the cook to discard the wilted lettuce after completing the dish. In the following recipe, the relatively large amount of broth as well as the short cooking time leaves the lettuce firm yet meltingly tender—there's no better companion to the peas.

MAKES 6 SERVINGS

- 2 tablespoons extra-virgin olive oil
- ½ cup finely chopped red onion
- 2 cups vegetable broth, preferably Basic Vegetable Broth (page 38) or low-sodium canned
- 1 medium head butter or Bibb lettuce, cut into 4 to 6 wedges, bound with kitchen string
- 3 large sprigs fresh mint, tied together with kitchen string
- ½ teaspoon sugar
- ¼ teaspoon dried lemon peel
- Salt and freshly ground black pepper, to taste
- 1 (16-ounce) bag frozen baby green peas, completely thawed

In a large nonstick skillet, heat the oil over medium heat. Add the onion and cook, stirring, until softened, about 3 minutes. Add the broth, lettuce, mint, sugar, lemon peel, salt, and pepper; bring to a brisk simmer over medium-high heat. Reduce the heat and simmer gently, uncovered, for 5 minutes, turning the lettuce wedges over halfway through cooking.

Add the peas and bring to a brisk simmer over medium-high heat. Reduce the heat and simmer gently, stirring occasionally, until the peas are cooked through and the lettuce is very tender, 3 to 5 minutes. With a slotted spoon, transfer the peas and lettuce to a serving dish. Remove the string from the lettuce; cover the dish and keep warm.

Return the skillet to the heat. Reduce the remaining liquid over high heat until about ½ cup remains. Remove and discard the mint sprigs. Pour the reduced broth over the vegetables; toss gently to combine. Serve warm.

PER SERVING

Calories 124 · Protein 8g · Total Fat 5g · Saturated Fat 1g · Cholesterol 0mg · Carbohydrate 13g · Dietary Fiber 5g · Sodium 259mg

Variation You can use fresh peas in this recipe, but make sure they are very young and quite fresh. Otherwise, increase their cooking time and either remove the lettuce early, or add it later.

Garlic-Mashed Potatoes with Olive Oil

While these heart-healthy mashed potatoes are probably not the ones your mother used to make, chances are you might like them as well, and maybe even better. Don't be alarmed at the thought of a dozen cloves of garlic in your mashed potatoes—cooking in this manner reduces them to a sweet puree remarkably reminiscent of butter.

MAKES 6 TO 8 SERVINGS

6 large baking potatoes (7 to 8 ounces each), peeled and quartered
1 large bay leaf
12 large cloves garlic, peeled
¼ cup hot vegetable broth, preferably Concentrated Vegetable Broth (page 37), or ¾ cup (or more) low-sodium canned broth reduced over high heat to ¼ cup
2 tablespoons extra-virgin olive oil
Salt, preferably the coarse variety, and freshly ground black pepper, to taste

Place the potatoes and bay leaf in a medium stockpot or large saucepan with salted water to cover; bring to a boil over high heat. Add the garlic cloves, reduce the heat to medium-high, and cook for 25 minutes, or until the potatoes are very tender. Drain well.

Transfer the mixture to a warm serving bowl; remove and discard the bay leaf. Mash briefly with a potato masher or a fork. Add the broth and oil and mash until the mixture is not quite smooth (add additional broth for a softer consistency). Season with salt and pepper. Serve at once.

PER SERVING

Calories 190 · Protein 5g · Total Fat 5g · Saturated Fat 1g · Cholesterol 0mg · Carbohydrate 33g · Dietary Fiber 3g · Sodium 76mg

Variation Top each serving with some warm Herbed Onion Confit (page 198).

New Potatoes with Herbes de Provence, Lemon, and Coarse Salt

Wild herbs grow in profusion throughout Provence. Herbes de Provence is a specific combination generally consisting of rosemary, thyme, basil, savory, chervil, mint, marjoram, oregano, and sometimes lavender. If you don't have some on hand, simply use dried rosemary; it's a safe bet. Try to get tiny new potatoes that are about 1½ inches in diameter for this dish. If they're much bigger, cut them in half before boiling.

MAKES 4 TO 6 SERVINGS

1½ pounds tiny new red potatoes, scrubbed and left whole
1 tablespoon extra-virgin olive oil
½ teaspoon herbes de Provence
½ teaspoon coarse salt
Juice of ½ medium lemon (about 1½ tablespoons)
Freshly ground black pepper, to taste

Place the potatoes in a large saucepan or medium stockpot with salted water to cover;

bring to a boil over high heat. Reduce the heat to a gentle boil and cook until the potatoes are just tender, about 10 minutes, depending upon size. Drain and set aside to cool slightly.

In a large nonstick skillet, heat the oil over medium-high heat. Add the herbes de Provence, and cook, stirring constantly, for about 10 seconds. Add the drained potatoes, coarse salt, and lemon juice; stir well to coat. Cook, tossing and stirring constantly, until the potatoes are heated through, 1 to 2 minutes. Season with pepper to taste. Serve immediately.

Advance Preparation You can boil the potatoes and let them stand for up to one hour at room temperature before completing the recipe. Or you can refrigerate the boiled potatoes overnight. Bring them to room temperature and finish the recipe.

PER SERVING

Calories 134 · Protein 3g · Total Fat 4g · Saturated Fat 1g · Cholesterol 0mg · Carbohydrate 24g · Dietary Fiber 2g · Sodium 243mg

Provençal Potato and Wild Mushroom Gratin

It was a native of the northern province of Picardy, Antoine-Auguste Parmentier, who first promoted the potato in France to stave off the effects of several disastrous wheat harvests in the late eighteenth century. While the Provençaux in the south still eat their pasta and bread with a gusto that one might expect from a people residing in the former "Provincia Romana," they continue to embrace the humble tuber with a passion unmatched on the Mediterranean. Indeed, the potato has virtually replaced grains as the most important year-round dietary staple in Provence, cropping up into countless soups, ragouts, tians, and gratins. Redolent of wild mushroom and garlic, the following gratin makes a splendid fall or winter dish.

MAKES 4 TO 6 SERVINGS

- ½ ounce dried porcini mushrooms, soaked in 1 cup hot water for 15 minutes
- ¼ cup vegetable broth, preferably Basic Vegetable Broth (page 38) or low-sodium canned
- 1½ pounds baking potatoes, unpeeled, sliced into ¼-inch-thick rounds
- 8 ounces white button mushrooms, thinly sliced
- 1 cup coarsely chopped fresh flat-leaf parsley
- 4 large cloves garlic, finely chopped
- Salt, preferably the coarse variety, and freshly ground black pepper, to taste
- 2 tablespoons extra-virgin olive oil
- Flat-leaf parsley sprigs for garnish (optional)

Preheat the oven to 350F (175C). Drain the porcini mushrooms, reserving the soaking liquid. Strain the soaking liquid through a coffee filter or paper towel—lined strainer. Reserve ½ cup, combine with the vegetable broth, and set aside. Rinse the porcini mushrooms thoroughly; chop coarsely and set aside.

Lightly oil a gratin or shallow baking dish large enough to hold the potatoes and mushrooms in a layer about 1½ inches deep. Place the potatoes, button mushrooms, porcini mushrooms, parsley, and garlic in the gratin; season with salt and pepper. Using your hands, toss well to combine. Arrange the mixture evenly, making the top as flat as possible. Slowly pour ½ cup of the reserved broth mixture over the top, then drizzle with 1½ tablespoons of the oil.

Bake, uncovered, for 30 minutes. Remove from the oven and, using a wide spatula, turn the potato mixture over. Pour the remaining reserved broth mixture over the top, then drizzle with the remaining oil. Bake for 20 to 30 minutes, or until the potatoes are tender and nicely browned. Garnish with the parsley sprigs, if desired, and serve at once.

PER SERVING

Calories 198 · Protein 6g · Total Fat 7g · Saturated Fat 1g · Cholesterol 0mg · Carbohydrate 30g · Dietary Fiber 4g · Sodium 52mg

Herbed Scalloped Potatoes, Provençal Style

Scalloped potatoes always seem special. It's hard to believe that this creamy Provençal-style variation of the famous pommes de terre Dauphinoises is made with not one drop of milk or cheese.

MAKES 6 SERVINGS

1¾ cups vegetable broth, preferably Basic Vegetable Broth (page 38) or low-sodium canned
4 cloves garlic, crushed
2 large fresh sage leaves
2 large bay leaves
6 black peppercorns
¼ teaspoon dried rosemary
¼ teaspoon dried thyme leaves
Salt, to taste
2 pounds russet potatoes, peeled, cut into ⅛-inch-thick slices
2 tablespoons extra-virgin olive oil

Combine the broth, garlic, sage, bay leaves, peppercorns, rosemary, thyme, and salt in a small saucepan; bring to a boil over high heat. Immediately remove the pan from the heat. Cover and let stand for 30 minutes to 1 hour.

Preheat the oven to 425F (220C). Lightly grease a shallow 2½-quart baking dish. Arrange the potatoes as flatly as possible in the dish. Strain the herbed broth over the potatoes, discarding the solids. (The potatoes will not be completely covered by the liquid.) Drizzle the tops of the exposed potatoes with half of the oil.

Bake, uncovered, for 20 minutes. Remove the dish from the oven. Using a wide spatula, turn the potatoes over, pressing down gently to immerse them as much as possible in the liquid. Drizzle the tops of the exposed potatoes with the remaining oil. Return to the oven and bake for 20 to 25 minutes, or until the potatoes are tender, the liquids are reduced, and the top is nicely browned. Serve at once.

Advance Preparation The herbed broth can be strained into a container and stored, covered, in

Cook's Tip

The liquid remaining in the baking dish should be of a creamy consistency. If the potatoes are done but too much thin liquid remains in the dish, remove some with a bulb baster.

the refrigerator for two or three days before completing the dish.

PER SERVING

Calories 168 · Protein 7g · Total Fat 5g · Saturated Fat 1g · Cholesterol 0mg · Carbohydrate 27g · Dietary Fiber 5g · Sodium 161mg

Roasted Greek Potatoes with Oregano and Lemon

Crispy on the outside, tender on the inside, these tangy golden wedges are delicious with any of the sandwiches (pages 198–206). They also team up well with the Green Beans with Sun-Dried Tomato and Black Olive Sauce (page 148) and Sicilian-Style Broccoli (page 140).

MAKES 6 SERVINGS

- 2 pounds large russet potatoes, unpeeled, quartered lengthwise
- 2 tablespoons extra-virgin olive oil
- 2 teaspoons dried oregano
- 2 large cloves garlic, finely chopped
- Salt, preferably the coarse variety, and freshly ground black pepper, to taste
- ½ cup vegetable broth, preferably Basic Vegetable Broth (page 38) or low-sodium canned
- ½ cup water, plus additional as necessary
- Juice of 1 medium lemon (about 3 tablespoons)

Preheat the oven to 450F (230C). Lightly oil a large shallow baking dish just large enough to hold the potatoes in a single layer. Add the potatoes and drizzle with the oil, tossing well to evenly coat. Sprinkle with the oregano, garlic, salt, and pepper. Toss again.

Combine the broth, ½ cup water, and lemon juice in a 2-cup measuring cup. Pour evenly over the potatoes. Roast, uncovered, for 50 minutes to 1 hour, or until the potatoes are tender and golden brown, stirring and turning the potatoes with a metal spatula several times during cooking, and adding water as necessary to the dish to prevent excessive sticking. Serve warm.

Advance Preparation The dish can be covered with foil and kept warm in a low oven for up to one hour before serving.

PER SERVING

Calories 139 · Protein 3g · Total Fat 5g · Saturated Fat 1g · Cholesterol 0mg · Carbohydrate 22g · Dietary Fiber 2g · Sodium 50mg

Roasted Rosemary Potatoes with Garlic

This perennial Italian favorite pairs up especially well with Roasted Green Beans with Slivered Almonds (page 147) or Roasted Asparagus with Mushrooms (page 138). They are also fine accompaniments to any of the sandwiches (pages 198–206).

MAKES 6 SERVINGS

- 2 pounds new red potatoes, left whole if small, halved or quartered if large
- 8 cloves garlic, peeled
- 2 tablespoons extra-virgin olive oil
- 1 tablespoon dried rosemary

Salt, preferably the coarse variety, and freshly ground black pepper, to taste

Preheat the oven to 400F (205C). Place the potatoes and garlic in a shallow baking dish large enough to hold them in a single layer. Drizzle with the oil and toss well to evenly coat. Sprinkle with the rosemary, salt, and pepper. Toss again.

Roast, uncovered, for 40 to 50 minutes, depending on size, turning halfway through cooking time, or until the potatoes are nicely browned and tender through the center. Serve hot.

PER SERVING

Calories 137 · Protein 3g · Total Fat 5g · Saturated Fat 1g · Cholesterol 0mg · Carbohydrate 22g · Dietary Fiber 2g · Sodium 8mg

Provençal Spinach Gratin

On the basis of the countless dishes for *épinards* that are found in the repertoire of Provençal cuisine, it's safe to say that the Provençaux eat their spinach. Among the many gratins, this creamy one is my favorite. MAKES 4 TO 6 SERVINGS

- 2 pounds fresh spinach, stems discarded, or 2 (10-ounce) bags ready-washed spinach leaves
- 1 tablespoon all-purpose flour, preferably unbleached
- ¼ cup vegetable broth, preferably Basic Vegetable Broth (page 38) or low-sodium canned
- ¼ cup finely chopped fresh flat-leaf parsley
- 2 tablespoons extra-virgin olive oil
- 2 cloves garlic, finely chopped
- Salt and freshly ground black pepper, to taste
- 2 tablespoons unseasoned dry bread crumbs

Preheat the oven to 425F (220C). Bring a large stockpot of water to a boil. Lightly oil a 10-inch pie plate and set aside.

Place half the spinach in a colander. Working in stages, pour half the boiling water over the spinach, turning the spinach with a wooden spoon until wilted. Press the spinach down in the colander with the back of the spoon to extract most of the liquid; transfer to a work surface. Repeat with the remaining spinach.

Coarsely chop the spinach and transfer to a large mixing bowl. Sprinkle with the flour and stir well to combine. Add the broth, parsley, 1 tablespoon of the oil, garlic, salt, and pepper; stir well to combine.

Transfer the spinach mixture to the prepared dish. Sprinkle evenly with the bread crumbs, then drizzle with the remaining oil. Bake for 20 minutes, or until the top is lightly browned and the mixture is sizzling. Serve hot.

Advance Preparation The assembled gratin can be held at room temperature for one hour before baking, or it can be covered and refrigerated for up to twenty-four hours.

PER SERVING

Calories 118 · Protein 6g · Total Fat 8g · Saturated Fat 1g · Cholesterol 0mg · Carbohydrate 10g · Dietary Fiber 4g · Sodium 170mg

Provençal Butternut Squash Gratin

If you are looking for a special yet simple squash dish to prepare for Thanksgiving, look no further. Prepared in this manner, the butternut variety never tasted so buttery and tender. The Provençaux can't seem to get enough of garlic, but as that might not be the case with some of your guests, the number of cloves to use has been left to your discretion. MAKES 6 SERVINGS

- 1 (3-pound) butternut squash, peeled, seeds and membranes removed, coarsely chopped
- 1 cup packed fresh flat-leaf parsley, chopped
- 2 to 6 large cloves garlic, finely chopped
- ¼ cup all-purpose flour, preferably unbleached
- ½ teaspoon ground sage
- ¼ teaspoon freshly grated nutmeg
- Salt and freshly ground black pepper, to taste
- ¼ cup vegetable broth, preferably Basic Vegetable Broth (page 38) or low-sodium canned
- 2 tablespoons extra-virgin olive oil

Preheat the oven to 350F (175F). Lightly oil a 2½-quart gratin or shallow casserole.

In a large bowl, combine the squash, parsley, and garlic. Sprinkle with the flour, sage, nutmeg, salt, and pepper; toss well to combine. Add the broth and 1 tablespoon of the oil; stir well to combine. Transfer to the prepared baking dish and drizzle with the remaining oil.

Bake for 50 to 60 minutes, stirring halfway through the cooking time, or until the top is nicely browned and the squash is meltingly tender. Serve hot.

Advance Preparation As peeling and chopping the squash is the most time-consuming step in this recipe, the peeled and chopped squash can be refrigerated in an airtight plastic bag or container overnight before using in the recipe. The assembled gratin can be held at room temperature for one hour before baking, or it can be covered and refrigerated for several hours before baking.

PER SERVING

Calories 160 · Protein 4g · Total Fat 5g · Saturated Fat 1g · Cholesterol 0mg · Carbohydrate 29g · Dietary Fiber 5g · Sodium 45mg

Spinach Sautéed with Raisins and Pine Nuts

Raisins and pine nuts are a classic Catalan combination, often appearing in spinach or rice dishes throughout both Spanish and French Catalonia. Similar recipes can be found in Italian cookbooks, as well. You can turn this recipe into a satisfying main course for two or three by serving it with Oven-Baked Spanish Saffron Rice with Pimiento (page 128). MAKES 4 SERVINGS

- 2 teaspoons extra-virgin olive oil
- 1 clove garlic, slightly crushed
- 1 pound fresh spinach, stems discarded, or 1 (10-ounce) bag ready-washed spinach leaves
- 2 tablespoons water

2 tablespoons raisins, soaked in warm water to cover for 10 minutes, drained
2 tablespoons pine nuts, lightly toasted (see Cook's Tip, page 121)
Salt and freshly ground black pepper, to taste

In a large nonstick skillet with a lid, heat the oil over medium heat. Add the garlic and cook, stirring constantly, until fragrant and golden, 3 minutes. With a slotted spoon, remove the garlic and discard. Add the spinach and sprinkle with the water; cover and cook for 1 minute. Uncover and cook, turning and stirring constantly, until all the leaves are just wilted, 1 to 2 minutes.

Remove the skillet from the heat. Add the raisins, pine nuts, salt, and pepper; toss well to combine. Serve immediately.

PER SERVING

Calories 76 · Protein 3g · Total Fat 5g · Saturated Fat 1g · Cholesterol 0mg · Carbohydrate 7g · Dietary Fiber 2g · Sodium 57mg

Variation For an Italian rendition, instead of spinach, use kale that has been stripped of stems and thick ribs, then cut into thin strips. Increase the cooking time slightly.

Sautéed Cherry Tomatoes with Mediterranean Herbs

Juicy cherry tomatoes, more often than not just an optional salad garnish, star in this sensational side dish, ideal in spring and early summer when the promising green tomatoes in the garden have barely shed their blossoms, but the fragrant young herbs offer immediate possibilities.

MAKES 4 TO 6 SERVINGS

1½ tablespoons extra-virgin olive oil
2 pints (4 cups) cherry tomatoes, stemmed if necessary
3 tablespoons finely chopped fresh basil, mint, tarragon, thyme, oregano, chives, parsley, cilantro, and/or chervil
Salt, preferably the coarse variety, and freshly ground black pepper, to taste

In a large nonstick skillet, heat the oil over medium-high heat. Add the tomatoes and cook, tossing and stirring often, until the skins begin to split, about 3 minutes. Do not overcook.

Remove from the heat and toss with the herbs; season with salt and pepper. Serve immediately.

PER SERVING

Calories 91 · Protein 2g · Total Fat 6g · Saturated Fat 1g · Cholesterol 0mg · Carbohydrate 10g · Dietary Fiber 2g · Sodium 19mg

Baked Tomatoes, Corsican Style

Wild and wonderful Corsica, the highly independent minded French island one hundred miles south of Provence and just north of Sardinia, has a cuisine much more in line with that of its Italian neighbors. Indeed, these meltingly tender stuffed tomatoes could easily be found basking in ovens throughout Italy. Don't be put off by the hour-plus cooking time, long roasting only intensifies their flavor.

MAKES 4 SIDE-DISH OR FIRST-COURSE SERVINGS

4 large ripe tomatoes (8 to 10 ounces each), cut in half horizontally; do not seed
Salt, preferably the coarse variety, and freshly ground black pepper, to taste
1 cup finely chopped fresh flat-leaf parsley
2 large cloves garlic, finely chopped
8 teaspoons extra-virgin olive oil

Preheat the oven to 450F (230C). Lightly oil a casserole just large enough to hold the tomatoes snugly. Sprinkle the cut sides of the tomato halves with salt and pepper. In a small bowl, combine the parsley and garlic. Stuff each tomato half evenly with the parsley mixture (about 2 tablespoons per half).

Arrange the tomatoes, overlapping them slightly, in the prepared dish. Drizzle each half with 1 teaspoon of the olive oil. Bake for 20 minutes. Reduce the heat to 350F (175C) and bake 1 hour longer, or until the tomatoes are very tender and caramelized. Serve slightly warm or at room temperature.

PER SERVING

Calories 136 · Protein 3g · Total Fat 10g · Saturated Fat 1g · Cholesterol 0mg · Carbohydrate 12g · Dietary Fiber 3g · Sodium 30mg

Baked Tomatoes, Sicilian Style

This recipe is yet another exercise in simplicity. Don't be dissuaded by the long cooking time, as these juicy Italian beauties only grow more flavorful and caramelized. For a nice contrast of taste and texture, you can conveniently cook these alongside the Baked Onions, Italian-Style (page 145), at the same temperature for a few minutes longer. To create a delicious dinner for four, serve one portion of each recipe over hot cooked rice, orzo, or couscous to absorb the delicious juices.

MAKES 4 SERVINGS

4 large ripe tomatoes (about 8 ounces each), cut in half horizontally, seeded
¼ cup unseasoned dry bread crumbs
½ teaspoon dried oregano
Freshly ground black pepper, to taste
Coarse salt, to taste
8 teaspoons extra-virgin olive oil

Preheat oven to 350F (175C). Lightly grease a shallow baking dish just large enough to hold the tomatoes. Turn the seeded tomato halves upside down on several layers of paper towels and drain for about 10 minutes. Arrange the drained tomato halves, cut side up, in the prepared dish.

In a small bowl, mix together the bread crumbs, oregano, and pepper. Fill the tomato halves with the bread crumb mixture (about ½ tablespoon each). Season with coarse salt. Drizzle each half with 1 teaspoon of the oil. Bake, uncovered, for 1½ hours, or until the tops are nicely browned and caramelized.

Let cool slightly before serving, or serve at room temperature. For best results, do not refrigerate.

PER SERVING

Calories 161 · Protein 3g · Total Fat 10g · Saturated Fat 1g · Cholesterol 0mg · Carbohydrate 18g · Dietary Fiber 3g · Sodium 66mg

Sautéed Zucchini and Mushrooms with Sun-Dried Tomatoes

Sun-dried tomatoes enliven simple zucchini and cultivated white mushrooms in this delicious side dish. To turn it into a delicious main course, toss with rice or couscous, and sprinkle with toasted pine nuts.

MAKES 4 SERVINGS

- 1 tablespoon plus 1 teaspoon extra-virgin olive oil
- 2 cloves garlic, finely chopped
- 2 small zucchini (about 4 ounces each), trimmed, cut in half crosswise, then cut lengthwise into ¼-inch-thick strips
- ½ pound white button mushrooms, stemmed and thinly sliced
- ¼ cup dry-packed sun-dried tomato halves, cut into thin strips with kitchen shears, soaked in warm water to cover for 15 minutes, drained
- 2 tablespoons vegetable broth, preferably Basic Vegetable Broth (page 38) or low-sodium canned
- 1 tablespoon chopped fresh basil (optional)
- Salt and freshly ground black pepper, to taste

In a large nonstick skillet, heat the oil over medium-high heat. Add the garlic and zucchini and cook, tossing and stirring often, for 3 minutes. Add the mushrooms, sun-dried tomatoes, broth, and basil, if using. Cook, tossing and stirring constantly, until the zucchini are crisp-tender and the mushrooms are softened and have just begun to release their liquid, 2 minutes.

Remove the skillet from the heat and season with salt and pepper. Serve at once.

PER SERVING

Calories 74 · Protein 3g · Total Fat 5g · Saturated Fat 1g · Cholesterol 0mg · Carbohydrate 7g · Dietary Fiber 2g · Sodium 91mg

Vegetable Main Dishes

Gratin of Young Artichokes and Olives

The Rhône River, originating in Switzerland and flowing southward through Provence into the Mediterranean, is the wellspring of France's fertile Rhône Valley, whose cuisine is a delightful mixture of rugged mountain and sultry sun. This delectable gratin, in which baby artichokes are nestled with onions, olives, and bread crumbs, then drizzled with olive oil, is a regional springtime specialty. MAKES 4 SERVINGS

- 3 tablespoons fresh lemon juice
- 12 small (egg-size) artichokes or 6 medium globe artichokes (about 6 ounces each)
- 1 cup soft plain white bread crumbs
- 4 tablespoons olive oil
- 3 medium onions (about 6 ounces each), thinly sliced
- 2 large cloves garlic, finely chopped
- ¼ cup Niçoise or other good-quality black olives, pitted and chopped
- ¼ cup finely chopped fresh flat-leaf parsley
- Salt and freshly ground black pepper, to taste
- ⅓ cup Concentrated Vegetable Broth (page 37), or 1 cup low-sodium canned vegetable broth reduced over high heat to ⅓ cup

Preheat the oven to 350F (175C). Fill a medium bowl with water and add the lemon juice. Set aside. With a sharp, serrated knife, cut about ½ inch off the top of each small artichoke, or about 1 inch off the medium ones. Pull off and discard the tough, dark green outer leaves to expose the pale green hearts. Trim the dark stem end of each artichoke. Quarter the small artichoke hearts, or cut the medium hearts lengthwise into 8 wedges. With a small spoon or your fingers, scrape out any prickly inner leaves. As you work, drop the artichokes into the lemon water to prevent browning.

Spread the bread crumbs in a single layer on a light-colored baking sheet (a dark surface tends to overbrown them). Toast in the oven until lightly browned, stirring once or twice, 3 to 5 minutes. Set aside. Set oven temperature to 425F (220C).

In a large nonstick skillet, heat 2 tablespoons of the oil over medium heat. Add the onions and cook, stirring often, for 3 minutes. Add the garlic and cook, stirring constantly, 2 minutes. Add the toasted bread crumbs and stir well to combine. Remove the skillet from the heat and add the olives, parsley, salt, and pepper, stirring well to combine. Set aside.

Brush a shallow 12 × 8-inch baking dish with half of the remaining oil. Drain the artichokes and pat dry with paper towels. Arrange one-third of the onion mixture in the prepared dish. Spread half the drained artichokes over the onion mixture. Repeat, ending with the remaining third of the onion mixture. Pour the broth carefully

Cook's Tip

If fresh artichokes are unavailable, 2 (8-ounce) packages frozen quartered artichoke hearts, completely thawed, can be substituted. Follow the cooking times for the small artichokes.

around the edges of the dish. Season the top lightly with salt and pepper, then drizzle with the remaining 1 tablespoon oil.

Cover the baking dish tightly with foil and bake for 20 minutes. Reduce the oven temperature to 350F (175C). Cook until the artichokes are almost cooked through and tender, about 10 minutes for the small, 15 to 20 minutes for the medium. Uncover the dish and bake for 10 minutes, or until the artichokes are tender when pierced with the tip of a sharp knife and the top is browned. (If the mixture appears too dry, add more broth as necessary around the edges of the dish.) Let cool slightly. Serve warm.

Advance Preparation The bread crumb and onion mixture can be prepared and refrigerated, covered, for up to twenty-four hours before assembling the gratin. The assembled gratin can be held for one hour at room temperature or covered and refrigerated for up to eight hours before baking. The cooked dish can be held for one hour at room temperature. Reheat, covered, in a low oven.

PER SERVING

Calories 319 · Protein 10g · Total Fat 18g · Saturated Fat 2g · Cholesterol 0mg · Carbohydrate 34g · Dietary Fiber 10g · Sodium 549mg

Greek-Style Artichoke and Bean Stew

The refreshing flavors of lemon, dill, and mint instill this stew with a decidedly Greek character. Traditionally made in the spring with fresh young fava, or broad beans, which are virtually impossible to come by in most areas of the United States, the following recipe uses more readily accessible lima beans, a standard substitute in many cookbooks, instead. If you are lucky enough to have access to fresh favas, see the Cook's Tip, page 162, for directions on preparing.

MAKES 4 SERVINGS

1 large lemon, halved
4 large globe artichokes (10 to 12 ounces each)
¼ cup extra-virgin olive oil
1 large red onion (about 10 ounces), coarsely chopped
4 cloves garlic, finely chopped
2 cups freshly shelled lima beans (3½ to 4 pounds unshelled), or 2 cups cooked frozen or drained and rinsed canned baby lima beans
2 cups vegetable broth, preferably Basic Vegetable Broth (page 38) or low-sodium canned
½ pound ripe tomatoes, peeled, seeded, and chopped
1 tablespoon finely chopped fresh dill
1 tablespoon finely chopped fresh mint
Salt and freshly ground black pepper, to taste
Fresh dill or mint sprigs (optional)

Fill a large bowl with water and add the juice from one lemon half. Cut off the stem of each artichoke flush to the base. With a serrated knife, cut about 2 inches from the tops. Bend back and pull off the tough, dark green outer leaves to expose the pale green hearts. Trim the base, if necessary. Quarter each artichoke heart. Remove the purple, thistlelike leaves and scrape out the hairy choke with a melon baller or grapefruit spoon. Drop each artichoke into the lemon water when you finish to discourage browning. Set aside.

In a large deep-sided skillet with a lid or a medium stockpot, heat the oil over medium-low heat. Add the onion and garlic and cook, stirring occasionally, until the onion is very tender, about 15 minutes.

Rinse and drain the artichokes in a colander, then add them to the skillet, along with the fresh beans, if using, broth, tomatoes, dill, mint, and juice from the remaining lemon half; season with salt and pepper. Bring to a brisk simmer over medium-high heat. Cover tightly, reduce the heat to medium-low, and simmer until the artichokes are just tender when pierced at the base with a sharp knife, 20 to 30 minutes. Add the cooked frozen or canned beans, if using, stirring well to combine.

Cook, covered, over medium-low heat, until the artichokes and fresh beans, if used, are completely tender, about 5 minutes. Uncover, increase the heat to medium-high, and cook, stirring occasionally, until the liquids are slightly reduced, 3 to 5 minutes. Serve warm, garnished with the dill or mint sprigs, if desired.

Advance Preparation The stew can be held, covered, for one hour over low heat before serving. The stew can be stored, covered, in the refrigerator for up to twenty-four hours. Reheat over low heat.

PER SERVING

Calories 340 · Protein 17g · Total Fat 14g · Saturated Fat 2g · Cholesterol 0mg · Carbohydrate 40g · Dietary Fiber 15g · Sodium 348mg

Cook's Tip

If you would like to make an authentic Greek broad bean and artichoke stew, use fresh young fava, or broad beans, which are typically available in Greek and Italian markets in the spring. (Both canned and cooked dried fava beans have an overly earthy flavor that does not work particularly well in this recipe.) To use fresh favas, select 3½ to 4 pounds of beans with flexible pods. Shell the beans, with each pound of unshelled favas yielding about ½ cup shelled. If the beans are young, it is not necessary to remove the outer skin of each bean. Cook as directed in the recipe for the freshly shelled lima beans.

Beans in a Bottle, Tuscan Style

Don't worry, no empty Chianti bottle or brick oven is required for this rendition of fagioli in fiasco, an old-fashioned Tuscan bean dish that used to be made on baking day. Re-created in a baking dish inside a modern oven, these meltingly tender beans can be eaten on their own, with a little lemon juice and olive oil drizzled over the top. They make a terrific dip or spread for bread. As an added treat, their wonderful aroma will perfume your home for hours. **MAKES 6 SERVINGS**

- 2 cups dried cannellini, Great Northern, or navy beans, soaked in 2 to 3 times their volume in water for a minimum of 8 hours, drained (or see Box, page 18 for quick-soak method)
- Hot water
- 2 tablespoons extra-virgin olive oil
- 3 large sage leaves
- 2 large cloves garlic, coarsely chopped
- Salt and freshly ground black pepper, to taste
- Lemon wedges, for serving (optional)
- Extra-virgin olive oil, for serving (optional)

Preheat the oven to 325F (165C). Place the drained beans in a 2-quart casserole. Add enough hot water to cover the beans by about ¼ inch. Stir in the oil, sage, and garlic. Cover the dish tightly with foil. With the tip of a sharp knife, puncture the foil in six places.

Bake for 2 to 2½ hours, or until the beans are very tender and creamy. Season with salt and pepper, stirring gently yet thoroughly to combine. Divide evenly among 6 small bowls and serve warm or at room temperature, with the lemon wedges and olive oil passed separately, if using.

Advance Preparation The cooled beans can be stored, covered, in the refrigerator for a few days, but will lose some of their creaminess. You may need to add some water or broth before reheating in a low oven.

PER SERVING

Calories 267 · Protein 16g · Total Fat 5g · Saturated Fat 1g · Cholesterol 0mg · Carbohydrate 41g · Dietary Fiber 10g · Sodium 11mg

Variation To serve as a dip or spread, place in a large bowl. Serve with bread sticks and/or toasted baguette rounds.

Cannellini Beans with Sautéed Kale

This classic Italian bean dish is often flavored with pancetta, a type of spicy Italian bacon, but a few vegetarian versions, such as the following, rely upon the far healthier combination of garlic, herbs, and spice. Escarole or curly endive, fellow members of the chicory family, can be used in place of the kale, if desired. **MAKES 4 SERVINGS**

- 2 tablespoons extra-virgin olive oil
- 1 large onion (10 to 12 ounces), cut lengthwise in half, thinly sliced crosswise
- 2 large cloves garlic, finely chopped
- 1 pound kale, stems removed and coarsely chopped
- 3 cups cooked cannellini beans (see Box, page 18) or 2 (15-ounce) cans cannellini, Great Northern, or navy beans, drained and rinsed
- ¼ teaspoon dried rubbed sage
- ¼ teaspoon dried oregano
- Pinch cayenne pepper, or to taste (optional)
- Salt and freshly ground black pepper, to taste

In a large nonstick skillet, heat the oil over medium heat. Add the onion and garlic and cook, stirring often, until the onion is wilted, about 5 minutes. Increase the heat to medium-high and add the kale in batches, tossing and stirring until wilted and bright green, 2 to 4 minutes. Reduce the heat to medium-low and add the beans, sage, oregano, cayenne (if using), salt, and pepper. Cook, stirring often, until all is heated through. Serve warm.

PER SERVING

Calories 333 · Protein 18g · Total Fat 8g · Saturated Fat 1g · Cholesterol 0mg · Carbohydrate 52g · Dietary Fiber 14g · Sodium 59mg

Braised Cabbage with Red Beans and Rice

Cabbage with red beans is a classic Italian combination, and it is often served with rice. This homey main dish is, to me, the epitome of comfort food. **MAKES 4 TO 6 SERVINGS**

- 2 tablespoons extra-virgin olive oil
- 1 small onion (about 4 ounces), chopped
- ¼ cup chopped carrot
- 8 cups shredded green cabbage (about 1 pound)
- 4 cups vegetable broth, preferably Basic Vegetable Broth (page 38) or low-sodium canned
- 1 cup arborio rice
- Salt and freshly ground black pepper, to taste
- 1½ cups cooked red kidney beans (see Box, page 18) or 1 (15-ounce) can red kidney beans, drained and rinsed

In a large deep-sided skillet with a lid or a medium stockpot, heat the oil over medium-low heat. Add the onion and carrot and cook, stirring occasionally, until softened, about 10 minutes.

Add the cabbage and 1 cup of the broth, tossing to combine. Cover and cook over medium-low heat for 20 minutes, stirring a few times. Add the remaining broth and bring to a boil over high heat. Add the rice, salt, and pepper. Reduce the heat to medium-low, cover, and cook until the rice is tender and most of the broth has been absorbed, 15 to 20 minutes.

Add the beans and cook, uncovered, stirring occasionally, until heated through, about 5 minutes. Serve warm.

PER SERVING

Calories 410 · Protein 23g · Total Fat 8g · Saturated Fat 1g · Cholesterol 0mg · Carbohydrate 64g · Dietary Fiber 10g · Sodium 556mg

Provençal Tian of Chickpeas, Eggplant, Tomatoes, and Olives

This gratin, or tian, from Provence makes an excellent quick, protein-packed meal when prepared with rinsed and drained canned chickpeas. Because the dish is on the spicy side, salting the eggplant cubes really isn't necessary. But if you'd rather, salt them and set in a colander for fifteen minutes while you preheat the oven and start on the tomato sauce, then rinse and pat dry with paper towels. **MAKES 4 TO 6 SERVINGS**

- 1 large eggplant (about 1 pound), cut into 1-inch cubes
- 2 tablespoons extra-virgin olive oil
- 1 medium onion (about 6 ounces), finely chopped
- 2 large cloves garlic, finely chopped
- 2 pounds ripe tomatoes, peeled, seeded, and chopped
- 6 sprigs fresh parsley
- 1 sprig fresh thyme
- 1 bay leaf
- Salt and freshly ground black pepper, to taste
- 3 cups cooked chickpeas (see Box, page 18) or 2 (15-ounce) cans chickpeas, drained and rinsed

½ teaspoon crushed red pepper flakes
½ teaspoon ground allspice
12 to 16 fresh basil leaves, shredded
¼ cup dry unseasoned bread crumbs
½ cup pitted Niçoise or other good-quality black olives

Preheat the oven to 400F (205C). Arrange the eggplant cubes in a single layer on a lightly oiled large baking sheet. Bake for 10 minutes, turning once halfway through cooking time. Remove from the oven and set aside.

Reduce the oven temperature to 375F (190C). Lightly oil a 12-inch gratin or 11 × 8-inch flameproof baking dish. Set aside.

Meanwhile, in a large nonstick skillet, heat 1 tablespoon of the oil over medium heat. Add the onion and cook, stirring, for 2 minutes. Add the garlic and cook, stirring, for 2 minutes. Add the tomatoes, parsley, thyme, bay leaf, salt, and pepper. Bring to a brisk simmer over medium-high heat. Reduce the heat to medium and cook, stirring often to prevent scorching, until most of the liquids have evaporated, about 15 minutes. Remove from the heat. Remove and discard the parsley, thyme, and bay leaf.

Add the eggplant, chickpeas, red pepper flakes, allspice, basil, and remaining 1 tablespoon oil to the skillet; stir well to combine. Transfer to the prepared gratin and sprinkle evenly with the bread crumbs, then scatter the olives over the top. Bake for about 25 minutes, or until hot and lightly browned.

Advance Preparation The sauce can be stored, covered, in the refrigerator for two days before using. The assembled gratin, without the bread crumbs, can be stored, covered, in the refrigerator for up to twenty-four hours before baking.

PER SERVING

Calories 459 · Protein 15g · Total Fat 19g · Saturated Fat 2g · Cholesterol 0mg · Carbohydrate 61g · Dietary Fiber 10g · Sodium 552mg

Eggplant Croquettes with Tomato Sauce

Croquettes are highly popular in Italian, French, and Spanish cuisine, but, alas, are frequently deep-fried. Not here, where these breaded eggplant cakes are baked to golden perfection in a hot oven. The following recipe, though lengthy, is a snap to make if you prepare the filling the night before.

MAKES 4 TO 6 SERVINGS

2 eggplants (about 1 pound each), halved lengthwise
2 tablespoons plus 1 teaspoon extra-virgin olive oil
1 cup soft unseasoned bread crumbs
1 cup packed fresh basil leaves, shredded
4 large cloves garlic, finely chopped
1 teaspoon coarse salt
Pinch cayenne red pepper (optional)
Freshly ground black pepper, to taste
About 1½ cups dry unseasoned bread crumbs
1 teaspoon dried oregano
2 cups Light Tomato Sauce (page 196), or purchased marinara sauce, warmed

Preheat the oven to 475F (245C). Rub the cut sides of the eggplant halves evenly with the 1 teaspoon oil. Place cut side down on a large ungreased baking sheet; prick the skin in several places with the tines of a fork. Bake for 15 to 20 minutes, or until the skin is beginning to shrivel. Place on several layers of paper towel to drain.

When cool enough to handle, remove the skin from the eggplant and transfer the flesh to a food processor fitted with the knife blade. Add the soft bread crumbs, basil, garlic, coarse salt, cayenne (if using), and black pepper. Process with on/off motions until smooth but not quite pureed. Transfer to a medium bowl; cover, and refrigerate for at least 1 hour.

Preheat the oven to 400F (205C). Lightly oil a baking sheet and set aside.

In a small bowl, combine the dry bread crumbs with the oregano. Shape the chilled eggplant mixture into 12 balls. Dip each ball in the dry bread crumb mixture. Using the palms of your hands, shape each ball into a loosely packed patty and place on the prepared baking sheet. Brush the tops evenly with 1 tablespoon of the oil. Bake for 10 minutes. Turn each patty and brush evenly with remaining 1 tablespoon oil. Bake for 10 minutes, or until nicely browned. Serve hot with the warmed sauce.

PER SERVING

Calories 458 · Protein 12g · Total Fat 18g · Saturated Fat 3g · Cholesterol 0mg · Carbohydrate 67g · Dietary Fiber 13g · Sodium 871mg

Variation Serve, sandwich-style, in small round rolls with the Tomato-Cognac Sauce (page 202).

Eggplant-Couscous Rolls with Black Olives and Minted Tomato Sauce

Because the rolls can be assembled well in advance, this dish is ideal for elegant yet carefree summer entertaining. If you don't have time to make the Light Tomato Sauce called for in this recipe, throw a tablespoon of chopped fresh mint into your favorite store-bought marinara sauce; no one will guess you didn't make it from scratch unless you tell them. Serve with a mixed green salad and pita bread.

MAKES 4 TO 6 SERVINGS

2 eggplants (about 1 pound each)
2 tablespoons extra-virgin olive oil
1¼ cups vegetable broth, preferably Basic Vegetable Broth (page 38) or low-sodium canned
3 tablespoons fresh lemon juice
¾ cup instant couscous
½ tablespoon fresh thyme leaves or ½ teaspoon dried
Pinch cayenne, or to taste (optional)
Salt, to taste
½ cup chopped kalamata or other good-quality black olives
3 tablespoons finely chopped fresh mint
Freshly ground black pepper, to taste
1 cup Light Tomato Sauce (page 196) or purchased marinara sauce, at room temperature
About 12 whole kalamata or other good-quality black olives
Shredded fresh mint leaves, for garnish (optional)

Preheat the oven to 400F (205C). Lightly oil 2 baking sheets and set aside.

Trim both ends of the eggplants. Stand one eggplant on end and remove most of the skin in thin slices. Repeat with the second eggplant. Cut each eggplant lengthwise into about 6 (⅜-inch-thick) slices. Brush evenly with 1½ tablespoons of the oil and arrange in a single layer on the prepared baking sheets. Bake for 12 to 15 minutes, turning once halfway through cooking, or until tender and lightly browned.

Meanwhile, in a medium saucepan, bring the broth and 1 tablespoon of the lemon juice to a boil. Stir in the remaining ½ tablespoon oil, couscous, thyme, cayenne (if using), and salt. Cover, remove from the heat, and let stand for 7 minutes, or until the broth is absorbed. Uncover, fluff with a fork, and let cool for a few minutes. Stir in the chopped olives, 2 tablespoons of the mint, and black pepper.

Lightly oil a 13 × 9-inch baking dish. Divide the couscous mixture evenly down the centers of the eggplant slices. Roll up the eggplant firmly around the filling, pushing back in any escaping filling as you roll. Place the rolls, seam side down, in the prepared dish. Cover with foil and bake for 10 minutes.

Stir the remaining mint into the sauce. Uncover the baking dish and spoon the sauce evenly over the top of each eggplant roll. Top each roll with a whole olive, skewering with a toothpick. Cover and bake for 10 minutes. Uncover and bake for 5 minutes, or until the sauce is heated through. Garnish with the shredded mint, if desired, and serve at once.

Advance Preparation The assembled filled rolls can be stored, covered, in the refrigerator for up to twenty-four hours before baking. Increase the initial baking time by five minutes.

PER SERVING

Calories 424 · Protein 12g · Total Fat 21g · Saturated Fat 2g · Cholesterol 0mg · Carbohydrate 50g · Dietary Fiber 10g · Sodium 865mg

Greek Ragout of Green Beans, Potatoes, and Vine-Ripened Tomatoes

This is a simple yet very satisfying stew I look forward to making again and again using vine-ripened tomatoes. But even if you've no tomatoes ripening on your windowsill, you can substitute one 28-ounce can of whole tomatoes, drained and coarsely chopped, and the following recipe will still be delicious. **MAKES 4 SERVINGS**

- ¼ cup extra-virgin olive oil
- 2 medium onions (6 to 8 ounces each), quartered and very thinly sliced
- 2 cloves garlic, finely chopped
- 2 pounds boiling potatoes, peeled and cut into 2-inch pieces
- 2 pounds vine-ripened tomatoes, cored and coarsely chopped
- ¾ pound trimmed fresh green beans
- ¼ cup vegetable broth, preferably Basic Vegetable Broth (page 38) or low-sodium canned
- ½ teaspoon dried oregano
- ¼ teaspoon sugar
- Salt and freshly ground black pepper, to taste
- Juice of half a medium lemon (about 1½ tablespoons)

In a large deep-sided skillet with a lid or a medium stockpot, heat the oil over medium-low heat. Add the onions and garlic and cook, stirring occasionally, until the onions are very tender, about 15 minutes. Add the potatoes, tomatoes, green beans, broth, oregano, sugar, salt, and pepper. Bring to a brisk simmer over medium-high heat. Reduce the heat, cover, and simmer gently for 1 hour, stirring occasionally, or until the vegetables are tender but not mushy.

Uncover the skillet and add the lemon juice, stirring well to combine. Increase the heat to medium-high and bring to a brisk simmer; cook, stirring occasionally and adjusting the heat to maintain a brisk simmer, until the liquids are reduced by about half, 5 to 10 minutes. Season with additional salt and pepper as necessary. Serve warm.

Advance Preparation Up until adding the lemon juice, the ragout can be held at room temperature for one hour before finishing the recipe. Or it can be covered and refrigerated overnight before completing and serving.

PER SERVING

Calories 370 · Protein 9g · Total Fat 15g · Saturated Fat 2g · Cholesterol 0mg · Carbohydrate 56g · Dietary Fiber 10g · Sodium 70mg

Eggplant Napoleons with Tomato and Orange Sauce, Catalan-Style

Like their Spanish brothers, the people of French Catalonia, from whom this recipe draws its inspiration, have a fondness for eggplants and tomatoes. Give your crop its last hurrah before the first frost sets in with this baked rendition of fried eggplant with sauce Catalane, a classic garlic and tomato sauce distinguished by the tang of Seville's bitter oranges. Serve with rice and a green salad for a lovely meal.

MAKES 4 SERVINGS

- 1 large eggplant (at least 6 inches long after trimming), cut into 20 (¼-inch-thick) rounds, sprinkled with salt, and set in a colander to drain for 30 minutes (salting is optional)
- 1 large red onion, sliced into 8 (¼-inch-thick) rounds
- 2½ tablespoons extra-virgin olive oil
- Salt, preferably the coarse variety, and freshly grated black pepper, to taste
- 8 cloves garlic, coarsely chopped
- 2½ pounds ripe tomatoes, peeled, seeded, and chopped
- 1½ tablespoons all-natural Seville-style (bitter) orange marmalade
- 6 teaspoons unseasoned dry bread crumbs
- 4 tablespoons chopped kalamata olives

Preheat the oven to 475F (245C). Rinse the drained eggplant under cold running water. Dry between paper towels.

Arrange the eggplant and onion slices on 2 lightly greased medium baking sheets. Brush the tops evenly with 2 tablespoons of the oil. Season with salt and pepper. Cover tightly with foil and bake for 20 minutes. Remove from the oven and uncover; set aside to cool. Reduce the oven temperature to 425F (220C).

Meanwhile, heat the remaining ½ tablespoon oil in a large nonstick skillet over medium heat. Add the garlic; cook until golden, stirring constantly, 2 to 3 minutes. Add the tomatoes, salt, and pepper. Increase the heat to medium-high and bring to a brisk simmer. Reduce the heat to low and simmer, uncovered, stirring occasionally, for 10 minutes. Stir in the marmalade. Simmer, stirring occasionally, until the mixture is reduced and thickened, 10 minutes. Cover and keep warm over very low heat.

Layer the reserved vegetables, sauce, and bread crumbs in 4 piles on one of the baking sheets in the following manner: 1 eggplant slice, ½ tablespoon sauce, ½ teaspoon bread crumbs, 1 eggplant slice, 1 onion slice, 1 eggplant slice, ½ tablespoon sauce, ½ teaspoon bread crumbs, 1 eggplant slice, 1 onion slice, 1 eggplant slice, ½ tablespoon sauce, and ½ teaspoon of bread crumbs. Sprinkle each stack with additional salt and pepper to taste. Garnish each stack with 1 tablespoon of the chopped olives. Place a bamboo skewer through each stack, if desired.

Bake for 7 to 10 minutes, or until all is heated through and the tops of the napoleons are lightly browned. To serve, divide remaining sauce evenly among 4 warmed serving plates. Arrange a napoleon on top. Serve immediately.

PER SERVING

Calories 311 · Protein 5g · Total Fat 18g · Saturated Fat 1g · Cholesterol 0mg · Carbohydrate 38g · Dietary Fiber 8g · Sodium 529mg

Stuffed Portobello Mushrooms with Sun-Dried Tomatoes and Basil

Sun-dried tomatoes lend piquancy to stuffings of all sorts in Italy. Though giant portobello mushrooms are not really Italian, they are ideal vehicles for this flavorful filling, which is also excellent as a stuffing for large globe artichokes. Served atop a ladle of Light Tomato Sauce or your favorite pasta sauce and garnished with a sprig of fresh basil, this entree is as elegant as it is delicious.

MAKES 4 SERVINGS

3 tablespoons extra-virgin olive oil
2 medium onions (about 6 ounces each), chopped
4 large cloves garlic, finely chopped
¼ cup packed oil-packed sun-dried tomatoes, drained and chopped
½ cup finely chopped fresh flat-leaf parsley
¼ cup finely chopped fresh basil
Salt and freshly ground black pepper, to taste
4 ounces day-old crusty Italian or French bread, crust included, coarsely ground (2½ to 3 cups)
1 cup vegetable broth, preferably Basic Vegetable Broth (page 38) or low-sodium canned
8 large portobello mushroom caps (about 2 ounces each)
8 teaspoons pine nuts (optional)
2 cups Light Tomato Sauce (page 196) or your favorite pasta sauce

Preheat the oven to 400F (205C). Lightly oil a shallow casserole large enough to hold the mushrooms in a single layer. Set aside.

In a large nonstick skillet, heat the oil over medium heat. Add the onions and garlic and cook, stirring, until the onion is softened and the garlic is fragrant, about 5 minutes. Remove the skillet from the heat and stir in the tomatoes, parsley, basil, salt, and pepper. Add the ground bread, stirring well to combine. Add ½ cup of the broth, stirring well to combine. With a wooden spoon, push the stuffing into 8 equal mounds.

Fill the mushrooms with equal portions of the stuffing. Transfer to the prepared casserole. Spoon 1 tablespoon of the remaining broth over each. Cover tightly with foil and bake for 45 minutes. Uncover and bake for 10 to 15 minutes, or until the tops are lightly browned and crusty. Sprinkle 1 teaspoon of the pine nuts, if using, over each mushroom cap for the last 5 minutes of cooking.

To serve, ladle ½ cup of the sauce onto each of 4 individual serving plates and top with 2 stuffed mushrooms. Spoon any juices remaining in the casserole equally around the mushrooms. Serve warm.

Advance Preparation The assembled stuffed mushrooms can be held for one hour at room temperature before baking, or stored, covered, in the refrigerator up to twelve hours before baking.

PER SERVING

Calories 391 · Protein 13g · Total Fat 19g · Saturated Fat 3g · Cholesterol 0mg · Carbohydrate 48g · Dietary Fiber 9g · Sodium 378mg

Orzo-Stuffed Peppers with Basil and Mint

Americans are increasingly discovering the versatility of orzo, a rice-shaped pasta that used to be sold only in specialty stores but is now found in most well-stocked supermarkets. Indeed, in many recipes, this quick-cooking pasta can be substituted for the longer cooking rice, and it will not harden in the refrigerator, as long-grain white rice will do. If you prefer, however, about 3½ cups of slightly undercooked white rice—preferably arborio, which will not harden in the refrigerator—can be used instead of the orzo in this recipe.

MAKES 4 SERVINGS

- 2½ tablespoons extra-virgin olive oil
- 1 medium onion (about 6 ounces), finely chopped
- 3 large cloves garlic, finely chopped
- 1½ pounds tomatoes, peeled, seeded, and chopped
- ¼ cup dry white wine
- Salt and freshly ground black pepper, to taste
- 8 ounces (about 1¼ cups) orzo, slightly undercooked according to package directions
- ¼ cup finely chopped fresh basil
- 2 tablespoons finely chopped fresh mint
- 2 tablespoons drained capers
- 2 tablespoons chopped black kalamata olives
- 4 large bell peppers (8 to 10 ounces each)
- 2 cups Light Tomato Sauce (page 196) or purchased pasta sauce

Preheat the oven to 400F (205C).

In a large nonstick skillet, heat 2 tablespoons of the oil over medium heat. Add the onion and cook, stirring, until softened but not browned, about 5 minutes. Add the garlic and cook, stirring, for 2 minutes. Add the tomatoes, wine, salt, and pepper. Bring to a boil over medium-high heat. Reduce the heat to medium and simmer briskly until the mixture has thickened and most of the liquids have evaporated, 15 to 20 minutes, stirring frequently to prevent scorching.

Remove the skillet from the heat and add the orzo, basil, mint, capers, and olives, stirring well to thoroughly combine. Taste and season with additional salt and pepper, if needed. Set aside.

Cut a lid off the stem end of each pepper and reserve. Remove the seeds and white membranes from each pepper shell. Brush the outsides of the lids and shells with the remaining ½ tablespoon of oil. Stuff each pepper shell lightly (do not pack) with equal amounts of the orzo mixture and top with its lid (lids will not close).

Place the stuffed peppers upright in a baking dish just large enough to hold them. Add enough water to the dish to measure ½ inch deep. Cover tightly with foil and bake for 50 to 60 minutes, or until the peppers are tender when pierced with the tip of a sharp knife. Remove the foil and bake for 5 minutes, or until the lids just begin to blister.

To serve, heat the tomato sauce. Ladle ½ cup warmed sauce on each of 4 heated serving plates. Arrange a pepper in the center of the sauce and serve.

Advance Preparation The assembled stuffed peppers can be stored, covered, in the refrigerator overnight before baking.

PER SERVING

Calories 544 · Protein 14g · Total Fat 18g · Saturated Fat 2g · Cholesterol 0mg · Carbohydrate 85g · Dietary Fiber 11g · Sodium 206mg

Tomatoes Stuffed with Herbed Rice, Provençal Style

Stuffed vegetables are legion on the Mediterranean, especially in Provence, where tomatoes are favored receptacles for all sorts of fillings. The following recipe makes a fine main course serving four, or an impressive first course or side dish serving eight. As the almost cooked grains of rice finish cooking inside juicy ripe tomatoes flavored with herbs and garlic, they absorb the delicious broth.

MAKES 4 MAIN-COURSE OR 8 SIDE-DISH SERVINGS

- 8 large ripe yet firm tomatoes (8 to 10 ounces each)
- Salt, preferably the coarse variety, to taste
- 1 cup long-grain white rice
- 1 large bay leaf
- ¼ cup plus 4 teaspoons extra-virgin olive oil
- ¼ cup coarsely chopped fresh basil leaves
- 3 large cloves garlic, finely chopped
- ¼ teaspoon dried thyme leaves
- Freshly ground black pepper, to taste
- 8 teaspoons pine nuts (optional)
- 8 whole fresh basil leaves (optional)

Cut a slice from the top of each tomato about ½ inch thick and reserve. Gently squeeze out the seeds from each tomato. Using a small sharp knife or a melon spoon, scoop out the pulp and reserve, discarding any white core. Lightly salt the inside of each tomato shell. Turn the shells upside down on several layers of paper towels and drain for 30 minutes.

Meanwhile, cook the rice with the bay leaf in 2 quarts boiling salted water in a large pot over high heat until not quite tender, 8 to 10 minutes. Drain well. Remove and discard the bay leaf.

Chop the reserved tomato pulp and place in a medium bowl. Add the rice, the ¼ cup oil, chopped basil, garlic, thyme, salt, and pepper; stir well to combine. Let set for 20 minutes at room temperature to allow the flavors to blend.

Preheat the oven to 350F (175C). Lightly oil a shallow baking dish just large enough to hold the tomatoes in a single layer. Set aside.

Sprinkle the insides of the drained tomatoes with a little pepper. Fill the tomatoes evenly with the rice mixture (do not pack down). Cover with the reserved tops. Arrange upright in the prepared dish. Brush the tops and sides of each tomato with a ½ teaspoon oil. Bake the tomatoes, uncovered, for 25 minutes. Remove and discard the lids. Sprinkle the top of each tomato with 1 teaspoon of the pine nuts, if using. Bake for 5 to 10 minutes, or until the tomatoes are soft but not falling apart and the nuts (if used) are lightly toasted.

Let the tomatoes cool slightly and serve warm, or serve at room temperature. Garnish with the basil leaves if desired.

Advance Preparation The assembled stuffed tomatoes can be held at room temperature for one hour before baking. The cooked stuffed tomatoes can be held at room temperature for one hour before serving. If you are making the arborio rice variation, the cooked stuffed tomatoes can be stored, covered, in the refrigerator for up to twelve hours and served either chilled or brought to room temperature, as the cooked grains of this variety will not harden in the refrigerator.

PER MAIN-COURSE SERVING

Calories 420 · Protein 7g · Total Fat 20g · Saturated Fat 3g · Cholesterol 0mg · Carbohydrate 58g · Dietary Fiber 5g · Sodium 40mg

Variation For a creamier version, substitute Italian arborio rice for the long-grain variety, and cook in the same manner.

Ratatouille with White Beans

Ratatouille is arguably the most famous of Provençal vegetable dishes, and with good reason—it's simply delicious. Typically served as a side or starter, it shines as a main course when paired with tender white beans. You can, of course, omit the beans and serve the ratatouille on its own. A great dish for company, it actually tastes better the day after it's been made.

MAKES 6 SERVINGS

- 1 pound eggplant (about 1 large), cut into 1- to 1½-inch cubes, sprinkled with salt, and set in a colander to drain for 30 minutes (salting is optional)
- 4 tablespoons extra-virgin olive oil
- 1 pound onions (about 2 medium), chopped
- 1 medium green bell pepper (about 6 ounces), cut into 1- to 1½-inch cubes
- 1 medium red bell pepper (about 6 ounces), cut into 1- to 1½-inch cubes
- 4 large garlic cloves, finely chopped
- 1 pound zucchini (about 2 medium), cut into 1- to 1½-inch cubes

¼ cup dry white wine
¾ cup vegetable broth, preferably Basic Vegetable Broth (page 38) or low-sodium canned
1½ pounds tomatoes (about 4 medium), peeled, seeded, and chopped
1 tablespoon tomato paste
1½ teaspoons fresh thyme leaves or ½ teaspoon dried
1½ teaspoons chopped fresh oregano or ½ teaspoon dried
¼ teaspoon whole coriander seeds, crushed
1 large bay leaf
Salt and freshly ground black pepper, to taste
4 cups cooked cannellini beans (see Box, page 18) or 2 (19-ounce) cans cannellini or other white beans, drained and rinsed
¼ cup finely chopped fresh basil
Pitted black olives (optional)
Whole fresh basil sprigs, for garnish (optional)

Rinse the drained eggplant under cold running water. Dry between paper towels and set aside.

In a large deep-sided skillet (a nonstick pan is not recommended) with a lid, heat 3 tablespoons of the oil over medium heat. Add the onions and cook, stirring, until softened, about 3 minutes. Stir in the bell peppers and garlic; cook, stirring often, for 2 to 3 minutes. Add the eggplant and cook, stirring often, for 2 to 3 minutes. Add the remaining 1 tablespoon oil and the zucchini and cook, stirring often, until the zucchini is barely tender, about 5 minutes.

Add the wine and broth. Bring to a boil over high heat, tossing and scraping the bottom of the skillet to loosen any brown bits. Reduce the heat to medium-high and stir in the tomatoes, tomato paste, thyme, oregano, coriander, and bay leaf; season with salt and pepper. Let come to a brisk simmer. Reduce the heat, cover, and simmer gently for 20 minutes, stirring occasionally.

Add the beans to the skillet, stirring well to combine. Cook, uncovered, until the vegetables are tender yet somewhat firm and the liquids have thickened, stirring occasionally, 10 to 15 minutes. Remove the skillet from the heat and stir in the chopped basil. Serve warm or at room temperature, garnished with the olives and basil sprigs, if desired.

Advance Preparation The cooled dish can be covered and refrigerated for up to three days. Return to room temperature or reheat in a low oven before serving.

Cook's Tip

While you can use a nonstick skillet, a standard skillet is preferred as it promotes sticking of the little brown bits of vegetables that impart so much flavor to the dish.

PER SERVING

Calories 350 · Protein 16g · Total Fat 10g · Saturated Fat 2g · Cholesterol 0mg · Carbohydrate 52g · Dietary Fiber 12g · Sodium 46mg

Italian Summer Vegetable Stew (Ciambotta)

This is a specialty of southern Italy, sometimes called giambotta or cianfotta, which, in homage to summer's bounty, is always made with garden-fresh ingredients. Serve this with lots of crusty Italian bread to sop up the delicious juices. It is also ideal spooned over a bed of polenta.

MAKES 4 SERVINGS

- 1 pound eggplant (about 1 large), cut into 1- to 1½-inch cubes, sprinkled with salt, and set in a colander to drain for 30 minutes (salting is optional)
- 4 tablespoons extra-virgin olive oil
- 1 large onion (10 to 12 ounces), chopped
- 1 stalk celery, finely chopped
- 1 medium green bell pepper (about 6 ounces), cut into thin strips
- 1 medium red bell pepper (about 6 ounces), cut into thin strips
- 4 large garlic cloves, finely chopped
- ¾ pound zucchini (about 2 medium), cut into ½-inch-thick rounds
- 1½ pounds vine-ripened tomatoes (about 4 medium), peeled, seeded, and chopped
- 1 pound potatoes, peeled and cut into 2-inch chunks
- 1 cup vegetable broth, preferably Basic Vegetable Broth (page 38) or low-sodium canned
- 1½ teaspoons finely chopped fresh oregano or ½ teaspoon dried
- Salt and freshly ground black pepper, to taste
- 1 cup packed fresh basil leaves, chopped

Rinse the drained eggplant under cold running water. Dry between paper towels and set aside.

In a large deep-sided skillet with a lid or a medium stockpot, heat 3 tablespoons of the oil over medium heat. Add the onion and celery and cook, stirring often, until softened, 3 to 5 minutes. Stir in the bell peppers and garlic; cook, stirring often, for 2 to 3 minutes. Add the eggplant and cook, stirring often, 2 to 3 minutes. Add the remaining 1 tablespoon oil and the zucchini and cook, stirring often, until the zucchini is barely tender, 5 to 8 minutes. Add the tomatoes, potatoes, broth, oregano, salt, and pepper, stirring well to combine. Bring to a brisk simmer over medium-high heat. Reduce the heat, cover, and simmer gently until all the vegetables are tender, 20 to 25 minutes, stirring occasionally. Stir in the basil just before serving. Serve hot.

Advance Preparation The stew, without the basil, may be held, covered, over low heat for one hour before serving. The stew may be refrigerated, covered, for up to three days. Reheat over low heat.

PER SERVING

Calories 332 · Protein 11g · Total Fat 15g · Saturated Fat 2g · Cholesterol 0mg · Carbohydrate 45g · Dietary Fiber 12g · Sodium 168mg

Swiss Chard Dolmas with Chickpeas

Grape leaves and spinach leaves are interchangeable with Swiss chard in this quintessential Middle Eastern favorite. Because fresh grape leaves are virtually impossible to come by for most Americans, including me, I prefer to use large fresh Swiss chard or spinach leaves instead of canned grape leaves. If you do use canned grape leaves, rinse them well under cold running water to remove the brine and skip the first step of the recipe, as they do not require softening.

MAKES 6 SERVINGS

- 24 to 30 large fresh Swiss chard or spinach leaves, washed and drained
- 3 tablespoons extra-virgin olive oil
- 1 medium onion (about 6 ounces), finely chopped
- 4 scallions, white and green parts, finely chopped
- 1 cup finely chopped fresh flat-leaf parsley
- 2 cups slightly undercooked white rice
- 1 cup cooked chickpeas (see Box, page 18) or ½ (19-ounce) can chickpeas, drained and rinsed
- 1 tablespoon finely chopped fresh mint
- Salt and freshly ground black pepper, to taste
- About 1 cup vegetable broth, preferably Basic Vegetable Broth (page 38) or low-sodium canned
- 2 tablespoons fresh lemon juice
- 1 recipe Light Tomato Sauce (page 196) or 2½ cups purchased tomato sauce, warmed

Bring a large stockpot filled with water to a boil. Quickly blanch each chard leaf by holding the stem and dipping in boiling water for 1 or 2 seconds. Transfer to paper towels to drain.

Remove the stems and transfer them to a cutting board. Finely chop and place the stems in a large deep-sided skillet with a lid. Add ½ tablespoon of the oil and toss well to thoroughly coat. Spread the stems evenly over the bottom of the skillet. Set aside.

In a medium nonstick skillet, heat the remaining oil over medium heat. Add the onion and scallions and cook, stirring, until softened but not browned, about 5 minutes. Add the parsley and cook, stirring, for 1 minute. Remove from the heat and add the rice, chickpeas, mint, salt, and pepper. Toss well to combine. Set aside.

Spread the drained chard leaves on a large work surface and place about 2 heaping tablespoons of the rice mixture on each stem end. Roll up, jelly-roll fashion, folding in the sides as you roll. Arrange the rolls, seam side down, in rows on top of the chard stems in the large skillet. (If they don't fit comfortably in a single layer, arrange another layer in the opposite direction over top.) Add the broth and lemon juice, adding more broth, if necessary, to almost cover the rolls. Place a plate slightly smaller than the diameter of the skillet on top of the rolls to weight them down during cooking. Bring to a gentle simmer over medium heat. Cover, reduce the heat, and simmer gently until the leaves are tender but still a bit firm, about 25 minutes.

With a slotted spoon, transfer to a large heated serving platter or individual serving plates. Serve hot, with the warmed tomato sauce drizzled over the top.

Advance Preparation The filling can be made up to twenty-four hours in advance and stored, covered, in the refrigerator. The stuffed rolls, without the broth and lemon juice added, can be refrigerated in the covered skillet for up to twelve hours before cooking. The cooked stuffed rolls can be held over very low heat, partially covered, for up to one hour; reduce the cooking time by about 5 minutes so that the chard leaves remain somewhat firm.

PER SERVING

Calories 360 · Protein 13g · Total Fat 14g · Saturated Fat 2g · Cholesterol 0mg · Carbohydrate 53g · Dietary Fiber 9g · Sodium 487mg

Zucchini Stuffed with Couscous, Golden Raisins, and Currants

These delicious main-course stuffed zucchini look especially pretty served with Sautéed Cherry Tomatoes with Mediterranean Herbs (page 157). If desired, you can halve the recipe and serve one stuffed zucchini half as a vegetable side dish or first course. If currants are unavailable, substitute with dark raisins. MAKES 4 SERVINGS

4 large zucchini (about 12 ounces each), trimmed and halved lengthwise
2½ tablespoons extra-virgin olive oil
1 medium onion (about 6 ounces), finely chopped
1 medium carrot (about 3 ounces), finely chopped
1 cup vegetable broth, preferably Basic Vegetable Broth (page 38) or low-sodium canned
1 teaspoon freshly grated lemon peel or ½ teaspoon dried
Salt and freshly ground black pepper, to taste
½ cup instant couscous
¼ cup golden raisins, soaked in water to cover for 10 minutes, drained
2 tablespoons zante currants, soaked in water to cover for 10 minutes, drained
¼ cup chopped fresh flat-leaf parsley
2 tablespoons chopped fresh chives or scallions, mostly green parts
Juice of ½ large lemon (about 2 tablespoons)
¼ teaspoon freshly grated nutmeg

Preheat the oven to 425F (220C). Lightly oil a baking sheet and set aside. Scoop out the insides from each zucchini half, leaving a ⅜-inch-thick shell. Rub the outsides of the zucchini shells with ½ tablespoon of the oil and set aside. Finely chop the insides and set aside.

In a large deep-sided skillet with a tight-fitting lid, heat the remaining 2 tablespoons oil over medium heat. Add the onion and carrot and cook, stirring frequently, until softened, about 5 minutes. Add the chopped zucchini and increase the heat to medium-high. Cook, stirring often, until most of the liquid released by the zucchini has evaporated, 10 to 15 minutes.

Add the broth, lemon peel, salt, and pepper; bring to a boil over high heat. Add the couscous, raisins, and currants. Cover and remove from the heat. Let stand for 8 to 10 minutes, or until the couscous has absorbed all the liquid.

Uncover and fluff the couscous mixture with a fork. Add the parsley, chives, lemon juice, and nutmeg, stirring well to combine. Taste and season with additional salt and pepper, if needed. Spoon the filling evenly into each zucchini shell and arrange on the prepared baking sheet. Bake for 25 to 30 minutes, or until the tops are lightly browned and the shells are tender when pierced with the tip of a sharp knife. Serve warm or at room temperature.

Advance Preparation A great buffet dish, the baked zucchini can sit for up to two hours at room temperature. They can also be stored, covered, in the refrigerator overnight. Bring to room temperature, or reheat, covered, in a low oven.

PER SERVING

Calories 290 · Protein 11g · Total Fat 9g · Saturated Fat 1g · Cholesterol 0mg · Carbohydrate 45g · Dietary Fiber 8g · Sodium 154mg

Breads

Mediterranean Breads, Pizza, Focaccia, Savory Pies, and Sandwiches

Of all the foods of the world, bread is surely the most basic. Of all the regions of the world, the Mediterranean holds the biggest breadbasket. It is here, many believe, where the miracle of mixing yeast and grain with warm salty water was first discovered. It is here, undoubtedly, where bread has been sustaining life since the beginning of recorded history, at the very least.

To this day, many housewives in rural areas still rise early to set the dough for their families' daily bread, then either bake the risen loaves at home or send them along to the "neighborhood oven." In village squares, dazzling arrays of freshly baked breads in various shapes and sizes are sold or bartered in open-air markets. On the streets, bread can often be bought or bartered from women storing loaves in cloth-covered baskets. In the cities, loaves of knotted, twisted, and braided specialties are advertised in bakery windows. Walk in, and savory pies tantalize from behind glass counters. Sandwiches are made on demand. Well outside of Naples or Nice, pizzerias abound. In its sheer abundance and in countless forms, bread can be gotten on the cheap from Beirut to Barcelona. Yet not to be wasted are the day-old scraps and pieces, thrown into soups, tossed into salads, or ground into crumbs. Not for sale are the starter doughs, lovingly nurtured like babies, some purportedly for as long as one hundred years. Not advertised are the bread maker's secrets, quietly passed on to the next generation, which steadfastly guards them for the next. Indeed, the Mediterranean peoples take their bread seriously.

Given such dedication, it's not surprising that bread making throughout the Mediterranean has evolved into an art form, one in which instinct and creativity combined with lots of hands-on practice are more important than cookbook knowledge or technique. But given that most of us are not natural-born bread makers with the experience of the ages behind us, the handful of recipes in this chapter requiring a yeasted dough made from scratch are as detailed, I think, as I could make them. While some offer both food processor and hand methods of kneading, you will find no bread machine adaptations here. With the busy cook in mind, however, one bread requires no kneading or rising time, and several of the pizza and focaccia recipes use either store-bought dough or quick-rising yeast. The recipes in the remaining sections, Savory Pies and Sandwiches, make use of commercially prepared doughs and ready-made breads. Indeed, many of the recipes in these categories could easily have been included in other chapters, but I thought they were most appropriately located here, as savory pies such as spanakopita and sandwiches such as panini are most often associated with breads.

One final suggestion about bread making, especially if you're new to it: Don't be afraid of it. Just do it. Even the pita, perhaps the trickiest of the bunch, is fun to make and will still be delicious if your loaves don't quite split into perfect pockets the first time. Of all the foods of the world, bread is surely the most forgiving.

Mediterranean Breads

Black Olive Bread

Olive bread in various forms can be found throughout the Mediterranean. This is a very basic recipe, made simply with unbleached white flour and my favorite black olive, the plump and juicy Greek kalamata. If you use the wrinkled, oil-cured Moroccan-style black olives, decrease the total amount of flour used for the dough by about ½ cup, then gradually add more, as needed.

MAKES 2 ROUND LOAVES, 12 SLICES EACH

FOR THE SPONGE:

1½ cups warm water (105–115F; 40–45C)
1 teaspoon active dry yeast
1½ cups unbleached all-purpose flour

FOR THE DOUGH:

1½ cups warm water (105–115F; 40–45C)
4 tablespoons extra-virgin olive oil
1 teaspoon salt
4¾ cups unbleached all-purpose flour, plus additional if necessary
¾ cup kalamata or other high-quality black olives, pitted and cut into bits (do not chop)

To make the sponge: Place the warm water in a large mixing bowl. Add the yeast, stirring until dissolved. With a wooden spoon, stir in the flour until well combined (a few lumps are okay). Cover with a damp kitchen towel and set aside to rise for 3 to 4 hours at a temperature of about 70F (20C).

To make the dough: Add warm water, 3 tablespoons of the oil, and the salt to the sponge, stirring well with a wooden spoon to combine. Add 2 cups of the flour, stirring well to combine. Gradually add 2 cups more of the flour, stirring well with the wooden spoon, then mixing with your hands. Spread the remaining ¾ cup of flour on a flat work surface. Turn out the dough and knead for about 15 minutes, incorporating all the flour on the work surface, or until a smooth and elastic dough is formed. If the mixture feels too sticky, knead in additional flour, 1 tablespoon at a time, until satiny.

Clean the mixing bowl and grease the bottom and sides with the remaining 1 tablespoon oil. Place the dough in the bowl, turning to coat with the oil. Cover the bowl with a damp kitchen towel and set aside to rise until doubled in bulk, about 2 hours at a temperature of about 70F (20C).

Turn the risen dough out onto a lightly floured work surface. Punch the dough down and knead gently to get rid of any air bubbles, about 1 minute. Spread the dough out and scatter the surface evenly with the olives. Gather the dough up into a ball and knead briefly to incorporate the olives evenly throughout. Divide the dough in half and form each half into a round loaf. Cover lightly with a damp kitchen towel and set aside for about 30 minutes to rise briefly.

Preheat the oven to 425F (220F). Place the loaves on an ungreased baking sheet and bake for 30 to 35 minutes, or until the crust is golden brown and the bread feels hollow when gently rapped.

Cool on a rack for at least 2 hours before slicing. Cut each loaf into 12 slices. The bread can be cooled completely, placed in freezer storage bags, and frozen up to 1 month.

PER SLICE

Calories 160 · Protein 3g · Total Fat 5g · Saturated Fat 0g · Cholesterol 0mg · Carbohydrate 25g · Dietary Fiber 1g · Sodium 207mg

Variation Substitute all or half of the olives with bits of well-drained oil-packed sun-dried tomatoes, which have been blotted between paper towels.

Whole-Wheat Pita Bread

This homemade pita bread is so different from the commercially packaged variety that you may wonder if the two are related, save for that mysterious pocket. But the mystery of forming pockets in Arab flatbread, also known as "pocket bread," is really no mystery at all once you get the hang of it. The pocket is literally the air that is trapped inside the loaves as the dough rises in the oven. The key is to allow this pocket to form by not creating tears in the balls of dough when you're stretching and rolling them; otherwise, this air will slowly escape, the loaves won't properly puff, and the pocket will be partially closed. To troubleshoot for tears, I find that using a heavy marble rolling pin and pushing the dough out with one's palms, instead of stretching with one's fingers, works best. But even if some of your baked pita needs a little help from a knife to separate into those pockets, a taste test between the "haves" and the "have-nots" will prove it really doesn't matter anyway!

MAKES ABOUT 8 (8-INCH) LOAVES

FOR THE SPONGE:

- 1¼ cups warm water (105–115F; 40–45C)
- 1 teaspoon active dry yeast
- 1½ cups whole-wheat flour

FOR THE DOUGH:

- 1¼ cups warm water (105–115F; 40–45C)
- 1 teaspoon salt
- 4½ cups unbleached all-purpose flour, plus additional, if necessary
- 1 teaspoon extra-virgin olive oil

To make the sponge: Place the warm water in a large mixing bowl. Add the yeast, stirring until dissolved. With a wooden spoon, stir in the flour until well combined (a few lumps are okay). Cover with a damp kitchen towel and set aside to rise for about 4 hours at a temperature of about 70F (20C).

To make the dough: Add the warm water and the salt to the sponge, stirring well with a wooden spoon to combine. Add 2 cups of the flour, stirring well to combine. Gradually add 1 cup more of the flour, stirring well with the wooden spoon, then mixing with your hands if mixture becomes too resistant. Spread half of the remaining flour on a flat work surface. Turn the yeast mixture out onto the work surface and sprinkle with the remaining flour. Knead for about 15 minutes, until all the flour has been incorporated and a smooth and elastic dough is formed. If mixture feels too sticky, knead in additional flour, 1 tablespoon at a time, until satiny.

Clean the mixing bowl and grease the bottom and sides with the oil. Place the dough in the bowl, turning to coat with the oil. Cover the bowl with a damp kitchen towel and set aside to rise until doubled in bulk, about 2 hours at a temperature of about 70F (20C).

Turn the risen dough out onto a lightly floured work surface. Punch the dough down and knead slightly to get rid of any air pockets. Form the dough into a long cylinder.

Using a sharp knife, slice the dough into 8 equal pieces. Form each piece into a ball (this is important). With your palms and a heavy rolling pin, roll and stretch each ball into a circle 7 to 8 inches in diameter. Set aside for about 20 minutes.

Meanwhile, preheat the oven to 425F (220C). Lightly oil 2 large baking sheets without sides. (If your sheets can't accommodate all the circles, bake in two stages.) Place the dough circles on the prepared sheets and bake for 7 to 10 minutes, or until the breads are puffed and very lightly browned. Remove from the oven and immediately place the breads on a kitchen towel, then cover with another. Let rest for 5 minutes. With your palms, press lightly on the towel to flatten the breads. Remove from the towels and transfer to a rack to cool. Serve within twelve hours for best results. The cooled bread can be placed in a freezer bag and frozen for up to one month.

PER LOAF

Calories 339 · Protein 11g · Total Fat 2g · Saturated Fat 0g · Cholesterol 0mg · Carbohydrate 70g · Dietary Fiber 5g · Sodium 269mg

Quick Sun-Dried Tomato Bread

Sourdough starters are nurtured like children—some for years—on the Mediterranean. If you don't tell, no one will ever know that the American trick to turning out in a mere forty-five minutes this delicious sourdoughlike bread, redolent of marinated sun-dried tomatoes, is a can of cold beer and some baking powder.

MAKES 1 LOAF; 12 SLICES

- **3 cups all-purpose flour, preferably unbleached**
- **3 tablespoons sugar**
- **1 tablespoon plus ¾ teaspoon baking powder**
- **1 (12-ounce) can cold beer**
- **¼ cup well-drained marinated sun-dried tomatoes, finely chopped, plus 2 tablespoons oil reserved from the tomatoes.**

Preheat the oven to 350F (175C). Lightly oil a 9 × 5-inch 5 loaf pan and set aside.

In a large mixing bowl, combine the flour, sugar, and baking powder. With a large spoon, stir in the beer and tomatoes; mix until thoroughly blended. Transfer the dough to the prepared pan. Bake for 30 minutes.

Remove the bread from the oven. Using a thin sharp-tipped knife, make several deep incisions to within 1 inch from the bottom of the bread. Slowly brush the reserved marinade oil evenly over the top of the bread. Return the pan to the oven and bake for 10 minutes, or until the top is nicely browned.

Let the bread stand in the pan for 10 minutes before removing from the pan. Serve warm or at room temperature, preferably within twelve hours of baking for best results. The cooled bread can be placed in a freezer bag and frozen for up to one month.

PER SLICE

Calories 163 · Protein 3g · Total Fat 3g · Saturated Fat 0g · Cholesterol 0mg · Carbohydrate 29g · Dietary Fiber lg · Sodium 122mg

Pizza and Focaccia

Basic Pizza Dough

This pizza dough can be mixed by hand or in a food processor.

MAKES 1 (14-INCH) PIZZA

- ¾ cup warm water (105–115F; 40–45C)
- ½ teaspoon sugar
- 1 package (about 1 tablespoon) active dry yeast
- 3 teaspoons extra-virgin olive oil
- 2 to 2¼ cups unbleached all-purpose flour
- ½ teaspoon salt

In a small bowl, combine the water and sugar. Sprinkle the yeast over the water and stir until the yeast is completely dissolved. When the mixture is foamy, whisk in 2 teaspoons of the oil and set aside.

To mix by hand: Place 1¼ cups flour and the salt in a large mixing bowl. Add the yeast mixture and stir with a large wooden spoon to thoroughly blend. Gradually add an additional ¾ cup of flour, stirring initially with the wooden spoon, then mixing with your hands. When the mixture pulls cleanly away from the sides of the bowl, turn out onto a lightly floured work surface. Knead the dough until smooth and elastic, about 8 minutes, adding the remaining flour as needed if the mixture feels too wet. Shape the dough into a ball.

To mix in a food processor: Place 2 cups of the flour and the salt in a food processor fitted with the metal blade. Process for 10 seconds to combine. With the machine running, slowly add the yeast mixture. Process until the dough begins to form a sticky mass, about 30 seconds. If the mixture feels too wet, gradually add the remaining flour as needed. Transfer the dough to a lightly floured work surface and knead until smooth and elastic, about 2 minutes. Shape the dough into a ball.

To finish the dough: Lightly grease the bottom and sides of a deep mixing bowl with the remaining teaspoon of oil. Place the dough in the oiled bowl, turning to coat with the oil. Cover with plastic wrap, then drape with a kitchen towel. Set aside in a draft-free warm area (about 70F, 20C) until doubled in bulk, 1 to 1½ hours. Turn the dough out onto a lightly floured work surface and knead briefly to remove any air pockets. Shape the dough into a ball. Cover with a kitchen towel and let rest for about 15 minutes before shaping and rolling as directed in the recipe.

PER ¼ OF DOUGH

Calories 282 · Protein 8g · Total Fat 4g · Saturated Fat 1g · Cholesterol 0mg · Carbohydrate 52g · Dietary Fiber 3g · Sodium 269mg

Quick Classic Pizza alla Marinara

When pizza came to America it put on a few pounds, mostly in the form of gooey four-cheese toppings and greasy, meat-lovers specials. In fact, traditional Neopolitan pizza, according to the True Neapolitan Pizza Association, is made with one of two classic sauces, marinara or Margherita. Marinara is nothing more than a simple sauce of tomatoes, olive oil, garlic, oregano, salt, and pepper, while the latter is essentially a marinara, minus the garlic and oregano, topped with a few slices of fresh mozzarella and whole basil leaves. This recipe for pizza alla marinara uses fresh store-bought pizza dough so that you can enjoy the simple, uncomplicated, real thing from Naples in less than one hour. If you'd rather make the dough from scratch, see the recipe on page 184.

MAKES 4 SERVINGS

Cornmeal for dusting (optional)
1 pound fresh or frozen pizza dough, thawed according to package directions if frozen
Flour for dusting
1½ tablespoons extra-virgin olive oil
¾ cup Classic Pizza Sauce (page 186)
4 to 6 large cloves garlic, slivered
About ½ teaspoon dried oregano
Salt, preferably the coarse variety, and freshly ground black pepper, to taste

Preheat the oven to 500F (260C). Set a rack on the lowest position. Sprinkle a 12- to 14-inch pizza pan with cornmeal, if desired, or lightly oil; set aside.

Turn the dough out onto a lightly floured work surface. Roll and stretch into a 12- to 14-inch circle. Transfer the dough to the prepared pan. Brush the dough with ½ tablespoon of the oil. Spread the pizza sauce evenly to within ½ inch of the edge of the crust. Distribute the garlic slivers evenly over the sauce. Sprinkle with the oregano, salt, and pepper. Drizzle the remaining oil evenly over the top.

Bake the pizza for 12 to 15 minutes, or until the bottom is crisp and the edges are browned. Cut into wedges and serve at once.

PER SERVING

Calories 365 · Protein 9g · Total Fat 12g · Saturated Fat 2g · Cholesterol 0mg · Carbohydrate 57g · Dietary Fiber 2g · Sodium 151mg

Classic Pizza Sauce

Though similar to the Light Tomato Sauce (page 196) without the herbs and onions, this sauce is cooked at a higher heat for a shorter period and should be much thicker after it is pureed. If not, be sure to reduce it to the recommended amount; a runny sauce might make the pizza crust a bit soggy.

MAKES ABOUT 1½ CUPS

- 2 tablespoon extra-virgin olive oil
- 3 cloves garlic, finely chopped
- 3 pounds tomatoes, cored and cut into ½-inch pieces, all the juices included, or 1 (28-ounce can) and 1 (14-ounce) can whole tomatoes, coarsely chopped, juices included ½ teaspoon salt, or to taste
- ½ teaspoon salt, or to taste
- ½ teaspoon sugar
- Freshly ground black pepper, to taste

In a large nonstick skillet, heat the oil over medium heat. Add the garlic and cook, stirring, for 30 seconds. Add the tomatoes and their juices, salt, sugar, and pepper. Bring to a simmer over high heat. Reduce the heat to medium and cook, uncovered, for 20 to 30 minutes, stirring occasionally, or until the tomatoes have reduced to a thick pulp.

Pass the sauce through the medium blade of a food mill. If there is much more than 1½ cups of pureed sauce, or if the mixture seems too watery, return it to the skillet.

Cook over medium heat, stirring constantly to avoid scorching, until the sauce is the desired consistency.

Advance Preparation The pizza sauce can be stored, covered, in the refrigerator for up to three days.

PER ABOUT ¼ CUP

Calories 97 · Protein 2g · Total Fat 5g · Saturated Fat 1g · Cholesterol 0mg · Carbohydrate 14g · Dietary Fiber 2g · Sodium 196mg

Cook's Tips

The amount of time it takes to cook tomatoes to the pulpy stage is largely dependent upon how ripe they are. If the mixture is still watery after 30 minutes, increase the heat to medium-high and cook, stirring constantly to avoid scorching, until the proper consistency is achieved, then puree.

A food mill is highly recommended over a food processor or blender for pureeing the cooked tomato mixture, because the latter tend to grind up the seeds, creating a bitter sauce. If you don't have a food mill, pulse the mixture in a food processor fitted with the plastic blade a few times, then push it through a coarse sieve.

Quick Tuscan-Style Pizza with White Beans, Tomatoes, and Basil

The following recipe uses store-bought pizza dough to deliver this Tuscan specialty in less than forty-five minutes. With meltingly tender beans smeared even on their pizza, it's no wonder that other Italians often refer to their fellow countrymen as *mangiafagioli* or "bean-eaters." Prebaking the pizza shell guards against a soggy top of the crust.

MAKES 4 SERVINGS

- Cornmeal for dusting (optional)
- 3 tablespoons extra-virgin olive oil
- 2 large cloves garlic, finely chopped
- 1½ cups cooked cannellini beans (see Box, page 18) or 1 (15-ounce) can cannellini or other white beans, drained and rinsed
- 6 tablespoons vegetable broth, preferably Basic Vegetable Broth (page 38) or low-sodium canned
- Salt and freshly ground black pepper, to taste
- ¼ cup finely chopped fresh basil
- Flour for dusting
- 1 pound fresh or frozen pizza dough, thawed according to the package directions if frozen
- 6 ounces ripe plum tomatoes (about 3), cut into ¼-inch-thick slices

Preheat the oven to 450F (230C). Sprinkle a 12- to 14-inch pizza pan with cornmeal, if desired, or lightly oil; set aside.

In a small saucepan, heat 1½ tablespoons of the oil over medium-low heat. Add the garlic and cook, stirring, for 2 minutes. Add the beans, broth, salt, and pepper. Bring to a simmer over medium-high heat. Reduce the heat to medium-low and cook, uncovered, stirring occasionally, until the mixture is thickened and very creamy, about 10 minutes. Stir in half of the basil and set aside.

Turn the dough out onto a lightly floured work surface. Roll and stretch into a 12- to 14-inch circle. Transfer the dough to the prepared pan. Prick the dough lightly all over with the prongs of a wet fork. Brush the dough with ½ tablespoon of the remaining oil. Bake on the middle rack for 4 minutes. Prick the dough all over with the prongs of a dry fork. Bake for 4 minutes.

Remove the pan from the oven. Set a rack on the lowest position. Spread the bean mixture evenly to within ½ inch of the edge of the crust. Distribute the tomato slices evenly over the bean mixture, then sprinkle lightly with additional salt and pepper. Drizzle the remaining oil evenly over top.

Bake for 10 to 15 minutes longer, or until the bottom of the crust is crisp and the edges are browned. Sprinkle with the remaining basil. Cut into wedges and serve at once.

PER SERVING

Calories 447 · Protein 15g · Total Fat 13g · Saturated Fat 2g · Cholesterol 0mg · Carbohydrate 67g · Dietary Fiber 7g · Sodium 60mg

Pizza with Caramelized Onion, Kalamata Olives, and Tomatoes

Topped with tender golden onions, juicy kalamata olives, and ripe plum tomatoes, pizza never tasted—or smelled—any better. Use this as a model for any of your favorite pizza toppings.

MAKES 4 SERVINGS

1 recipe Basic Pizza Dough (page 184)
Cornmeal for dusting (optional)
1 tablespoon plus 2 teaspoons extra-virgin olive oil
1 pound onions, halved lengthwise, then thinly sliced crosswise
½ teaspoon dried rosemary leaves
½ teaspoon sugar
Salt, preferably the coarse variety, and pepper, to taste
8 ounces plum tomatoes (about 4), sliced into ¼-inch-thick rounds
12 to 16 pitted kalamata olives, halved lengthwise

Prepare the basic pizza dough as directed.

Preheat the oven to 500F (260C) with the oven rack set at the lowest position. Sprinkle a 12- to 14-inch pizza pan with cornmeal if desired or lightly oil; set aside.

In a large nonstick skillet, heat the 1 tablespoon oil over medium-low heat. Add the onions, rosemary, and sugar; cook, uncovered, stirring occasionally, until the onions are very tender and light golden, 25 to 30 minutes. Season with salt and pepper. Set aside.

Place the ball of the pizza dough on a lightly floured work surface. With your palms, flatten into a thick circle. Using a rolling pin and your fingers, gently roll and stretch into a 14-inch circle, adding more flour to the work surface as necessary to prevent sticking. Transfer the dough to the prepared pan.

Distribute the onion mixture evenly to within ½ inch of the edge of the dough. Arrange the tomatoes in a circular pattern over the onion mixture. Place the olives, cut side down, evenly on top. Season with salt and pepper, then drizzle with the remaining oil.

Bake for 12 to 15 minutes, or until the edges are golden brown and the bottom of the crust is crisp. Cut into wedges and serve at once.

PER SERVINGS

Calories 415 · Protein 9g · Total Fat 13g · Saturated Fat 1g · Cholesterol 0mg · Carbohydrate 65g · Dietary Fiber 5g · Sodium 456mg

Quick Catalan-Style Pizza with Peppers, Tomatoes, and Onion

Inspired by the small, thin-crusted pizzas known as cocas, made in Spanish Catalonia, these quick-cooking individual pizzas are conveniently made with store-bought dough. Cocas almost always feature fresh vegetables and rarely contain cheese. While tomatoes, bell peppers, and onions are a classic Catalan combination, you can vary the vegetables according to taste, so long as they're fresh. If making six pizzas, use the greater amount of vegetables listed in the recipe.

MAKES 4 TO 6 INDIVIDUAL PIZZAS

- 6 or 8 ounces plum tomatoes (3 or 4), seeded and chopped
- 6 or 8 ounces onion (about 1 medium or 1 large), finely chopped
- 4 or 6 ounces red bell pepper (1 small or 1 medium), finely chopped
- 1 jalapeño chile pepper, seeded and finely chopped
- 1 tablespoon finely chopped fresh flat-leaf parsley
- 1 tablespoon finely chopped fresh cilantro (optional)
- Pinch regular salt
- 2 (1-pound) packages fresh or frozen pizza dough, thawed according to package directions if frozen
- Cornmeal for dusting
- 3 tablespoons extra-virgin olive oil
- 4 cloves garlic, finely chopped
- 1 teaspoon sweet paprika
- ½ teaspoon sugar
- Freshly ground black pepper, to taste
- Dried oregano, to taste
- Coarse salt, to taste

Preheat the oven to 400F (205C). Lightly oil 2 large baking sheets and set aside. In a medium bowl, combine the tomatoes, onion, bell pepper, jalapeño chile, parsley, cilantro (if using), and salt. Set aside while you prepare the dough.

Turn each dough out onto a large work surface lightly dusted with cornmeal. Divide each dough into 2 or 3 equal balls. Roll each ball out to an oval about ¼-inch thickness. Arrange the pizza ovals on the prepared baking sheets. Brush the ovals evenly with 1 tablespoon of the oil.

Drain the vegetables briefly in a colander, and return to the bowl. Add the remaining oil, garlic, paprika, sugar, and pepper; toss well to combine. Divide the vegetable mixture evenly among the crusts, leaving a ¼-inch border. Sprinkle with oregano and coarse salt.

Bake in the middle of the oven for 5 minutes. Reduce the heat to 300F (150C) and bake for 20 to 25 minutes, or until the vegetables are tender and the crust is golden. Serve at once.

PER SERVING

Calories 632 · Protein 16g · Total Fat 16g · Saturated Fat 2g · Cholesterol 0mg · Carbohydrate 106g · Dietary Fiber 3g · Sodium 14mg

Quick-Rise Focaccia Dough

Ready to be topped in just about thirty minutes, it uses quick-acting yeast and a warm oven in which to rise. MAKES 1 (12 × 7-INCH) LOAF

- 2¼ to 2½ cups all-purpose unbleached flour
- 1 package (about 1 tablespoon) quick-acting/rapid-rise yeast
- ½ teaspoon salt
- 1 cup very warm water (120–130F; 50–55C)
- 1 tablespoon extra-virgin olive oil

Preheat the oven to 200F (95C). Lightly grease a 12 × 7-inch or 12 × 8-inch shallow baking dish and set aside.

In a large bowl, combine 1½ cups of the flour, yeast, and salt. Stir in the warm water and oil. Gradually stir in ½ cup of the remaining flour. Turn the yeast mixture out onto a lightly floured work surface and knead for about 10 minutes, incorporating the additional flour as needed, or until a smooth and elastic dough is formed. Shape the dough into a ball. Cover with a kitchen towel and let rest for 10 minutes.

Transfer the dough to the prepared baking dish; press and stretch evenly along the bottom. Set the baking dish on a large baking sheet. Dampen the kitchen towel and drape over the baking dish. Place in the preheated oven and immediately turn off the heat. Let set for 20 minutes, or until the dough has risen to about twice its height. Remove from the oven.

Remove the kitchen towel and the baking sheet. The dough is ready to be topped and baked as directed in the recipe.

PER ¼ OF DOUGH

Calories 305; · Protein 8g; · Total Fat 4g · Saturated Fat 1g · Cholesterol 0mg · Carbohydrate 57g · Dietary Fiber 3g · Sodium 269mg

Provençal-Style French Bread Pizza with Caramelized Onion, Broccoli, and Niçoise Olives

I created this quick recipe when I realized too late that the pizza dough I'd intended to use was still in the freezer, but a long arm of baguette stretched across the top of my refrigerator. I don't know how "French" French bread pizza really is, but no matter: the things that make this dish Provençal are the caramelized onions, olives, and herbs. The broccoli adds color as well as vitamin C, calcium, and iron. The pizza smells great as it bakes and tastes even better.

MAKES 4 SERVINGS

- 2 tablespoons extra-virgin olive oil
- ¾ pound onions, halved lengthwise, then thinly sliced crosswise
- ½ teaspoon herbes de Provence or dried rosemary
- Pinch sugar
- Salt, preferably the coarse variety, and freshly ground black pepper, to taste
- 2 cups bite-size pieces fresh or frozen broccoli florets
- 1 (about 24-inch-long) fresh French baguette, cut in half crosswise
- 1 clove garlic, halved
- ¼ cup Niçoise or kalamata olives, pitted

In a large nonstick skillet, heat 1 tablespoon of the oil over medium-low heat. Add the onions, herbes de Provence, and sugar; cook, uncovered, stirring occasionally, until the onions are very soft and light golden, 25 to 30 minutes. Season with salt and pepper. Set aside.

While the onions are cooking, preheat the oven to 350F (175C). In a medium stockpot or saucepan large enough to accommodate a 9-inch steaming basket, put 1 inch of water. Place the steaming basket in the pot and add the broccoli. Bring to a boil over high heat. Cover tightly, reduce the heat to medium, and steam until the broccoli is softened but still firm, 3 to 5 minutes. Carefully remove the steamer from the pan and set aside to cool.

Slice each baguette half lengthwise in half, not cutting all the way through. Open each half out carefully, leaving the "hinge" intact (this helps them keep their balance on the baking sheet). Rub each cut side with the flat sides of the halved garlic. Arrange the opened bread halves, crust side down, on an ungreased baking sheet. Spoon the onion mixture evenly over the tops, leaving the hinged area free. Arrange the broccoli and olives evenly on the onions, then drizzle evenly with the remaining oil.

Bake for 10 minutes, or until the bread is toasted and the onion is beginning to brown and caramelize. Cut each half through the hinge, and serve at once.

Advance Preparation The onions can be cooked and held at room temperature for up to one hour before assembling and baking the pizza.

PER SERVING

Calories 338 · Protein 8g · Total Fat 13g · Saturated Fat 1g · Cholesterol 0mg · Carbohydrate 47g · Dietary Fiber 5g · Sodium 676mg

Variation Omit the halved garlic, replace the broccoli with 2 or 3 thinly sliced plum tomatoes, and spread one recipe of Pistou Sauce (for pizza, page 61) evenly over the bread (about 2 tablespoons per piece) before topping with the onions and remaining ingredients. Bake as directed in the recipe, and serve garnished with a few shredded fresh basil leaves, if desired.

Classic Focaccia with Rosemary, Olive Oil, and Coarse Salt

This is perhaps the most basic of focaccia recipes, delicious in its simplicity. Served with vegetable soup or a green salad, it becomes a satisfying main course for four. Cut into eighths, it becomes a lovely appetizer. Use it as a model for any of your favorite focaccia or pizza toppings.

MAKES 4 MAIN-COURSE OR 8 APPETIZER SERVINGS

- 1 recipe Quick-Rise Focaccia Dough (page 189)
- 2 tablespoons extra-virgin olive oil
- 1 tablespoon dried rosemary leaves, or more to taste
- 1 teaspoon coarse salt, or to taste

Prepare the quick-rise focaccia dough as directed. Preheat the oven to 400F (205C).

With two wet fingertips, make several indentations across the top of the dough at regular intervals. Brush the dough evenly with the oil, then sprinkle with the rosemary and sea salt.

Bake for 20 to 25 minutes, or until lightly golden. Cut into wedges and serve warm or at room temperature, preferably within a few hours of baking for the best results. The cooled focaccia can be wrapped in plastic wrap, then foil, and frozen for up to one month.

PER MAIN-COURSE SERVING

Calories 368 · Protein 8g · Total Fat 11g · Saturated Fat 2g · Cholesterol 0mg · Carbohydrate 58g · Dietary Fiber 3g · Sodium 739mg

Quick Focaccia with Artichokes and Sun-Dried Tomatoes

This recipe uses commercially prepared frozen bread dough so that you can enjoy homemade focaccia in just about one hour, but you must remember to thaw the dough, then set it in the refrigerator overnight to rise. Use the following as a model for any number and combination of toppings.

MAKES 4 TO 6 MAIN-COURSE OR 8 APPETIZER SERVINGS

- 1 (1-pound) frozen packaged bread dough, thawed at room temperature according to package directions, set in the refrigerator to double in bulk overnight or up to 24 hours
- 2 ounces (about ¼ cup packed) oil-packed sun-dried tomatoes, drained, cut in half, 1 tablespoon oil reserved
- 1 tablespoon extra-virgin olive oil
- 2 cloves garlic, finely chopped
- 4 ounces marinated artichoke hearts, drained (about ½ packed cup), thinly sliced lengthwise
- Dried oregano, to taste
- Salt, preferably the coarse variety, and freshly ground black pepper, to taste

Preheat the oven to 200F (95C). Lightly oil a shallow 12 × 8-inch baking dish.

Transfer the risen refrigerated dough to the prepared dish; press and stretch evenly along the bottom. Set the baking dish on a large baking sheet. Dampen a kitchen towel and drape over the baking dish. Place in the preheated oven and immediately turn off the heat. Let set for 20 minutes. Uncover and let set for an additional 5 minutes. Remove from the oven. Turn the oven setting to 425F (220C).

Remove the kitchen towel and baking sheet. With two wet fingertips, make several indentations across the top of the dough at regular intervals. In a small bowl, combine the reserved marinade oil with the extra-virgin olive oil. Brush evenly over the dough. Distribute the garlic evenly over the dough, then arrange the artichokes evenly on top. Season with oregano, salt, and pepper.

Bake on the middle rack for 12 minutes. Remove from the oven and reduce the oven temperature to 300F (150C). Place the rack on its lowest setting. Working quickly, place the dried tomatoes among the artichokes. Immediately return to the oven and bake for about 15 minutes, or until the crust is golden. Let cool slightly before cutting into squares, and serving warm or at room temperature, preferably within 12 hours of baking for best results. The cooled focaccia can be wrapped in plastic wrap, then foil, and frozen for up to 1 month.

PER MAIN-COURSE SERVING

Calories 390 · Protein 11g · Total Fat 12g · Saturated Fat 2g · Cholesterol 0mg · Carbohydrate 60g · Dietary Fiber 4g · Sodium 649mg

Savory Pies

Greek Lenten Spinach Pie

Spanakopita, the famous Greek spinach savory pie, is almost always made with eggs and cheeses, but not in religious Greek Orthodox homes during the Lenten fast, when consumption of any animal product is forbidden. The use of commercial phyllo dough renders this Lenten variation remarkably easy to assemble and pop in the oven anytime of the year.

MAKES 6 SERVINGS

- 2 pounds spinach with stems, stems discarded, washed, or 2 (10-ounce) bags fresh ready-washed spinach leaves
- 4 tablespoons plus ½ teaspoon extra-virgin olive oil
- 1 medium onion (6 to 8 ounces), chopped
- 2 large cloves garlic, finely chopped
- ¼ teaspoon crushed fennel seeds
- Salt and freshly ground black pepper, to taste
- 2 tablespoons finely chopped fresh flat-leaf parsley
- 2 tablespoons finely chopped fresh dill
- 1 tablespoon all-purpose flour, preferably unbleached
- ½ teaspoon sugar
- ⅛ teaspoon freshly grated nutmeg
- 12 sheets phyllo dough, thawed according to package directions

Bring a large stockpot filled with salted water to a boil over high heat. Working in two batches, add the spinach and blanch for 2 to 3 minutes, or until just wilted. Using tongs or a large slotted spoon, transfer to a colander.

Rinse under cold running water and drain. With your hands, squeeze out as much liquid as possible. Transfer to a cutting board and coarsely chop. Set aside.

In a large skillet, preferably nonstick, heat 2 tablespoons of the oil over medium-low heat. Add the onion and garlic and cook, stirring occasionally, until softened, about 10 minutes. Add the chopped spinach and fennel and season lightly with salt and pepper. Increase the heat to medium and cook, stirring frequently, until the moisture released from the spinach has evaporated, 7 to 10 minutes. Add the parsley, dill, flour, sugar, and nutmeg. Cook, stirring constantly, for 2 minutes. Season with additional salt and pepper as necessary. Set aside to cool.

Preheat the oven to 375F (190C). Lightly grease the bottom and sides of a 10-inch round cake pan or straight-sided tart pan. Working quickly, arrange a sheet of phyllo dough in the pan, pressing lightly against the bottom and sides, leaving the excess dough to drape over the sides. (As you work, keep remaining phyllo sheets covered with a damp kitchen towel to retain their moisture.) Except for the overhanging dough, brush the dough evenly with ½ teaspoon of the remaining oil. Layer, then oil, 5 more sheets in this manner, placing each sheet slightly crosswise to the one below.

After the sixth layer is in place, spoon the cooled spinach mixture into the pie, spreading with the back of the spoon to make a smooth surface. Repeat the layering process with the remaining 6 sheets of phyllo. When the final layer is in place and has been oiled, trim off the excess pastry with kitchen shears or scissors, leaving about 1½ inches of pastry extending beyond the rim of the pan. Brush the excess edge of the pastry with water, then roll inwards to form a border around the rim of the pie. Brush the border with the remaining ½ teaspoon of oil. Bake for 35 to 40 minutes, or until the top of the pie is golden and crisp. Serve warm.

Advance Preparation The filling can be stored, covered, in the refrigerator for up to twenty-four hours before assembling the pie. The assembled pie can be covered well with plastic wrap and refrigerated for several hours, or overnight, before baking. The baked pie can be held for one hour at room temperature, but is best eaten soon after baking when the crust is still quite crisp. To restore some of the crispiness, reheat in a low oven just before serving. Refrigerated leftovers will still taste good when reheated, but the bottom crust will remain on the soggy side.

PER SERVING

Calories 238 · Protein 6g · Total Fat 12g · Saturated Fat 2g · Cholesterol 0mg · Carbohydrate 28g · Dietary Fiber 3g · Sodium 261mg

Variation

Lenten Hortópitta

Substitute one-third of the spinach with escarole, curly endive, kale, dandelion greens, or any other bitter greens.

Polenta Pie with Wild Mushroom Filling

Appearing with increasing frequency on upscale restaurant menus these days, polenta is nothing more than a savory cornmeal porridge dating back to ancient Roman times. Those days, of course, it was made not from corn but typically from farro, an ancient strain of soft wheat, and was strictly plebian fare. Thanks to the introduction of corn from the Americas, coarse-ground cornmeal found its way into the polenta of northern Italians, who quickly took a shining to the golden grain. Although rather bland on its own, polenta is the perfect foil for many spicy or rich sauces and stews. Filled with a warm and fragrant wild mushroom ragout, this pie is an especially welcome respite on a cold winter's night. It's also a great make-ahead company dish that can be assembled up to a day before baking.

MAKES 6 TO 8 SERVINGS

½ ounce dried porcini mushrooms, soaked in 1 cup hot water for 20 minutes
3 tablespoons plus 1 teaspoon extra-virgin olive oil
1 small red onion (about 4 ounces), finely chopped
4 large cloves garlic, finely chopped
1 pound white button mushrooms, thinly sliced
½ cup dry red wine
1½ tablespoons tomato paste
½ teaspoon dried rosemary
Salt and freshly ground black pepper, to taste
3 cups water
3 cups vegetable broth, preferably Basic Vegetable Broth (page 38) or low-sodium canned

2 cups polenta (coarse-ground yellow cornmeal), regular or instant variety
2 cups Light Tomato Sauce (page 196) or your favorite pasta sauce, heated
8 small sprigs fresh rosemary or fresh flat-leaf parsley (optional)

Drain the mushrooms in a strainer, reserving the soaking liquid. Rinse the mushrooms thoroughly with cold water, then drain. Coarsely chop and set aside. Line the strainer with a coffee filter or paper towel and strain the soaking liquid; set aside.

In a large nonstick skillet, heat 1 tablespoon of the oil over medium-low heat. Cook the onion until slightly softened, stirring, about 3 minutes. Add half the garlic and increase the heat to medium. Cook, stirring, for 1 minute. Add the button mushrooms and cook, stirring, for 2 minutes, or until the mushrooms begin to give off their own liquid. Add the porcini mushrooms, their strained soaking liquid, wine, tomato paste, rosemary, salt, and pepper. Bring to a boil over medium-high heat. Reduce the heat to medium and cook, uncovered, stirring occasionally, until the liquids are almost completely reduced, about 20 minutes. Set aside.

Preheat the oven to 375F (190C). Lightly oil a 10- or 11-inch pie plate; set aside.

If using regular polenta: In a medium stockpot placed on a back burner (the polenta tends to sputter), bring the water and broth to a boil over high heat. Slowly add the polenta, stirring constantly with a long-handled wooden spoon. Reduce the heat to low and stir in 2 tablespoons of the remaining oil, remaining garlic, and salt. Cover and cook, stirring occasionally, until tender and thickened, about 15 minutes. Remove from the heat and let stand, covered, for 5 minutes.

If using instant polenta: In a medium stockpot placed on a back burner, combine the water, broth, polenta, 2 tablespoons of the remaining oil, remaining garlic, and salt to taste. Bring to a boil over high heat; immediately reduce the heat to medium and cook, stirring often with a long-handled wooden spoon, for 5 minutes.

Immediately spoon half the polenta into the prepared pie plate, pressing down with the back of a large spoon to form a smooth surface. Spoon the mushroom filling on top, spreading to within ½ inch of the outside edge of the polenta. Carefully spoon the remaining polenta over the filling, using your fingers to evenly spread and the back of a large spoon to form a smooth surface. Brush the top evenly with the 1 teaspoon oil.

Cover with foil and bake for 30 minutes. Remove the foil and bake for 15 minutes, or until the top is lightly browned. Remove from the oven and let rest for 15 minutes. Cut into wedges and transfer to warmed serving plates. Spoon the warm sauce evenly over each serving. Garnish with the rosemary or parsley, if desired. Serve at once.

Advance Preparation The mushroom filling can be stored, covered, in the refrigerator for up to eight hours before using in the recipe. The assembled pie can be stored, covered, in the refrigerator for up to twenty-four hours before baking.

PER SERVING

Calories 404 · Protein 15g · Total Fat 11g · Saturated Fat 1g · Cholesterol 0mg · Carbohydrate 63g · Dietary Fiber 12g · Sodium 344mg

Light Tomato Sauce

The following recipe produces a light yet flavorful tomato sauce, ideal for many of the instances in this book where a simple pasta sauce is called for. To double the recipe, use a stockpot or Dutch oven and increase the cooking time slightly.

MAKES ABOUT 2½ CUPS

- 2 tablespoons extra-virgin olive oil
- 1 medium onion (about 6 ounces), finely chopped
- 3 large cloves garlic, finely chopped
- 3½ pounds vine-ripened tomatoes, cored and coarsely chopped, accumulated juices included, or 2 (28-ounce) cans whole tomatoes, preferably plum, drained and coarsely chopped, 1 cup juices reserved
- 1 tablespoon tomato paste
- 12 large basil leaves, shredded, or 1 teaspoon dried oregano
- ½ teaspoon sugar
- Salt and freshly ground black pepper, to taste

In a large deep-sided skillet with a lid, heat the oil over medium-low heat. Add the onion and cook, stirring often, until softened and translucent, 7 to 10 minutes. Add the garlic and increase the heat to medium; cook, stirring, for 1 minute. Add the tomatoes and their juices, tomato paste, basil, sugar, salt, and pepper; bring to a boil over medium-high heat. Reduce the heat to medium-low and simmer, uncovered, stirring frequently to prevent scorching, until the tomatoes have cooked down to a thick mass, 30 to 45 minutes for fresh tomatoes, a bit longer for canned. Remove the pan from the heat. Cover and let stand for 15 minutes.

Pass the sauce through the medium blade of a food mill. If the sauce appears too thin, return it to medium-low heat and cook, stirring often, until it is the desired consistency.

Advance Preparation The sauce will keep, covered, in the refrigerator for up to three days, or it can be frozen in freezer containers for three to four months.

PER ½ CUP

Calories 130 · Protein 3g · Total Fat 7g · Saturated Fat 1g · Cholesterol 0mg · Carbohydrate 18g · Dietary Fiber 4g · Sodium 53mg

Variations For a chunkier version that requires no pureeing and yields about 4 cups cooked sauce, peel and seed the tomatoes before coarsely chopping and cooking as directed to a thick consistency.

For a chunkier, fiber-rich version of the pureed recipe, add back half of the seeds and skins to the pureed sauce.

Cook's Tip

A food mill is highly recommended over a food processor or blender for pureeing the cooked tomato mixture, because they tend to grind up the seeds, creating a bitter sauce. If you don't have a food mill, pulse the mixture in a food processor fitted with the pastry blade a few times, then push it through a coarse sieve.

Sun-Dried Tomato Pesto

Outstanding tossed with any pasta, this also makes a fine topping for crostini or bruschetta or filling for broiled mushrooms. Like the pesto on page 107, it is meant to be thinned with pasta cooking liquid or vegetable broth.

MAKES ABOUT 1½ CUPS

1 cup packed fresh basil
1 cup packed fresh flat-leaf parsley
¼ cup pine nuts
¼ cup oil-packed sun-dried tomatoes, drained
2 tablespoons extra-virgin olive oil
4 large cloves garlic, finely chopped
½ teaspoon coarse salt, or to taste

Combine all the ingredients in a food processor fitted with the metal blade or in a blender; process or blend until a smooth paste is formed.

Advance Preparation The pesto can be stored, tightly covered, in the refrigerator for up to five days.

PER TABLESPOON

Calories 24 · Protein 1g · Total Fat 2g · Saturated Fat 0g · Cholesterol 0mg · Carbohydrate 1g · Dietary Fiber 0g · Sodium 44mg

Linguine Tart with Sun-Dried Tomato Pesto

Do they make such tarts in Italy? Maybe, maybe not, but everyone knows they make linguine, pesto sauce, and sun-dried tomatoes, the main components of this delicious dish. If you're short on time, skip preparations for the "tart shell," and serve the linguine and sauce with baguette or Italian bread.

MAKES 4 SERVINGS

1½ tablespoons extra-virgin olive oil
2 cloves garlic, finely chopped
32 to 38 (¼-inch-thick) baguette rounds
10 ounces uncooked linguine
1 cup Sun-Dried Tomato Pesto (opposite)

Preheat the oven to 400F (205C). In a small saucepan, heat the oil over medium heat. Add the garlic and cook, stirring, for 1 minute. Remove from the heat and set aside.

Line the bottom and sides of a lightly oiled 10-inch pie plate with the bread rounds, placing the bread upright against the rim of the plate to make a scalloped border. Brush the bread evenly with the garlic-flavored oil. Scatter any remaining garlic evenly along the bottom. Bake for 5 minutes, or until the bread is just beginning to brown. Remove from the oven and set aside. Reduce the heat to 350F (175C).

Meanwhile, cook the linguine according to the package directions until barely cooked al dente. Reserve ¼ cup of the cooking liquid and drain the pasta well. Transfer to a large bowl and add the pesto and the reserved cooking liquid; toss well to thoroughly combine. Pour the linguine mixture into the pie plate, pressing firmly with the back of a large spoon or spatula until packed down.

Bake for 15 minutes, or until the exposed bread is nicely browned around the edges and the top of the pasta mixture is lightly browned. Cut into 4 wedges and serve at once.

PER SERVING

Calories 513 · Protein 16g · Total Fat 16g · Saturated Fat 2g · Cholesterol 0mg · Carbohydrate 78g · Dietary Fiber 4g · Sodium 440mg

Sandwiches

Herbed Onion Confit

In southwestern France, *confit* typically refers to duck, goose, or pork that has been preserved by slowly cooking in its own fat. When the mixture is cooled and solid, it is used as a spread on bread. Throughout the Mediterranean Languedoc and French Catalonia, a similar technique is often applied to the ubiquitous onion, with meltingly tender results. This condiment also makes a fine topping for mashed potatoes or vegetarian burgers.

MAKES ABOUT 8 SERVINGS

2 tablespoons extra-virgin olive oil
1½ pounds onions, cut into ½-inch-thick slices
4 large cloves garlic, finely chopped
1 teaspoon sugar
¼ teaspoon dried thyme leaves
¼ teaspoon dried oregano
Salt and freshly ground black pepper, to taste

Preheat the oven to 425F (220C). Grease a baking sheet with a rim with half of the oil. Arrange the onions in a single layer on the sheet. Sprinkle the garlic, sugar, thyme, oregano, salt, and pepper evenly over the top. Drizzle evenly with the remaining oil. Cover tightly with foil and bake for 25 minutes.

Remove the baking sheet from the oven and uncover. With a spatula, turn the onions over, separating into small rings. Cover tightly and return to the oven for 25 to 30 minutes, or until the onions are meltingly tender and easily broken apart. Break the onions apart with the edge of the spatula. Let cool slightly and serve warm or at room temperature.

Advance Preparation The cooled confit can be refrigerated, covered, for two or three days before bringing to room temperature and using.

PER SERVING

Calories 67 · Protein 1g · Total Fat 4g · Saturated Fat 1g · Cholesterol 0mg · Carbohydrate 8g · Dietary Fiber 2g · Sodium 3mg

Variation Substitute shallots for the onions.

Bagels with Eggplant Spread

The bagel, of course, was perfected by Jewish bakers of Polish and Russian descent who brought it to Long Island, New York, from where it traveled to become an indispensable item at breakfast, lunch, brunch, and snack tables all across North America. But while the bagel might not exactly be a Mediterranean invention, the following eggplant spread, a perfect topping for the toasted bread, most definitely is. Serve as brunch, lunch, or snack.

MAKES 6 TO 8 SERVINGS

1 large eggplant (about 1¼ pounds)
1 small red bell pepper (about 4 ounces)
2 tablespoons plus 1 teaspoon extra-virgin olive oil
1 medium red onion (about 6 ounces), cut into eighths
¼ cup packed flat-leaf parsley
¼ cup packed fresh basil leaves
Juice of ½ large lemon (about 2 tablespoons)
1 tablespoon tomato paste
2 cloves garlic, finely chopped
Pinch cayenne, or to taste
Salt and freshly ground black pepper, to taste
6 to 8 bagels, plain, whole wheat, or oat bran, halved and lightly toasted

Preheat the oven to 400F (205C). Pierce the eggplant in several places with the tines of a fork. Rub the eggplant and the bell pepper with the 1 teaspoon oil. Place the eggplant and bell pepper on an ungreased baking sheet. Roast for 40 to 45 minutes, turning frequently with tongs, or until the eggplant is collapsed and the pepper is blistered and beginning to char. Carefully stem the eggplant, cut in half lengthwise, and drain, cut side down, on several layers of paper towel. Place the bell pepper in a paper bag; twist closed and leave for 20 minutes.

When the eggplant is cool enough to handle, strip away and discard the skin. Cut the flesh into chunks and set aside. Peel off the skin of the pepper with your fingers or with a small pairing knife. Cut lengthwise in half, removing the core, ribs, and seeds, then cut each half lengthwise in half.

Place the eggplant, bell pepper, remaining oil, onion, parsley, basil, lemon juice, tomato paste, garlic, cayenne, salt, and pepper in a food processor fitted with the metal blade. Process with on/off motions until not quite smooth (do not puree). Transfer to a serving bowl and let stand at room temperature for 30 minutes to allow the flavors to blend.

Serve at room temperature, accompanied with the toasted bagel halves. Or cover and refrigerate for at least 1 hour and serve chilled.

Advance Preparation The eggplant spread can be stored, covered, in the refrigerator for up to twenty-four hours. Serve chilled or return to room temperature before serving.

PER SERVING

Calories 285 · Protein 9g · Total Fat 7g · Saturated Fat 1g · Cholesterol 0mg · Carbohydrate 48g · Dietary Fiber 5g · Sodium 406mg

"Golden Slipper" Ciabatta Sandwich with Roasted Yellow Pepper and Caramelized Onion

Ciabatta (*cha-báhta*) is the Italian word for "slipper," which is the shape this delightful Tuscan flatbread typically assumes. According to legend, a baker in Tuscany, under the influence of too much wine, mistakenly added too much water to the morning bread mix. Thus the rather flat, oblong loaf with its characteristic crispy crust and cloudlike interior was born. Available at Italian bakeries and many major supermarkets, it is the ideal bread for a gourmet sandwich such as this, although regular Italian bread or plain focaccia will work as well. If you can't find yellow bell peppers, any color can be substituted—jarred roasted red peppers are great in a pinch. These sandwiches are especially delicious served with a bowl of Tomato-Rice Soup (page 47) or Tomato-Fennel Soup (page 46).

MAKES 4 MAIN-COURSE OR 8 APPETIZER SERVINGS

½ cup vegetable broth, preferably Basic Vegetable Broth (page 38) or low-sodium canned
2 tablespoons extra-virgin olive oil
8 large fresh sage leaves
3 cloves garlic, peeled and lightly crushed
1 medium yellow onion (6 to 8 ounces), thinly sliced
1 large yellow bell pepper (about 8 ounces), roasted, peeled, and sliced into thin strips (see Cook's Tip, page 201)
1 teaspoon balsamic vinegar
Salt and freshly ground black pepper, to taste
1 (12-ounce) loaf ciabatta, Italian bread, or plain focaccia, split horizontally in half

In a medium skillet with a lid, combine the broth, oil, sage, and garlic; bring to a brisk simmer over medium heat. Cover and remove from the heat. Let stand for 20 to 30 minutes. Remove the sage, squeezing out the excess liquid, and the garlic; discard.

Preheat the oven to 350F (175C). Add the onion to the skillet and cook over medium heat, stirring often, until the onion is golden and most of the liquid has evaporated, about 10 minutes. Remove from the heat and add the roasted pepper, vinegar, salt, and pepper; toss well to combine.

Arrange the pepper and onion mixture evenly over the bottom half of the bread. Cover with the top half and wrap the sandwich tightly in foil;

Cook's Tip

Roasted Peppers To quickly roast bell peppers when called for in recipes, adjust the oven rack to about 4 inches from the heating element and preheat the oven to broil. Trim the top and bottom off the pepper and cut in half lengthwise. Remove the seeds and inner white membranes or ribs. Slice each half lengthwise into 3 even strips. Arrange the pepper strips, cut side down, on an ungreased baking sheet. Broil until partially charred, about 5 minutes. Place in a paper bag, twist tightly to close, and leave for 20 minutes. Peel off the skins with your fingers or with a small sharp knife. Cut into desired lengths.

transfer to a baking sheet. Bake for 15 minutes, or until all is nicely heated through. Remove the foil and bake for 5 minutes, or until the top of the bread is crispy. Cut crosswise into 4 or 8 equal pieces and serve at once.

PER MAIN-COURSE SERVING

Calories 347 · Protein 11g · Total Fat 10g · Saturated Fat 2g · Cholesterol 0mg · Carbohydrate 54g · Dietary Fiber 5g · Sodium 565mg

French Bread Panini with Grilled Eggplant, Herbed Onion Confit, and Tomato-Cognac Sauce

Although panini are grilled Italian sandwiches, they are popular in France, as well, where they are often made with baguette bread. While I don't own a panini-maker, and my sandwich grill is too small, I've found that using my palms, perhaps a heavy rolling pin, and an outdoor or stovetop grill to create the characteristic flattened shape and grill marks—before filling the sandwiches, that is—simulates either type of panini quite well. If you don't have time to prepare the onion confit and tomato-cognac sauce, substitute for them with sautéed or grilled onions and your favorite tomato sauce—or ketchup!

MAKES 4 SERVINGS

- 1 eggplant (about 1 pound)
- Salt
- 1 loaf French baguette (about 10 ounces)
- 2 tablespoons olive oil
- 1 clove garlic, halved
- Freshly ground black pepper, to taste
- Herbed Onion Confit (page 198), warm or at room temperature
- Tomato-Cognac Sauce (page 202), warm, cold, or at room temperature

Trim both ends of the eggplant and stand upright on the flattest end. Remove most of the skin in thin slices. Cut eggplant lengthwise into 2 equal halves. Place one half, cut side down, on a cutting board. With one hand resting on top of the eggplant, make 4 equal parallel cuts with a large sharp knife. Repeat with the other half. (You should have a total of 8 long eggplant slices each about ½ inch thick.) Sprinkle the eggplant slices liberally with salt and place in a colander to drain for 30 minutes. Rinse under cold running water and drain well between paper towels. (Do not skip this step.)

Meanwhile, prepare a medium-hot charcoal or gas grill, or preheat a broiler. If broiling, position the oven rack about 4 inches from the heat source; lightly oil a large baking sheet and set aside. Or place a stovetop grilling pan with grids over medium-high heat.

Trim about ½ inch from either end of the baguette and discard. Using a heavy rolling pin or the palms of your hands, flatten the baguette on a cutting board until it is about 1 inch thick. Divide crosswise into 4 equal pieces. Working parallel to the cutting board, slice each piece in half without cutting all the way through. Open out, cut side down, and flatten again. Set aside until needed.

Brush the eggplant slices on both sides evenly with half of the oil. If broiling, arrange the eggplant on the prepared baking sheet. Otherwise, place the eggplant directly on the grill. Grill or broil until lightly browned, 2 to 3 minutes per side; if grilling, rotate clockwise with a wide metal spatula a few times on each side to prevent scorch marks. Remove from heat source. Sprinkle lightly with salt and pepper; keep warm while grilling the bread.

Grill or broil the baguette pieces on both sides until nicely toasted, keeping them spread open. Arrange the baguette pieces, cut sides up, on a work surface. Rub the tops with the cut sides of the garlic. Top the bottom half with two eggplant slices, folding them if necessary to fit the length of the bread. Close the sandwich. Repeat with the remaining baguette pieces. Serve at once, with the confit and sauce passed separately.

PER SERVING

Calories 279 · Protein 7g · Total Fat 9g · Saturated Fat 1g · Cholesterol 0mg · Carbohydrate 43g · Dietary Fiber 4g · Sodium 435mg

Variation

Tomato Concassé

Substitute tomato concassé, a Provençal garnish of raw tomatoes often mixed with a little fresh basil and olive oil, for the tomato-cognac sauce. To make enough concassé for four sandwiches, peel, seed, and coarsely chop 4 small vine-ripened tomatoes. Place in a colander, sprinkle with a little salt, and let drain for about 15 minutes. Transfer to a small bowl and add about 1 tablespoon finely chopped basil, 1 teaspoon olive oil, and salt and freshly ground black pepper to taste. Spoon equal amounts of the concassé evenly over the grilled eggplant sandwiches.

Tomato-Cognac Sauce

This is like glorified ketchup, and it makes a delicious topping for grilled zucchini or vegetarian burgers as well. **MAKES ABOUT ½ CUP**

- ½ cup diced canned tomatoes, undrained
- 2 tablespoons tomato ketchup
- 2 teaspoons cognac or brandy
- 1 tablespoon water
- Salt and freshly ground black pepper, to taste
- 1 teaspoon extra-virgin olive oil

In a small saucepan, combine the tomatoes, ketchup, cognac, water, salt, and pepper. Bring to a boil over high heat; immediately reduce the heat to low and simmer gently, uncovered, for 3 minutes. Cool slightly and transfer to a food processor fitted with the metal blade or to a blender. Add the oil and process or blend until a smooth puree is formed. Season with additional salt and pepper as necessary. Serve warm, cold, or at room temperature.

PER TABLESPOON

Calories 14 · Protein 0g · Total Fat 1g · Saturated Fat 0g · Cholesterol 0mg · Carbohydrate 2g · Dietary Fiber 0g · Sodium 46mg

Grilled Mediterranean Vegetable Panini

From eggplant to zucchini, many of the Mediterranean's most popular vegetables are featured in these delicious grilled sandwiches. If using a charcoal or gas grill, a fine-meshed vegetable grid is recommended here. Otherwise, it's best to use a stovetop grill or the broiler. To mimic the appearance of a sandwich pressed in a panini-maker, flatten the bread with a heavy rolling pin before grilling, and only grill one side, if desired.

MAKES 6 SERVINGS

- 1 small eggplant (about 8 ounces)
- 3 tablespoons extra-virgin olive oil
- 1 medium fennel bulb (about 12 ounces), trimmed, cored, and cut lengthwise into 8 wedges
- 2 small zucchini (about 4 ounces each), cut into ½-inch-thick rounds
- 1 medium red bell pepper (about 6 ounces), cut lengthwise into eighths
- 1 medium red onion (about 6 ounces), cut into ½-inch-thick rounds
- 4 small plum tomatoes (about 2 ounces each), cored and cut lengthwise into quarters
- Juice of ½ large lemon (about 2 tablespoons)
- Dried oregano, to taste
- Salt, preferably the coarse variety, and freshly ground black pepper, to taste
- 12 large slices Italian bread (about 1¼ ounces each)
- 1 large clove garlic, halved

Cut the eggplant into ½-inch-thick rounds, sprinkle with salt, and set in a colander to drain for 30 minutes. (Do not skip this step.)

Prepare a medium-hot charcoal or gas grill, or preheat a broiler. Position the grill rack or oven rack 4 to 6 inches from the heat source. If grilling, lightly oil a vegetable grid and set aside. If broiling, lightly oil a large baking sheet and set aside. Or place a stovetop grilling pan with grids over medium-high heat.

Rinse the eggplant slices under cold running water and drain well between paper towels; set aside.

Reserve 1 tablespoon of the oil. Brush the eggplant, fennel, zucchini, bell pepper, and onion on all sides with 2 tablespoons of the oil, reserving about ½ teaspoon for the tomatoes. If grilling, brush the rounded undersides of the quartered tomatoes with the reserved ½ teaspoon oil. If broiling, brush the flat cut sides with the oil.

Grill or broil the vegetables until browned and tender, working in batches as necessary. As a general rule, cook the fennel for 4 to 5 minutes per side, the red pepper for 3 to 4 minutes per side, and the eggplant, zucchini, and onion for 2 to 3 minutes per side. Grill or broil the tomatoes for about 2 minutes, cut sides up. Place the vegetables on a large baking sheet as they finish cooking.

When all the vegetables are done, drizzle with the lemon juice and the remaining 1 tablespoon of oil. Sprinkle with the oregano, salt, and pepper. Toss gently with a large spatula to combine. Cover with foil and keep warm while grilling the bread.

Grill or broil the bread on both sides until nicely toasted. Rub one side of each slice with the cut sides of the garlic. Divide the vegetables evenly among 6 slices of the toasted bread, garlic-rubbed sides up. Top each with a slice of toasted bread, garlic-rubbed side down. Serve at once.

PER SERVING

Calories 310 · Protein 9g · Total Fat 10g · Saturated Fat 2g · Cholesterol 0mg · Carbohydrate 49g · Dietary Fiber 7g · Sodium 450mg

Pita Stuffed with Eggplant Salad

Spilling over with the best of summer's bounty, these pita halves provide edible pockets for the wealth of eggplants and tomatoes in your garden. Good served at room temperature, they're perfect for stashing away in your picnic basket, then savoring outdoors. For optimal flavor, use kalamata, gaeta, or other high-quality black olives found in the deli sections of most supermarkets—the bland canned variety will result in a disappointing sandwich. MAKES 4 SERVINGS

- 1 medium eggplant (about ¾ pound)
- 2 tablespoons extra-virgin olive oil
- 1 medium onion (about 6 ounces), chopped
- 1 large clove garlic, finely chopped
- ½ pound tomatoes, cored, seeded, and coarsely chopped
- 1 tablespoon tomato paste
- 1 tablespoon red wine vinegar
- 1 teaspoon fresh thyme leaves or ½ teaspoon dried
- 1 teaspoon chopped fresh mint or ½ teaspoon dried
- ¼ teaspoon dried oregano
- Salt and freshly ground black pepper, to taste
- ½ cup black olives, preferably kalamata, pitted and halved
- 1 tablespoon drained capers
- 2 tablespoons chopped fresh flat-leaf parsley
- 2 tablespoons chopped fresh cilantro
- 4 (6-inch) pita breads, halved

Cut the eggplant into ½-inch cubes, sprinkle with salt, and set in a colander to drain for 30 minutes. (If time doesn't permit, omit salting and draining eggplant that is to be stewed or baked with several ingredients, as any bitterness is typically masked by the other flavors.) Rinse the drained eggplant under cold running water. Dry between paper towels and set aside.

In a medium nonstick skillet, heat the oil over medium heat. Add the eggplant, onion, and garlic and cook, stirring often, until softened and lightly colored, about 5 minutes. Add the tomatoes, tomato paste, vinegar, thyme, mint, oregano, salt, and pepper. Cook, stirring occasionally, until the eggplant is tender, the mixture is thickened, and the liquids are greatly reduced, about 15 minutes.

Remove from the heat and stir in the olives, capers, parsley, and cilantro. Season with addi-

Cook's Tip

To pit olives: Place each olive on its side and place the flat side of a large knife over it. Using your palm, strike the knife swiftly; the olive usually splits in half and the pit pops out.

tional salt and pepper as necessary. Let cool to room temperature. Or cover and refrigerate for at least 2 hours and serve chilled. Stuff each pita half with eggplant salad and serve.

Advance Preparation The eggplant salad can be stored, covered, in the refrigerator for up to two days before assembling the sandwiches.

PER SERVING

Calories 356 · Protein 8g · Total Fat 16g · Saturated Fat 1g · Cholesterol 0mg · Carbohydrate 48g · Dietary Fiber 4g · Sodium 855mg

Provençal Marinated Vegetable Sandwich

Pan bagnat **means bathed bread, but this specialty of Provence is actually a hearty stuffed-loaf sandwich, where the bread is typically pulled out and a tangy mixture of both fresh and marinated vegetables put in. While it's true that anchovies or tuna are often included, the two ingredients essential to an authentic sandwich are juicy tomatoes and garlicky vinaigrette. Be creative with the following recipe, if you choose. Also, pan bagnat are meant to be on the soggy side—if that idea doesn't appeal to you, serve them after just thirty minutes of marinating.**

MAKES 4 SERVINGS

1 (about 24-inch-long) fresh French baguette
2 tablespoons red wine vinegar
2 tablespoons extra-virgin olive oil
2 teaspoons Dijon mustard
2 cloves garlic, finely chopped
1 large tomato (about 8 ounces), cored, seeded, and chopped
1 medium red bell pepper (about 6 ounces), chopped
½ medium red onion (about 4 ounces), finely chopped
2 ounces marinated quartered artichoke hearts, drained (about ¼ cup packed) and chopped
2 tablespoons chopped pitted black olives, preferably kalamata
2 tablespoons drained capers
2 tablespoons finely chopped fresh flat-leaf parsley
Salt and freshly ground black pepper, to taste

Cut the bread in half lengthwise. Pull most of the crumbs from both halves, leaving ½-inch-thick shells. If desired, save the crumbs for another use such as fresh bread crumbs.

In a large bowl, whisk together the vinegar, oil, mustard, and garlic. Stir in the tomato, bell pepper, onion, artichokes, olives, capers, and parsley; season with salt and pepper. Spoon the vegetable mixture into the bottom bread shell and replace the top. Cut in half crosswise. Wrap each half tightly in plastic wrap and refrigerate for at least 30 minutes or up to 2 hours (the bread might become overly soggy if left longer), turning a few times to evenly moisten the top and bottom of the bread.

To serve, cut each half crosswise into 2 equal pieces.

PER SERVING

Calories 354 · Protein 9g · Total Fat 11g · Saturated Fat 2g · Cholesterol 0mg · Carbohydrate 55g · Dietary Fiber 5g · Sodium 699mg

Desserts

Spectacular Fruit Compotes, Parfaits, Sorbets, Granitas, and More!

In the Mediterranean, dessert is an understated affair, a simple conclusion to a satisfying meal that desires no grand finale. Usually fruit, either raw or cooked, fulfills this wish. Sometimes slices of raw fruit are dressed in sugar syrup or drizzled with liqueur, left to marinate, and called a macédoine or macedonia. If cooked in this syrup, the dish becomes a compote. Baked with a crumbly, crunchy nut topping, it's a gratin; baked over pastry, it's a tart. Other times, fruit may be pureed and frozen into ice crystals to make a granita, or further blended to form a smooth sorbet. For more formal occasions, it might be layered attractively in parfaits, or left whole, then poached, braised, or baked in wine. No matter how it's prepared or presented, fruit never steals the show.

Not surprisingly, fruit finds its way into the more elaborate desserts that appear around the holidays, like the aromatic Spiced Apple and Almond Cake from Israel or the rich Panforte, studded with mixed dried and candied fruits, from Italy. So does olive oil. And if you do serve the Greek Currant Cake, redolent of citrus and cinnamon, moist with extra-light olive oil, and glazed with a Grand Marnier syrup, take care—it just might steal the show.

Apples Baked in Red Wine

This artless Provençal recipe elevates the ordinary baked apple to the sublime and represents French cuisine at its finest. **MAKES 4 SERVINGS**

- 4 medium tart baking apples (about 6 ounces each), such as Granny Smith, cored with base intact
- 8 teaspoons apricot preserves
- 2 teaspoons sugar
- 4 pinches plus ¼ teaspoon ground cinnamon
- 1 cup dry red wine, such as a Côtes du Rhône or Beaujolais
- ½ teaspoon chopped dried orange peel

Preheat the oven to 400F (205C). Fill each apple with 2 teaspoons of the preserves, then sprinkle with ½ teaspoon of the sugar and a pinch of the cinnamon. Pour the wine in an 8- or 8½-inch pie plate. Add the orange peel and the remaining cinnamon and stir to combine. Arrange the apples upright in the plate.

Bake, uncovered, for 40 to 45 minutes, or until the skins begin to split and the flesh is fork-tender but not mushy. Transfer each apple to a small shallow serving dish. Strain the cooking liquid into a glass measuring cup; pour equal portions around each apple. Serve at once.

Advance Preparation The assembled stuffed apples can be stored, covered, in the refrigerator for two to three hours before baking.

PER SERVING

Calories 146 · Protein 1g · Total Fat 0g · Saturated Fat 0g · Cholesterol 0mg · Carbohydrate 28g · Dietary Fiber 3g · Sodium 46mg

Apples Poached in White Wine

Like the French, Italians adore fresh fruits simmered in wine. While the French typically reserve pears or peaches for poaching in their world-class wines, and apples for baking or stewing in compotes, in Italy no such restrictions apply. The optional garnish of dried cranberries or cherries and mint leaves is especially attractive around the holidays. **MAKES 4 TO 6 SERVINGS**

- 2 cups dry white wine
- ½ cup sugar
- 4 medium Golden Delicious apples (about 6 ounces each), peeled, cored, and quartered
- 1 cinnamon stick
- 1 tablespoon pure vanilla extract
- ½ teaspoon dried chopped lemon peel
- Dried cranberries or dried cherries (optional)
- Whole mint leaves (optional)

In a large nonreactive saucepan, heat the wine and sugar over medium heat, stirring until the sugar dissolves. Add the apples, cinnamon stick, vanilla extract, lemon peel, and enough water to cover the apples; bring to a simmer over medium-high heat. Reduce the heat to low, cover, and cook, turning occasionally, until the apples are just tender when pierced with a thin sharp knife, about 10 minutes. With a slotted spoon, transfer the apples to a serving bowl.

Reduce the remaining poaching liquid over high heat until about ½ cup of syrup remains, about 15 minutes. Remove the cinnamon stick and pour the syrup over the apples; let cool to room temperature. Serve at room temperature, garnished with the optional cranberries or cherries and mint leaves, if desired. Or refrigerate for at least 1 hour and serve chilled.

Advance Preparation The apples and syrup can be stored, covered, in the refrigerator for up to three days.

PER SERVING

Calories 270 · Protein 1g · Total Fat 1g · Saturated Fat 0g · Cholesterol 0mg · Carbohydrate 48g · Dietary Fiber 5g · Sodium 14mg

Fresh Apricot Compote with Ginger and Spearmint

Apricots, both fresh and dried, figure prominently in Moroccan desserts. This versatile compote can be enjoyed on its own or tossed with other fruits such as berries, peaches, melon, pineapple, or bananas. Sweet, juicy apricots are essential for the success of this recipe. If you can't locate them, use three (15¼-ounce) cans well-drained peeled whole apricots.

MAKES 4 TO 6 SERVINGS

- 3 pounds fresh ripe apricots
- ⅓ cup water
- 3 tablespoons sugar
- ¾ teaspoon pure vanilla extract
- ¾ teaspoon ground ginger
- 1½ tablespoons apricot brandy or orange-flavored liqueur (optional)
- 3 tablespoons chopped fresh spearmint or other mild mint
- 1½ tablespoons chopped crystallized ginger

Bring a medium stockpot filled with water to a boil over high heat; drop in the apricots and boil for 20 seconds. Drain and rinse under cold running water. Peel off the skins, cut in half lengthwise, and remove pits; cut each half lengthwise into 2 equal pieces.

Combine the water, sugar, vanilla, and ground ginger in a large saucepan; bring to a simmer over medium-high heat, stirring. Add the apricots and return to a simmer.

Immediately reduce the heat to medium-low and cook, uncovered, for 8 to 10 minutes, stirring occasionally, or until the fruit is tender but not falling apart and the liquid is syrupy. Remove from the heat and stir in the brandy or liqueur, if using. Let cool to room temperature.

Just before serving, toss the compote gently with the mint and crystallized ginger. Serve at room temperature. Or refrigerate for at least 1 hour and serve chilled.

Advance Preparation The compote can be stored, covered, in the refrigerator for up to three days.

PER SERVING

Calories 207 · Protein 5g · Total Fat 1g · Saturated Fat 0g · Cholesterol 0mg · Carbohydrate 46g · Dietary Fiber 6g · Sodium 7mg

Macédoine of Cantaloupe with Anise

The term *macédoine,* not surprisingly, comes from Macedonia, where the custom of steeping fruit in alcohol probably began as a means of preservation. Today, it has come to refer to any fresh or cooked fruit marinated or drizzled with a liqueur or liqueur-flavored syrup. Light and refreshing, the combination of ripe, fragrant cantaloupe soaked in anisette is a favorite in Spain, Italy, and French Catalonia. MAKES 4 TO 6 SERVINGS

1 medium cantaloupe, halved and seeded
½ cup anisette or other anise-flavored liqueur

With a sharp pairing knife, remove the rind from the cantaloupe; cut the fruit into 1-inch chunks. Place the fruit in a medium serving bowl and pour in the anisette; toss gently to coat. Cover with plastic wrap and refrigerate for at least 30 minutes, tossing occasionally.

Serve chilled.

Advance Preparation The dish can be stored, covered, in the refrigerator for up to twenty-four hours before serving.

PER SERVING

Calories 159 · Protein 1g · Total Fat 0g · Saturated Fat 0g · Cholesterol 0mg · Carbohydrate 22g · Dietary Fiber 1g · Sodium 12mg

Macedonia of Fall Fruit

Combining fresh fruit with preserves is a common practice in Italian cuisine. Not only do the preserves help the fresh fruit maintain its freshness and color, but with an added splash of liqueur or citrus juice, they also provide an instant sauce that is delicious. MAKES 4 TO 6 SERVINGS

1 large apple, peeled, cored, and thinly sliced
1 large ripe firm pear, peeled, cored, and thinly sliced
1 large ripe banana, peeled and thinly sliced
1 tablespoon fresh lemon juice
¼ cup orange marmalade
¼ cup apricot preserves
2 tablespoons fresh orange juice, or 1 tablespoon Grand Marnier, Triple Sec, or other orange liqueur and 1 tablespoon fresh orange juice
1 cup seedless grapes
1 large seedless orange, peeled and segmented
1 small grapefruit, peeled and segmented

Place the apple, pear, and banana in a large serving bowl. Add the lemon juice, tossing gently yet thoroughly to combine.

Place the marmalade, preserves, and orange juice in a small bowl; stir well to combine. Add to the serving bowl along with the grapes, orange, and grapefruit; stir gently yet thoroughly to combine. Cover and refrigerate for at least 1 hour. Serve chilled.

Advance Preparation The dish can be stored, covered, in the refrigerator for up to twenty-four hours before serving.

PER SERVING

Calories 252 · Protein 2g · Total Fat 1g · Saturated Fat 0g · Cholesterol 0mg · Carbohydrate 66g · Dietary Fiber 6g · Sodium 24mg

Variation A garnish of shredded coconut, toasted if you prefer, is delicious here.

Provençal Mixed Fresh Fruit Compote with Mint

Refreshing and light, this stewed mixed fruit dish is possible in late summer when the grapes are being harvested, the last of the season's peaches are at their juiciest, and the first pickings of crisp apples arrive at the markets. If pears are available, they can be added, as well, along with a splash of liqueur, brandy, or eau-de-vie for good measure.

MAKES 4 TO 6 SERVINGS

1 cup water
½ cup sugar
Juice of 1 large lemon (about 4 tablespoons)
2 strips fresh lemon peel
1 pound ripe peaches, peeled, pitted, and sliced
1 pound apples (such as Golden or Red Delicious), peeled, cored, and sliced
½ pound seedless white, red, or black grapes
¼ cup fresh mint leaves, chopped

In a large nonreactive saucepan, bring the water, sugar, lemon juice, and lemon peel to a boil over high heat. Add the fruits, and reduce the heat to a gentle simmer. Cook, uncovered, stirring and turning the fruit a few times until the fruits are tender but not falling apart, 10 to 15 minutes. With a slotted spoon, transfer the fruits to a shallow serving bowl and set aside.

Meanwhile, bring the cooking liquid to a boil over medium-high heat. Cook until reduced and syrupy, about 5 minutes. Pour the resulting syrup over the fruits and let cool to room temperature. Cover the compote and refrigerate for at least 1 hour. Serve chilled, garnished with the chopped mint just before serving.

Advance Preparation The compote, without the mint garnish, can be stored, covered, in the refrigerator for up to two days.

PER SERVING

Calories 226 · Protein 1g · Total Fat 1g · Saturated Fat 0g · Cholesterol 0mg · Carbohydrate 59g · Dietary Fiber 6g · Sodium 6mg

Italian White Grape Ice

A granita is an Italian ice, similar to sorbet, only coarser in texture, made with fruit juice or coffee. This subtle white grape recipe easily doubles as an elegant palate-cleanser between courses or as a refreshing finale to a grand meal. It's also great after pizza or a bowl of soup.

MAKES 6 DESSERT SERVINGS OR 12 TO 16 BETWEEN-COURSE SERVINGS

1 cup water
½ cup sugar
1 (2-pound) bunch seedless green grapes, rinsed, drained, and stemmed
1½ cups chilled white grape juice

Combine the water and sugar in a small saucepan; bring to a simmer over medium heat. Cook, stirring constantly, until the sugar is completely dissolved. Remove the pan from the heat and let cool to room temperature. Cover and refrigerate for at least 1 hour. Meanwhile, place a shallow metal 2½-quart container (such as a large cake pan) in the freezer to chill.

Arrange the grapes in a food processor fitted with the metal blade; process until smooth and pureed. Strain through a fine-meshed strainer into a large bowl, pressing down hard with the back of a large wooden spoon to extract all the liquids. Discard the solids. Add the grape juice and chilled sugar mixture to the strained puree; stir until well blended. Pour into the chilled metal pan.

Place the pan in the freezer for 30 to 60 minutes, or until ice crystals form around the edges. Stir the ice crystals into the center of the pan and return to the freezer. Repeat every 30 minutes, or until all of the liquid is crystallized but not frozen solid, about 3 hours.

To serve, scoop the granita into chilled dessert bowls or goblets. (If the granita has become too hard, scrape it with a large metal spoon to break up the ice crystals.) Serve at once.

Advance Preparation The granita can be stored, covered, for up to four days in the freezer, during which it will freeze solid. To serve, either allow the granita to thaw in the refrigerator until you can scrape the crystals, or break it up into chunks and process with on/off motions in a food processor fitted with the metal blade until fairly smooth.

PER DESSERT SERVING

Calories 198 · Protein 1g · Total Fat 1g · Saturated Fat 0g · Cholesterol 0mg · Carbohydrate 52g · Dietary Fiber 2g · Sodium 5mg

Italian Lemon Ice

Lemon granita is easily the most popular of all Italian ices, and with good reason. On a hot summer's day, no refreshment beats its tangy, revitalizing taste. On a dreary winter's day, a spoonful instantly lifts the spirits.

MAKES 4 TO 6 SERVINGS

- 3 cups water
- 1 cup sugar
- Pinch salt
- 1 cup fresh lemon juice (juice of about 6 medium lemons)
- 1½ teaspoons finely grated fresh lemon peel (about the peel from 1 medium lemon)
- 2 teaspoons lemon extract

Combine 2 cups of the water with the sugar in a medium nonreactive saucepan; bring to a simmer over medium heat. Cook, stirring constantly, until the sugar is completely dissolved. Add the salt, stir, and remove the pan from the heat. Stir in the remaining water and let cool to room temperature. Cover and refrigerate for a minimum of 1 hour. Meanwhile, place a shallow metal 2½-quart container (such as a large cake pan) in the freezer to chill.

Add the lemon juice, lemon peel, and extract to the chilled sugar mixture; stir until well blended. Pour into the chilled metal pan.

Place the pan in the freezer for 30 to 60 minutes, or until ice crystals form around the edges. Stir the ice crystals into the center of the pan and

Cook's Tip

Use a nutmeg grater to grate the lemon peel.

return to the freezer. Repeat every 30 minutes, or until all of the liquid is crystallized but not frozen solid, about 3 hours.

To serve, scoop the granita into chilled dessert bowls or goblets. (If the granita has become too hard, scrape it with a large metal spoon to break up the ice crystals.) Serve at once.

Advance Preparation The granita can be stored, covered, for up to four days in the freezer, but it will have become frozen solid. To serve, either allow the granita to thaw in the refrigerator until you can scrape the crystals, or break it up into chunks and process with on/off motions in a food processor fitted with the knife blade until fairly smooth.

PER SERVING

Calories 212 · Protein 0g · Total Fat 0g · Saturated Fat 0g · Cholesterol 0mg · Carbohydrate 55g · Dietary Fiber 0g · Sodium 1mg

Macedonia of Melon in a Mint Syrup

This refreshing melon dish is a serene way to end a spicy meal. You can make this using cantaloupe or honeydew alone, but together, they make an attractive combination.

MAKES 4 TO 6 SERVINGS

- ½ cup water
- ½ cup dry white wine
- ¼ cup sugar
- 2 to 3 tablespoons chopped fresh mint leaves
- ½ teaspoon chopped dried orange peel
- ¼ cup fresh orange juice
- 4 cups mixed (1-inch) cubes or balls cantaloupe and honeydew melon (about 1½ pounds)
- Fresh whole mint leaves (optional)

In a small nonreactive saucepan, bring the water, wine, sugar, mint, and orange peel to a brisk simmer over medium heat, stirring often until the sugar dissolves. Reduce the heat slightly and simmer, stirring occasionally, until the mixture is reduced to about ¾ cup, 10 to 15 minutes. Strain the mixture into a small bowl, discarding the solids. Set aside to cool to room temperature.

Add the orange juice to the cooled syrup, stirring well to combine. Place the melon in a large serving dish or divide evenly among 4 individual dessert dishes. Pour the syrup evenly over the melon; turn the fruit gently to combine. Serve at room temperature, garnished with the mint leaves, if desired. Or refrigerate for at least 1 hour and serve chilled.

Advance Preparation The mint syrup, without the orange juice, can be refrigerated, covered, for up to three days.

PER SERVING

Calories 135 · Protein 1g · Total Fat 0g · Saturated Fat 0g · Cholesterol 0mg · Carbohydrate 29g · Dietary Fiber 1g · Sodium 18mg

Peaches Poached in Red Wine

In the major wine-producing regions of the Mediterranean, namely France, Spain, and Italy, peaches are regularly poached in red wine. With its fondness for grand presentation, France has a penchant for poaching the fruit whole. If you prefer, halve and pit the peaches, reducing the cooking time by about five minutes. In Provence, a Côtes du Rhône might be used, but any dry, simple red wine will work well in this recipe.

MAKES 4 SERVINGS

- 4 medium ripe but firm peaches, peeled
- 2 cups dry red wine
- ½ cup sugar
- Pinch ground cinnamon
- 1 teaspoon crème de pêches or other peach-flavored liqueur (optional)

Arrange the peaches in a noncreative saucepan just large enough to hold them in a single layer. Add the wine, sugar, cinnamon, and enough water to completely cover the peaches. Bring to a boil over medium-high heat. Reduce the heat and simmer gently, uncovered, until fork-tender but still firm, about 20 minutes, turning the peaches in the liquid a few times. Remove the peaches with a slotted spoon and set aside to cool to room temperature.

Reduce the poaching liquid over medium-high heat until reduced to about 1 cup. Remove the saucepan from the heat and let the liquid cool to room temperature. Stir in the liqueur, if using.

Arrange the peaches in individual dessert dishes; spoon the syrup evenly over each serving. Serve at room temperature. Or cover with plastic wrap and refrigerate for at least 3 hours, and serve chilled.

Advance Preparation The dish can stand at room temperature for one or two hours before serving. The completely cooled dish can be stored, covered, in the refrigerator for up to twenty-four hours.

PER SERVING

Calories 219 · Protein 1g · Total Fat 0g · Saturated Fat 0g · Cholesterol 0mg · Carbohydrate 37g · Dietary Fiber 2g · Sodium 76mg

Cook's Tip

To peel the peaches, bring a medium stockpot filled with water to a boil over high heat; drop in the peaches and boil for 20 seconds. Drain and rinse under cold running water. Peel off the skins.

Peach and Blackberry Parfait with Raspberry Coulis

Forget the temperamental custards and short-lived soufflés; fruit, and lots of it, is the choice par excellence for dessert in most French homes, particularly in Provence where it grows in abundance. The addition of either crème de cassis or crème de pêches, though optional, renders this pretty parfait elegant enough for a special dinner party. Though not a Provençal fruit, blueberries can easily be substituted for the blackberries, if desired.

MAKES 4 SERVINGS

- 4 small ripe peaches (about 4 ounces each), unpeeled, thinly sliced
- ¾ cup Raspberry Coulis (opposite)
- 2 cups fresh blackberries
- ¼ cup crème de cassis, crème de pêches, or other fruit liqueur (optional)

Alternate three layers of peaches, raspberry coulis, blackberries, and liqueur (if using) in 4 glass parfait dishes or large wine goblets. Serve at room temperature, or cover and refrigerate for at least 1 hour and serve chilled.

PER SERVING

Calories 173 · Protein 2g · Total Fat 1g · Saturated Fat 0g · Cholesterol 0mg · Carbohydrate 44g · Dietary Fiber 7g · Sodium 5mg

Raspberry Coulis

Fruit coulis is a versatile sauce made throughout France that can be used with any number of fruit and dessert dishes. Strawberries or blackberries can be substituted for the raspberries, or a combination may be used. If fresh fruit is unavailable, two cups thawed frozen unsweetened fruit, juices included, can be used.

MAKES ABOUT 1½ CUPS

- 2 cups (1 pint) fresh raspberries, rinsed and drained
- ⅓ cup superfine sugar
- 1 tablespoon fresh lemon juice

Puree all the ingredients in a food processor fitted with the metal blade or in a blender, until very smooth. If desired, pass the mixture through a food mill or fine-meshed sieve to remove the seeds. Serve at room temperature or chilled.

Advance Preparation The sauce can be stored, covered, in the refrigerator for up to three days or frozen in an airtight container for up to two months.

PER ¼ CUP

Calories 64 · Protein 0g · Total Fat 0g · Saturated Fat 0g · Cholesterol 0mg · Carbohydrate 16g · Dietary Fiber 2g · Sodium 0mg

Baked Stuffed Pears

The graceful pairing of pears and chocolate is a time-honored tradition in Italian cooking. The following recipe can be made a day in advance and then gently reheated in a low oven—perfect for those special occasions when you want to serve a dessert that impresses without the stress of last-minute preparation. As one stuffed pear half is more than sufficient after a big meal, the recipe can easily serve eight.

MAKES 4 GENEROUS OR 8 SMALL SERVINGS

- 4 large ripe firm Bosc pears, cut in half lengthwise
- ½ cup soft white bread crumbs
- ½ cup plus 1 tablespoon sugar
- ⅓ cup blanched almonds, toasted (see Cook's Tip, page 121)
- 2 tablespoons unsweetened cocoa powder
- 1 tablespoon marsala or sherry
- ½ cup dry white white
- ½ cup pear or apple juice

Preheat the oven to 350F (175C). Lightly oil a baking dish just large enough to hold the pears in a single layer.

With a melon baller, scoop out the cores and about 1 teaspoonful of flesh from the centers of each pear half. Place the pear flesh, bread crumbs, the ½ cup sugar, almonds, cocoa, and marsala in a food processor fitted with the metal blade. Process until very smooth.

Fill the pear halves evenly with the stuffing, and place in the prepared baking dish. Sprinkle the pears evenly with the 1 tablespoon sugar. Combine the wine and juice in a glass measuring cup; pour around the pears.

Bake for 40 to 45 minutes, uncovered, or until the pears are tender when pierced with the tip of a sharp knife. Serve warm.

Advance Preparation The baked stuffed pears can be stored, covered, in the refrigerator for up to twenty-four hours. Reheat, covered, in a low oven.

PER WHOLE PEAR

Calories 335 · Protein 4g · Total Fat 7g · Saturated Fat 1g · Cholesterol 0mg · Carbohydrate 64g · Dietary Fiber 6g · Sodium 36mg

Braised Pears in Red Wine

These beautiful, buttery braised pears are simply delicious. Served with their stems intact, they are the quintessence of elegance. In Provence, they might be braised in Côtes du Rhône, and in Italy, Barolo, but any good-quality domestic dry red wine, such as a California Merlot or Cabernet Sauvignon, will work well in this recipe.

MAKES 6 SERVINGS

- 6 large, ripe yet firm Bosc pears, peeled, stems intact
- 1½ cups dry red wine
- ½ cup water
- ½ cup sugar
- Juice of ½ large lemon (about 2 tablespoons)
- 1 cinnamon stick, 3 or 4 inches long, halved

Cut a thin level horizontal slice from the bottom of each pear so that they easily stand upright; set aside. In a medium stockpot, combine the wine, water, sugar, lemon juice, and cinnamon. Bring to a boil over high heat. Remove from the heat and carefully stand the pears upright in the pot.

Return the pot to the heat and bring to a brisk simmer over medium-high heat. Reduce the heat, cover, and simmer gently until the pears are very tender but not falling apart, 1 to 1½ hours, basting with the liquids occasionally. With a slotted spoon, transfer the pears to a serving platter or individual serving dishes.

Meanwhile, boil the cooking liquid over high heat until syrupy and reduced to about ½ cup. Remove and discard the cinnamon pieces. Spoon the syrup evenly over the pears; let cool to room temperature.

Serve at room temperature. Or cover and refrigerate for at least 1 hour and serve chilled.

Advance Preparation The pears can be stored, covered, in the refrigerator for up to twenty-four hours before serving.

PER SERVING

Calories 206 · Protein 1g · Total Fat 1g · Saturated Fat 0g · Cholesterol 0mg · Carbohydrate 43g · Dietary Fiber 4g · Sodium 38mg

Strawberry Sorbet

Smoother than granita, or Italian ice, sorbets are immensely popular in both Italy and France. Possessing a relatively low seed content for a berry, strawberries lend themselves particularly well to the following recipe. Raspberries or blackberries can be substituted when strawberries are out of season, but you might want to press them through a fine-meshed strainer after pureeing for a finer-textured sorbet. Then again, you might welcome the extra fiber!

MAKES 4 TO 6 SERVINGS

- ¾ cup sugar
- ½ cup water
- ¼ cup white grape juice
- 4 cups sliced fresh ripe strawberries
- ¾ cup dry white wine, chilled
- 1 to 2 tablespoons Grand Marnier or other orange liqueur (optional)
- 1 tablespoon fresh lemon juice

Combine the sugar, water, and grape juice in a small saucepan; bring to a simmer over medium heat. Cook, stirring constantly, until the sugar is completely dissolved. Remove the pan from the heat and let cool and let cool to room temperature. Transfer to the refrigerator to chill for at least 1 hour.

Place the strawberries in a food processor fitted with the metal blade or in a blender. Process or blend until smooth and pureed. Add the chilled sugar mixture, wine, liqueur (if using), and lemon juice; process or blend until thoroughly combined. Transfer to a covered container and refrigerate until well chilled, 2 to 3 hours.

Freeze in an ice-cream maker according to the manufacturer's directions. Or pour into 2 (16-

cube) plastic ice cube trays and freeze until solid, 4 to 6 hours. Just before serving, add the cubes to a food processor fitted with the metal blade. (To remove the cubes more easily, dip the bottom of the ice cube tray briefly in tepid water.) Process until smooth. Serve at once.

Advance Preparation After freezing, the frozen sorbet cubes can be transferred into plastic freezer storage bags and stored for up to four days in the freezer without loss of the fresh flavor.

PER SERVING

Calories 229 · Protein 1g · Total Fat 1g · Saturated Fat 0g · Cholesterol 0mg · Carbohydrate 51g · Dietary Fiber 3g · Sodium 5mg

Macedonia of Strawberries in Red Wine Syrup

Strawberries are always a favorite conclusion to a spring or summer meal in Italy. Use any dry, slightly fruity red wine in the following recipe.

MAKES 4 TO 6 SERVINGS

- 1½ cups dry red wine
- 6 tablespoons sugar
- 1 cinnamon stick
- 1½ teaspoons chopped dried orange peel
- 3 cups (1½ pints) fresh ripe strawberries, washed, hulled, and sliced
- Chopped fresh mint (optional)

In a small nonreactive saucepan, combine the wine, sugar, cinnamon stick, and orange peel. Bring to a boil over medium-low heat. Cook, stirring occasionally, until the mixture is syrupy and reduced by about half. Remove from the heat and let cool to room temperature.

Place the strawberries in a shallow serving bowl. Remove the cinnamon stick from the cooled syrup and discard. Pour the syrup over the strawberries, tossing gently to combine. Cover with plastic wrap and chill in the refrigerator a minimum of 1 hour. Serve chilled, garnished with the chopped mint, if desired.

Advance Preparation The wine syrup can be made up to three days in advance and stored, covered, in the refrigerator. The completed dish can be stored, covered, in the refrigerator for up to twenty-four hours.

PER SERVING

Calories 174 · Protein 1g · Total Fat 1g · Saturated Fat 0g · Cholesterol 0mg · Carbohydrate 29g · Dietary Fiber 3g · Sodium 58mg

Strawberry Parfait with Bananas, Grapes, and Grappa

This simple yet sophisticated parfait is for adults only. Indeed, grappa is a potent Italian spirit, distilled from the residue of grapes left behind in the wine press after the juice has been extracted from the wine. Kirsch, a clear cherry brandy, is a fine substitute.

MAKES 4 SERVINGS

- ¼ cup sugar
- ¼ cup grappa or kirsch

Juice from 1 large lemon (about ¼ cup)
1 pint (2 cups) strawberries, hulled and sliced crosswise
1 cup seedless white grapes, halved lengthwise
1 large banana, sliced crosswise
Mint sprigs for garnish (optional)

In a small nonreactive saucepan, combine the sugar, grappa, and lemon juice. Heat over low heat, stirring often, until the sugar is just dissolved. Remove from the heat and let cool for at least 15 minutes.

Distribute one-third of the strawberries among 4 glass parfait dishes or wine goblets. Do the same with the grapes and bananas. Top each with about 1 tablespoon of the syrup. Repeat the layering twice more. Cover and refrigerate for at least 1 hour. Served chilled, garnished with mint sprigs, if desired.

Advance Preparation The parfaits can be stored, covered, in the refrigerator for up to twelve hours before serving.

PER SERVING

Calories 164 · Protein 1g · Total Fat 1g · Saturated Fat 0g · Cholesterol 0mg · Carbohydrate 32g · Dietary Fiber 3g · Sodium 5mg

Plum Tart in Phyllo

Plums thrive along the Rhône River heading toward Provence. The most highly prized ones in Provençal markets are the smaller purple plums called prunes—often known as Italian prunes in American markets—and greengages, or *reines-claudes*. Although this tart is typically made with the smaller variety, the larger red ones, if nicely ripened, also work well.

MAKES 6 SERVINGS

6 sheets phyllo dough, defrosted according to package directions
3½ teaspoons mild vegetable oil, such as canola
1½ pounds ripe plums, halved and pitted if small, quartered if large
3 tablespoons sugar
¼ teaspoon ground cinnamon

Preheat the oven to 375F (190C). Lightly coat the bottom and sides of a 10-inch tart pan with vegetable spray or oil. Working quickly, arrange a sheet of phyllo dough in the pan, pressing lightly against the bottom and sides, leaving the excess dough to drape over the sides. (As you work, keep remaining phyllo sheets covered with a damp kitchen towel to retain their moisture.) Except for the overhanging dough, brush the dough evenly with ½ teaspoon of the oil. Layer, then oil, the remaining 5 sheets in this manner, placing each sheet slightly crosswise to the one below.

Trim off the excess pastry with kitchen shears or scissors, leaving about 1½ inches of pastry extending beyond the rim of the pan. Brush the excess edge of the pastry with water, then roll up into an attractive border. Brush the border with the ½ teaspoon remaining oil. Gently press the dough against the bottom and sides of the pan.

Prick the bottom lightly with the tines of a fork. Bake for 5 minutes.

Remove the tart pan from the oven and sprinkle 1 tablespoon of the sugar evenly over the bottom of the crust. Arrange the plums on the crust, cut side up. In a small bowl, combine the remaining sugar with the cinnamon; sprinkle evenly over the plums. Bake the tart for 25 to 30 minutes, or until the plums are fork-tender and the crust is lightly browned. (If crust is browning too quickly before the plums are done, cover the tart loosely with foil for the last 5 minutes or so of cooking.) Serve warm or at room temperature.

Advance Preparation The tart can be held for several hours at room temperature, but is best eaten within a few hours after baking while the crust is still quite crisp. To restore some of the crispiness, reheat in a low oven just before serving. If at all possible, do not refrigerate, as the crust will inevitably grow soggy.

PER SERVING

Calories 163 · Protein 2g · Total Fat 5g · Saturated Fat 0g · Cholesterol 0mg · Carbohydrate 30g · Dietary Fiber 2g · Sodium 91mg

Variation For a Middle Eastern variation, substitute ripe fresh figs for the plums.

Panforte

Though *panforte* means "strong bread," it is actually a thin and rich fruitcake whose flavor is distinguished by the use of many spices. A specialty of Siena, and traditionally eaten at Christmas, it is enjoyed throughout Italy any time of the year. Naturally, recipes abound. Some call for even more spice, and honey is typically used to make the sugar syrup. But I find that the following combination of spice and the use of the milder-tasting light corn syrup produce a cake that's just right for American taste buds. For the real Italian experience, serve panforte with a cup of strong black coffee or espresso.

MAKES 12 SERVINGS

- ½ cup all-purpose unbleached white flour
- 2 tablespoons unsweetened cocoa powder
- 1 teaspoon ground cinnamon
- ¼ teaspoon ground coriander
- ¼ teaspoon freshly grated nutmeg
- ¼ teaspoon ground cloves
- Pinch ground white pepper
- 1¼ cups coarsely chopped dried figs
- 1 cup coarsely chopped walnuts
- ½ cup coarsely chopped blanched almonds
- ½ cup coarsely chopped candied orange peel
- ½ cup coarsely chopped candied citron
- ⅔ cup sugar
- ⅔ cup light corn syrup
- Confectioners' sugar

Preheat the oven to 300F (150C). Grease the bottom and sides of a 9-inch springform pan. Cut a 9-inch circle of waxed paper or parchment paper; place in bottom of pan and grease. Set aside.

In a small bowl, place the flour, cocoa, cinnamon, coriander, nutmeg, cloves, and white pepper; stir well to combine. In a large bowl, combine the figs, walnuts, almonds, orange peel, and citron. Add the flour mixture, stirring well to break up any lumps.

In a small saucepan, combine the sugar and corn syrup. Cook over medium-low heat, stirring occasionally, until the syrup forms a firm ball when dropped into cold water, or reaches 245F (120C) on a candy thermometer. Immediately pour the syrup into the fruit and nut mixture; stir quickly until the flour is thoroughly moistened.

Spoon the batter into the prepared pan. Press into an even layer with the back of a large spoon. Bake for 45 minutes. (Do not test for doneness. As brownies do, the cake will firm as it cools.) Let cool completely in the pan on a rack.

Remove the sides of the springform pan and invert the cake onto a plate lined with a piece of waxed paper. Remove the bottom and peel off the paper circle. Set a cake plate over the top, and turn the cake right side up. Sprinkle with confectioners' sugar.

PER SERVING

Calories 358 · Protein 5g · Total Fat 9g · Saturated Fat 1g · Cholesterol 0mg · Carbohydrate 71g · Dietary Fiber 5g · Sodium 71mg

Spiced Apple and Almond Cake

On a crisp fall day, perfume and warm your home with the scents of apples, almonds, and spice as you make this dark, moist cake from Israel—especially nice with a cup of coffee or tea.

MAKES 12 SERVINGS

- 4 cups peeled, cored, and coarsely chopped Golden Delicious apples (about 4 medium)
- 1¾ cups sugar
- ½ teaspoon chopped dried lemon peel
- ½ cup canola or other mild vegetable oil
- ½ cup red currant jelly, at room temperature
- ½ teaspoon pure vanilla extract
- ½ teaspoon almond extract
- 2 cups all-purpose flour, preferably unbleached
- 2 teaspoons baking soda
- 1 teaspoon ground cinnamon
- ½ teaspoon freshly grated nutmeg
- ½ teaspoon salt
- 1 cup chopped blanched almonds
- Confectioners' sugar (optional)

Preheat the oven to 350F (175C). Grease a 13-by-9-inch baking pan. In a large bowl, combine the apples, sugar, and lemon peel; let stand for 15 minutes.

Add the oil, jelly, vanilla extract, and almond extract to the apple mixture; stir until the jelly is well dissolved.

In another large bowl, sift together the flour, baking soda, cinnamon, nutmeg, and salt. Gradually stir into the apple mixture. Add the almonds, stirring well to combine. Pour into the

Cook's Tip

The long rectangular shape of the baking pan is important to prevent this moist yet crumbly cake, leavened only with baking soda, from sinking in the center. If you don't own a 13 × 9-inch baking pan, disposable aluminum pans in this popular size are stocked regularly in supermarkets. Because the disposable pan has a flimsy bottom, it's best to set it on a cookie sheet while baking for easy removal from the oven. With potholders in each hand to grasp either long side, transfer the pan from the cookie sheet to a rack to cool. Otherwise, the pan's bottom might bend and cause the uncooled cake to crack.

prepared pan and bake until a toothpick inserted in the center comes out clean, 45 to 50 minutes.

Let the cake cool in the pan on a wire rack. When completely cooled, sprinkle with confectioners' sugar, if desired. Cut into squares and serve.

Advance Preparation The completely cooled cake can be covered with foil and stored at room temperature for up to two days.

PER SERVING

Calories 367 · Protein 4g · Total Fat 14g · Saturated Fat 1g · Cholesterol 0mg · Carbohydrate 60g · Dietary Fiber 2g · Sodium 306mg

Caramelized Apple Tart with Aniseed

The affinity of apples and aniseed is apparent in the first forkful of this golden and delicious open-faced pie, inspired by the flat rustic-edged tarts of Provence. The Golden Delicious apple is ideal here, but Red Delicious (so long as they're truly ripe) or Gala apples can also be used with satisfying results. MAKES 8 SERVINGS

PÂTE BRISÉE WITH ANISEED:

1 cup plus 2 tablespoons all-purpose flour
⅓ cup extra-light olive oil or other mild vegetable oil such as canola
1½ tablespoons sugar
1 teaspoon aniseeds, lightly crushed
¼ teaspoon salt
2 to 3 tablespoons ice water

FILLING:

9 tablespoons sugar
4 large Golden Delicious apples, peeled, cored, and cut into very thin slices
2 tablespoons canola oil

Make the pâte brisée: In a food processor fitted with the metal blade, combine the flour, oil, sugar, aniseeds, and salt; pulse a few times until combined. With the motor running, add water through the feed tube and process until the dough almost forms a ball.

With lightly floured fingers, gather the dough into a ball and flatten into a thick, even disk; cover with plastic wrap and refrigerate for at least 30 minutes or up to 2 days. (If refrigerated longer than 1 hour, let stand at room temperature 10 to 15 minutes before rolling.)

Preheat the oven to 425F (220C). Lightly oil a 12-inch pizza pan or a large baking sheet without sides; set aside.

On a lightly floured work surface using a lightly floured rolling pin, roll out the pâte brisée to a 12-inch circle. (Dough should be about ⅛ inch thick.) Place the circle of dough on the prepared pan. Prick lightly with a fork in several places.

Sprinkle dough with 2 tablespoons of the sugar. Leaving a 1-inch border of dough, arrange the apple slices in overlapping concentric circles, working from the outside edge to the center of the tart. With a fork, blend the oil with 4 tablespoons of the sugar. With your fingers, distribute the sugar mixture evenly over the apples. Fold the dough border over the apples to form a rustic edge on the tart.

Bake the tart in the middle of the oven for 10 minutes. Remove from the oven and sprinkle 2 tablespoons of the sugar evenly over the top. Return to the lower third of the oven and bake for 10 to 15 minutes, or until lightly golden. Remove from the oven and preheat the oven to broil.

Sprinkle the tart with the remaining 1 tablespoon of sugar. Broil on the middle rack until the tops of the apples are nicely browned and caramelized, turning the pan frequently to promote even browning, 2 to 3 minutes. Serve warm or at room temperature.

Advance Preparation The pâte brisée can be covered in plastic wrap and refrigerated for up to two days before using. The completely cooled baked tart can be stored, covered, at room temperature for two days or refrigerated for up to four days. If refrigerated, reheat in a low oven for the best results.

PER SERVING

Calories 263 · Protein 2g · Total Fat 13g · Saturated Fat 1g · Cholesterol 0mg · Carbohydrate 36g · Dietary Fiber 2g · Sodium 69mg

Variation Substitute half or all of the apples with ripe, yet firm fresh pears, cored, peeled, and sliced.

Provençal Cherry and Almond Gratin

Fruit gratins are among the most common of all French home-style desserts. It is the cherries and almonds, both major crops of Provence, that define this delicious dish as Provençal. While the crumbly and crunchy nut topping is traditionally worked with butter, thrifty cooks in a pinch also use less expensive vegetable shortening with its longer shelf life. Feel free to substitute any summer berry for the cherries, and either walnuts, pine nuts, or pecans for the almonds.

MAKES 4 TO 6 SERVINGS

- 1 pound fresh sweet cherries, pitted
- ¼ cup plus 2 tablespoons sugar
- ¼ cup all-purpose flour
- 2 tablespoons vegetable shortening, cut into small pieces
- ¼ cup chopped almonds

Preheat the oven to 450F (230C). Lightly grease an 8½- or 9-inch pie plate. Arrange the pitted cherries in a single layer on the bottom.

Sprinkle evenly with the 2 tablespoons of sugar. Set aside.

In a small bowl, combine the remaining sugar, flour, shortening, and almonds. Using your fingertips, pinch and toss until the mixture resembles coarse meal. Sprinkle the sugar-nut topping evenly over the cherries, leaving a ½-inch border of fruit exposed. Gently pat the topping into the fruit.

Cover the gratin tightly with foil and bake for 15 minutes. Remove the foil and reduce the heat to 375F (190C). Bake for 15 to 20 minutes, or until the topping is golden and the fruit is bubbling. Serve warm or at room temperature.

Advance Preparation The assembled gratin can be held at room temperature for about one hour before baking. The cooked gratin can be stored, covered, in the refrigerator for up to three days, and it can be reheated in a low oven. It will still be delicious, but the topping will have lost some of its crunchiness.

PER SERVING

Calories 246 · Protein 3g · Total Fat 10g · Saturated Fat 3g · Cholesterol 0mg · Carbohydrate 44g · Dietary Fiber 3g · Sodium 2mg

Variation For a particularly pretty winter combination, core and thinly slice 3 medium unpeeled apples (about 6 ounces each) of varying color, preferably a Red Delicious, a Golden Delicious, and a Granny Smith. Working from the outside of the pie plate to the center, pack alternating apple slices, peel side up, in a circular fashion. Add ¼ teaspoon ground cinnamon to the topping, if desired. Proceed as directed in the recipe, adding 5 minutes to the initial covered baking time.

Greek Currant Cake

This is a most amazing cake, chock-full of tiny currants and fragrant with citrus and cinnamon. Don't be hesitant about using olive oil in a dessert—the extra-light variety is very subtle in taste and lends this dessert its characteristic crunchy crust and moist center. Although not traditional, the optional orange glaze variation, listed below, is a sophisticated touch for any special occasion.

MAKES 12 SERVINGS

- 2½ cups plus 2 tablespoons all-purpose unbleached flour
- 1 tablespoon ground cinnamon
- 1 teaspoon baking soda
- Pinch salt
- 2 cups dried zante currants
- ½ cup golden raisins
- ⅓ cup fresh orange juice (1 medium orange)
- 3 tablespoons fresh lemon juice (1 medium lemon)
- 2 teaspoons grated orange peel (peel of 1 medium orange)
- 1½ teaspoons grated lemon peel (peel of 1 medium lemon)
- 2 teaspoons brandy
- 1 teaspoon pure vanilla extract
- ¾ cup plus 2 tablespoons extra-light olive oil
- 1½ cups sugar
- Confectioners' sugar (optional)

Preheat the oven to 350F (175C). Grease and flour a 10-inch round springform cake pan and set aside.

In a large bowl, sift together the flour, cinnamon, baking soda, and salt. (Or combine in a food processor fitted with the plastic blade, then transfer to a large bowl.) Add the currants and raisins, stirring well to evenly combine. Set aside.

Cook's Tip

Setting the cake pan over a pizza pan or similar device is essential to prevent an oven fire, as the oil (not the batter) tends to escape through the bottom edge of a springform pan. If you use foil, make sure you use two sheets to compensate for any tears. If you prefer, line the bottom and sides of the prepared pan with waxed paper or parchment, then grease again. After you've removed the sides of the pan from the cooled cake, peel off any exposed paper.

In a small bowl, combine the orange juice, lemon juice, orange peel, lemon peel, brandy, and vanilla; set aside.

Pour the oil into another large bowl. With an electric mixer on high speed, gradually beat in the sugar. When all the sugar has been incorporated, gradually beat in the citrus juice mixture on low speed.

Gradually add the flour mixture to the oil mixture, stirring well with a wooden spoon after each addition. Spoon the batter into the prepared pan, then place on a pizza pan or a circle of a double thickness of foil with a raised edge.

Bake for 50 to 60 minutes, or until a knife inserted in the center almost comes out clean (this is a very moist cake, with a texture similar to a brownie). If the cake is browning too quickly after 45 minutes, cover loosely with foil and bake until done. Let cool completely in the pizza pan or foil on a wire rack before transferring to a cake plate and removing the sides. Sprinkle with confectioners' sugar, if using, and serve.

Advance Preparation The completely cooled cake can be covered with foil and stored at room temperature for up to three days.

PER SERVING

(without the orange glaze):

Calories 377 · Protein 3g · Total Fat 16g · Saturated Fat 2g · Cholesterol 0mg · Sodium 107mg · Carbohydrate 56g · Dietary Fiber 2g

Variation Instead of sprinkling with confectioners' sugar, pierce the top of the unmolded cooled cake with the tines of a large two-pronged fork and brush with the following glaze, letting it drip down the sides. Cover the cake and let it rest for a few hours to allow the flavors to penetrate. Decorate the top of the cake with candied orange peel, if desired.

Orange Glaze

½ cup fresh orange juice
½ cup sugar
1 tablespoon Grand Marnier or other orange liqueur

In a small nonreactive heavy-bottomed saucepan, bring the juice and sugar to a boil over medium heat. Reduce the heat slightly and boil gently until mixture forms a light syrup and reduces to about ½ cup, 7 to 10 minutes, stirring occasionally. Cool slightly and stir in the liqueur. Use while warm.

PER ABOUT 2 TEASPOONS

Calories 42 · Protein 0g · Total Fat 0g · Saturated Fat 0g · Cholesterol 0mg · Carbohydrate 10g · Dietary Fiber 0g · Sodium 0mg

Meals in Minutes

Suggested Weeknight Menus Ready in Less than an Hour for the Busy Cook, plus Appetizer and Dessert Suggestions for Weekend Entertaining

If your hectic weeknight schedule dictates that dinner be ready in under an hour, consider the following menus. The average preparation and cooking time for an entree plus a side dish, first course, or salad is approximately forty-five minutes. For relaxed weekend entertaining, appetizer and dessert options have also been provided.

Spring and Summer Menus for Four

Polenta Crostini with Caponata (optional, page 17)
Sicilian Bread and Tomato-Basil Soup (page 40)
Romaine, Red Onion, and Chickpea Salad with Orange Vinaigrette (page 79)
Strawberry Sorbet (optional, page 217)

Hummus with Roasted Red Pepper and Cilantro with assorted raw vegetables (optional, page 18)
Lebanese Bread Salad (double recipe, page 84)
Moroccan Carrot Soup (page 42)
Macedonia of Melon in Mint Syrup (optional, page 213)

Roasted Eggplant Salad (optional, page 14) with Garlic-Herb Pita Toasts (optional, page 26)
Zucchini-Lemon Couscous with pine nuts (page 101)
Sautéed Cherry Tomatoes with Mediterranean Herbs (page 157)
Romaine, Red Onion, and Chickpea Salad with Orange Vinaigrette (page 79)
Pita bread
Fresh Apricot Compote with Ginger and Spearmint (optional, page 209)

Bruschetta with Tomatoes and Basil (optional, page 5)
Rotelle with Mixed Summer-Vegetable Sauce (page 119)
Salad of Bitter Greens and Pine Nuts with Classic Italian Vinaigrette (page 71)
Italian or French bread
Strawberry Parfait with Bananas, Grapes, and Grappa (optional, page 218)

Tomatoes Persillade (optional, page 27)
Arborio Rice with Roasted Peppers, Basil, Pine Nuts, and Olives (page 122)
Romaine Salad with Lemon-Date Dressing (page 80)
Italian or French bread
Peaches Poached in Red Wine (optional, page 214)

Roasted Red Pepper and Zucchini Salad (optional, page 75)
Quick Tuscan-Style Pizza with White Beans, Tomatoes, and Basil (page 187)
Salad of Bitter Greens and Pine Nuts with Classic Italian Vinaigrette (page 71)
Italian Lemon Ice (optional, page 212)

Eggplant Roll-Ups with Pesto (optional, page 73)
Tuscan Bread Salad (page 85)
Simple Mediterranean Vegetable Soup (page 48)
Strawberry Parfait with Bananas, Grapes, and Grappa (page 218)

Hummus with Roasted Red Pepper and Cilantro with assorted raw vegetables (optional, page 18)
Pita Stuffed with Eggplant Salad (page 204)
Morrocan Potato Salad (page 77)
Fresh Apricot Compote with Ginger and Spearmint (optional, page 209)

Broiled Mushrooms with Pesto (optional, page 19)
Polenta with Stewed Peppers and Tomatoes (page 132)
Romaine, Red Onion, and Chickpea Salad with Orange Vinaigrette (page 79)
Italian or French bread
Strawberry Parfait with Bananas, Grapes, and Grappa (optional, page 218)

Stuffed Zucchini, Niçoise Style (half recipe, optional, page 32)
Herbed Risotto with Tomato and Basil, Provençal-Style (page 128)
Mesclun Salad with Classic French Vinaigrette (page 72)
French bread
Peach and Blackberry Parfait with Raspberry Coulis (optional, page 215)

Provençal Eggplant Caviar with assorted raw vegetables (optional, page 15)
Gratin of Macaroni, Tomatoes, Basil, and Olives (page 111)
Romaine Salad with Roasted Garlic Vinaigrette (page 78)
French bread
Peaches Poached in Red Wine (optional, page 214)

Tomatoes à la Provençale (optional, page 29)
French Bread Panini with Grilled Eggplant, with grilled or sautéed onions to replace the onion confit (page 201)
Romaine Salad with Roasted Garlic Vinaigrette (page 78)
Italian Lemon Ice (optional, page 212)

Provençal Eggplant Caviar with assorted raw vegetables (optional, page 15)
Provençal Marinated Vegetable Sandwich (page 205)
New Potato and Young Green Bean Salad (page 76)
Provençal Mixed Fresh Fruit Compote with Mint (optional, page 211)

Crostini with Tomatoes, Capers, and Thyme (optional, page 10)
Italian Summer Vegetable Stew (page 174)
Romaine, Red Onion, and Chickpea Salad with Orange Vinaigrette (page 79)
Italian or French bread
Strawberry Parfait with Bananas, Grapes, and Grappa (optional, page 218)

Provençal Eggplant Caviar with assorted raw vegetables (optional, page 15)
Capellini with Fondue de Tomatoes (page 98)
Romaine, Red Onion, and Chickpea Salad with Orange Vinaigrette (page 79)
French bread
Peach and Blackberry Parfait with Raspberry Coulis (page 215)

Polenta Crostini with Caponata (optional, page 17)
Ligurian Bread Salad with Vegetables (page 86)
Asparagus Soup with Thyme (page 39)
Italian Lemon Ice (optional, page 212)

Spring and Summer Menus for Four to Six

Italian Sweet and Sour Baby Cipolline Onions (optional, page 24)
Spring Vegetable Risotto (page 130)
Salad of Bitter Greens and Pine Nuts with Classic Italian Vinaigrette (page 71)
Strawberry Sorbet (optional, page 217)

Spanish Sweet and Sour Pearl Onions in Tomato-Raisin Sauce (optional, page 25)
Provençal Tian of Chickpeas, Eggplant, Tomatoes, and Olives (page 164)
Romaine Salad with Roasted Garlic Vinaigrette (page 78)
Provençal Mixed Fresh Fruit Compote with Mint (optional, page 211)

Stuffed Artichokes, Niçoise Style (optional, page 3)
Vermicelli Nests with Chickpeas, Spinach, and Tomato (page 121)
Mesclun Salad with Classic French Vinaigrette (page 72)
French bread
Provençal Cherry and Almond Gratin (optional, page 223)

Bruschetta with Tomatoes, Black Olives, and Marinated Artichokes (optional, page 6)
Linguine with Pesto, Potatoes, and Green Beans (page 110)
Mesclun Salad with Classic French Vinaigrette (page 72)
Italian or French bread
Italian Lemon Ice (optional, page 212)

Roasted Eggplant Salad (optional, page 14) with Garlic-Herb Pita Toasts (optional, page 26)
Couscous with Seven-Vegetable Tagine (page 100)
Romaine Salad with Lemon-Date Dressing (page 80)
Pita bread
Fresh Apricot Compote with Ginger and Spearmint (page 209)

Zucchini Marinated with Sherry Vinegar and Mint (optional, page 31)
Quick Catalan-Style Pizza with Peppers, Tomatoes, and Onion (page 188)
Romaine Salad with Lemon-Date Dressing (page 80)
Macédoine of Cantaloupe with Anise (optional, page 210)

Italian Sweet and Sour Baby Cipolline Onions (optional, page 24)
Linguine with Tomato-Pesto Sauce (page 110)
Mixed Green Salad with Fresh Herb Vinaigrette (page 71)
Italian or French bread
Strawberry Sorbet (page 217)

Hummus with Roasted Red Pepper and Cilantro with assorted raw vegetables (optional, page 18)
Couscous with Peas, Lettuce, and Mint (page 99)
Asparagus with Black Olives and Orange Vinaigrette (page 139)
Pita bread
Strawberry Sorbet (page 217)

Italian Sweet and Sour Baby Cipolline Onions (optional, page 24)
Penne with Sweet Pepper and Tomato Sauce (page 116)
Salad of Bitter Greens and Pine Nuts with Classic Italian Vinaigrette (page 71)
Italian or French bread
Macedonia of Strawberries in Red Wine Syrup (optional, page 218)

Spanish Sweet and Sour Pearl Onions in Tomato-Raisin Sauce (optional, page 25)
Quick Farmer's Paella (page 124)
Mixed Green Salad with Fresh Herb Vinaigrette (page 71)
Italian or French bread
Macedonia of Strawberries in Red Wine Syrup (optional, page 218)

Spring and Summer Menus for Six

Bruschetta with Cannellini Beans, Bitter Greens, and Tomatoes (optional, page 4)
Fettuccine with Spicy Raw Tomato, Herb, and Caper Sauce (page 104)

Romaine Salad with Lemon-Date Dressing (page 80)
Italian or French bread
Macedonia of Strawberries in Red Wine Syrup (optional, page 218)

Tunisian Roasted Vegetable Salad (optional, page 82) with Garlic-Herb Pita Toasts (optional, page 26)
Provençal Couscous Tabbouleh Salad (page 90)
Moroccan Carrot Soup (page 42)
Pita bread
Provençal Cherry and Almond Gratin (optional, page 223)

Bruschetta with Cannellini Beans, Bitter Greens, and Tomatoes (optional, page 4)
Pasta Primavera with Roasted Vegetables, Basil, and Olives (page 114)
Romaine Salad with Roasted Garlic* Vinaigrette (page 78)
Italian or French bread
Macedonia of Strawberries in Red Wine Syrup (page 218)
*Roast the garlic with the vegetables.

Broiled Mushrooms with Pesto (optional, page 19)
Grilled Mediterranean Vegetable Panini (page 203)
Romaine Salad with Roasted Garlic Vinaigrette (page 78)
Italian Lemon Ice (optional, page 212)

Fall and Winter Menus for Four

Garlic Puree with Croutons (optional, page 12)
Bouillabaisse of Spinach, Potatoes, Chickpeas, and Saffron (page 50)
Fennel, Orange, and Black Olive Salad (page 69)
French bread
Apples Baked in Red Wine (optional, page 208)

Crostini with Pureed White Beans and Sautéed Wild Greens (optional, page 9)
Penne with Porcini Mushroom Sauce (page 115)
Radicchio and Butter Lettuce Salad with Toasted Walnuts (page 78)
Italian bread
Apples Poached in White Wine (optional, page 208)

Wild Mushroom Spread with Croutons (optional, page 13)
Eggplant Napoleons with Tomato and Orange Sauce, Catalan Style (page 168)
Cooked rice
Spinach Sautéed with Raisins and Pine Nuts (page 156)
French or Italian bread
Caramelized Apple Tart with Aniseed (page 222)

Crostini with Radicchio, Balsamic Vinegar, and Olive Oil (optional, page 10)
"Enraged" Penne (page 117)
Spinach and Orange Salad with Pine Nuts and Raisins (page 81)
Italian or French bread
Italian Lemon Ice (optional, page 212)

Wild Mushrooms in Garlic Sauce (optional, page 22)
Quick Classic Pizza alla Marinara (page 185)
Red Kidney Bean and Mixed Green Salad (page 67)
Italian Lemon Ice (page 212)

Crostini with Radicchio, Balsamic Vinegar, and Olive Oil (optional, page 10)
Quick Tuscan-Style Minestrone Soup (page 57)
Fennel, Orange, and Black Olive Salad (page 69)
Italian or French bread
Italian White Grape Ice (optional, page 211)

Wild Mushrooms in Garlic Sauce (optional, page 22)
Cannellini Beans with Sautéed Kale (page 163)
Orange, Cucumber, and Red Onion Salad with Aniseed (page 74)
Italian or French bread
Italian Lemon Ice (optional, page 212)

Mushrooms Stuffed with Bread Crumbs, Parsley, and Garlic (optional, page 21)
Sicilian-Style Broccoli, Potato, and Parsnip Soup (page 41)
Classic Bruschetta with Olive Oil, Garlic, and Coarse Salt (page 6)
Romaine, Red Onion, and Chickpea Salad with Orange Vinaigrette (page 79)
Spiced Apple and Almond Cake (optional, page 221)

Wild Mushrooms in Garlic Sauce (optional, page 22)
Sicilian Barley Soup (page 40)
Radicchio and Butter Lettuce Salad with Toasted Walnuts (page 78)
Italian or French bread
Macedonia of Fall Fruit (optional, page 210)

Crostini with Black Truffle Sauce (optional, page 11)
Rice Salad with Saffron and Green Olives (page 89)
Tomato-Fennel Soup (page 46)
Italian or French bread
Baked Stuffed Pears (optional, page 216)

Baked Black Olives with Herbes de Provence and Anise (optional, page 22)
Provençal Zucchini-Rice Soup with Winter Pistou (page 63)
Warm Wild Mushroom and Frisée Salad (page 73)
Italian or French bread
Plum Tart in Phyllo (optional, page 219)

Wild Mushroom Spread with Croutons (optional, page 13)
Spaghettini with Green Sauce (page 117)
Radicchio and Butter Lettuce Salad with Toasted Walnuts (page 78)
Italian or French bread
Apples Baked in Red Wine (optional, page 208)

Baked Black Olives with Herbes de Provence and Anise (optional, page 22)
Linguine Tart with Sun-Dried Tomato Pesto (page 197)
Warm Wild Mushroom and Frisée Salad (page 73)
Italian or French bread
Baked Stuffed Pears (optional, page 216)

Marinated Button Mushrooms with White Wine, Cloves, and Saffron (optional, page 20)
Catalan Rice Salad with Sherry-Tomato Vinaigrette (page 83)
Sicilian-Style Broccoli and Parsnip Soup (page 41)
Italian or French bread
Apples Baked in Red Wine (optional, page 208)

Provençal Chickpea Puree with assorted raw vegetables (optional, page 7)
Provençal-Style French Bread Pizza with Caramelized Onion, Broccoli, and Niçoise Olives (page 190)
Warm Wild Mushroom and Frisée Salad (page 73)
Italian White Grape Ice (optional, page 211)

Baked Black Olives with Herbes de Provence and Anise (optional, page 22)
Garlic Soup with Potatoes, Italian Style (page 44)
Classic Bruschetta with Olive Oil, Garlic, and Coarse Salt (page 6)

Red Kidney Bean and Mixed Green Salad (page 67)
Italian Lemon Ice (optional, page 212)

Fall and Winter Menus for Four to Six

Wild Mushroom Spread with Croutons (optional, page 13)
Conchiglie with Green and Black-Eyed Peas, Pearl Onions, and Basil (page 98)
Radicchio and Butter Lettuce Salad with Toasted Walnuts (page 78)
Italian or French bread
Braised Pears in Red Wine (optional, page 216)

Green Olive and Almond Tapenade with croutons (optional, page 24)
Orzo Pilaf with Peas, Pearl Onions, and Roasted Red Peppers (page 113)
Arugula and Mushroom Salad with Lemon Vinaigrette (page 67)
Italian or French bread
Braised Pears in Red Wine (page 216)

Mushrooms Stuffed with Bread Crumbs, Parsley, and Garlic (optional, page 21)
Pasta and Bean Soup (page 58)
Radicchio and Butter Lettuce Salad with Toasted Walnuts (page 78)
Italian or French bread
Panforte (optional, page 220)

Assorted Vegetables in Charmoula Sauce (optional, page 30)
Rice Pilaf with Currants, Golden Raisins, and Pine Nuts (page 127)
Tunisian Beet Salad with Harissa (page 68)
Pita bread
Plum Tart in Phyllo (optional, page 219)

Classic Bruschetta with Olive Oil, Garlic, and Coarse Salt (optional, page 6)
Braised Cabbage with Red Beans and Rice (page 164)
Arugula and Mushroom Salad with Lemon Vinaigrette (page 67)
Italian or French bread
Apples Poached in White Wine (optional, page 208)

Marinated Button Mushrooms with White Wine, Cloves, and Saffron (optional, page 20)
Rice and Lima Beans with Sofregit (page 125)
Spinach and Orange Salad with Pine Nuts and Raisins (page 81)
Italian or French bread
Caramelized Apple Tart with Aniseed (optional, page 222)

Assorted Vegetables in Charmoula Sauce (optional, page 30)
Bulgur Pilaf with Dried Fruits (page 97)
Moroccan Orange and Black Olive Salad (page 74)
Pita bread
Plum Tart in Phyllo (optional, page 219)

Crostini with Black Truffle Sauce (double recipe) (optional, page 11)
Farfalle with Sautéed Radicchio, Fennel, and Toasted Walnuts (optional, page 103)
Spinach and Orange Salad with Pine Nuts and Raisins (without nuts, page 81)
Italian or French bread
Braised Pears in Red Wine (optional, page 216)

Mushrooms Stuffed with Bread Crumbs, Parsley, and Garlic (optional, page 21)

Italian-Style Brown Rice Salad (page 88)
Tomato-Fennel Soup (page 46)
Italian or French bread
Macedonia of Fall Fruit (optional, page 210)

Wild Mushrooms in Garlic Sauce (optional, page 22)
Quick Focaccia with Artichokes and Sun-Dried Tomatoes (page 192)
Spinach and Orange Salad with Pine Nuts and Raisins (page 81)
Italian White Grape Ice (optional, page 211)

Fall and Winter Menus for Six

Mushrooms Stuffed with Bread Crumbs, Parsley, and Garlic (optional, page 21)
"Golden" Spaghetti with Olives and Raisins (page 120)
Romaine Salad with Roasted Garlic Vinaigrette (page 78)
Italian or French bread
Braised Pears in Red Wine (optional, page 216)

Black Olive Tapenade with croutons (optional, page 23)
Spaghettini with Walnut-Garlic Sauce (page 120)
Arugula and Mushroom Salad with Lemon Vinaigrette (page 67)
Italian or French bread
Apples Poached in White Wine (optional, page 208)

Mushrooms Stuffed with Bread Crumbs, Parsley, and Garlic (optional, page 21)
Orecchiette with Broccoli Rabe (page 112)
Orange, Cucumber, and Red Onion Salad with Aniseed (page 74)
Italian or French bread
Panforte (optional, page 220)

Crostini with Pureed White Beans and Sautéed Wild Greens (optional, page 9)
Ditali with Cauliflower* (page 102)
Spinach and Orange Salad with Pine Nuts and Raisins (page 81)
Italian or French bread
Braised Pears in Red Wine (optional, page 216)
*Follow Cook's Tip for toasting bread crumbs separately.

Bibliography

Brennan, Georgeanne. *The Food and Flavor of Haute Provence.* San Francisco: Chronicle Books, 1997.

Casale, Anne. *Lean Italian Meatless Meals.* New York: Ballantine Books, 1995.

Casas, Penelope. *Tapas: The Little Dishes of Spain.* New York: Knopf, 1985.

Charial-Thuilier, Jean-Andre. *Bouquet de Provence.* New York: Clarkson N. Potter, Inc., 1990.

David, Elizabeth. *French Provincial Cooking.* New York: Harper & Row, 1962.

Ferrary, Jeannette, and Louise Fiszer. *Jewish Holiday Feasts.* San Francisco: Chronicle Books, 1995.

Forbes, Leslie. *A Table in Tuscany.* San Francisco: Chronicle Books, 1991.

Grogan, Bryanna Clark. *Nonna's Italian Kitchen: Delicious Home-style Vegan Cuisine.* Summertown, TN: Book Publishing Company, 1998.

Hazan, Marcella. *Essentials of Classic Italian Cooking.* New York: Knopf, 1992.

Jenkins, Nancy Harmon. *The Mediterranean Diet Cookbook.* New York: Bantam Books, 1994.

Johnston, Mireille. *The Cuisine of the Sun.* New York: Random House, 1976.

Kochilas, Diane. *The Food and Wine of Greece.* New York: St. Martin's Press, 1990.

Loomis, Susan Herrmann. *The French Farmhouse Cookbook.* New York: Workman Publishing, 1996.

Olney, Richard. *Simple French Food.* New York: Antheneum, 1983.

Pupella, Eufemia Azzolina. *Sicilian Cookery.* Florence: Casa Editrice Bonechi, 1996.

Rodin, Claudia. *A Book of Middle Eastern Food.* New York: Vintage, 1974.

Shulman, Martha Rose. *Mediterranean Light.* New York: Bantam Books, 1989.

Shulman, Martha Rose. *Provençal Light.* New York: Bantam Books, 1994.

Slomon, Evelyne. *French Country Light Cooking.* New York: Perigee Books, 1993.

Torres, Marimar. *The Spanish Table.* New York: Doubleday, 1986.

Wells, Patricia. *Bistro Cooking.* New York: Workman Publishing, 1989.

Wolfert, Paula. *Mediterranean Cooking.* New York: HarperPerennial, 1994.

Wolfert, Paula. *Mediterranean Grains and Greens.* New York: HarperCollins, 1998.

Metric Conversion Charts

When You Know	Symbol	Comparison to Metric Measure Multiply By	To Find	Symbol
teaspoons	tsp	5.0	milliliters	ml
tablespoons	tbsp	15.0	milliliters	ml
fluid ounces	fl. oz.	30.0	milliliters	ml
cups	c	0.24	liters	l
pints	pt.	0.47	liters	l
quarts	qt.	0.95	liters	l
ounces	oz.	28.0	grams	g
pounds	lb.	0.45	kilograms	kg
Fahrenheit	F	5⁄9 (after subtracting 32)	Celsius	C

Fahrenheit to Celsius

F	C
200–205	95
220–225	105
245–250	120
275	135
300–305	150
325–330	165
345–350	175
370–375	190
400–405	205
425–430	220
445–450	230
470–475	245
500	260

Liquid Measure to Liters

¼ cup	=	0.06 liters
½ cup	=	0.12 liters
¾ cup	=	0.18 liters
1 cup	=	0.24 liters
1¼ cups	=	0.30 liters
1½ cups	=	0.36 liters
2 cups	=	0.48 liters
2½ cups	=	0.60 liters
3 cups	=	0.72 liters
3½ cups	=	0.84 liters
4 cups	=	0.96 liters
4½	=	1.08 liters
5 cups	=	1.20 liters
5½ cups	=	1.32 liters

Liquid Measure to Milliliters

¼ teaspoon	=	1.25 milliliters
½ teaspoon	=	2.50 milliliters
¾ teaspoon	=	3.75 milliliters
1 teaspoon	=	5.00 milliliters
1¼ teaspoons	=	6.25 milliliters
1½ teaspoons	=	7.50 milliliters
1¾ teaspoons	=	8.75 milliliters
2 teaspoons	=	10.0 milliliters
1 tablespoon	=	15.0 milliliters
2 tablespoons	=	30.0 milliliters

Index

About the Author

Donna Klein is a food writer whose work has appeared in *The Washington Post, Vegetarian Gourmet, Veggie Life, The Herb Companion, Victorian Decorating and Lifestyles* and, most frequently, *The Yoga Journal*. Having traveled to France, Spain, and Morocco and studied French regional cooking at Le Cordon Bleu, Paris, she combines a knowledge and passion for Mediterranean cooking with a strong sensibility for vegetarian tastes and health concerns.

A native of Philadelphia and graduate of St. Joseph's University, Ms. Klein has resided in the Washington, D.C., suburbs for several years with her husband and their two daughters. *The Mediterranean Vegan Kitchen* is her first cookbook.